The Evolution of European Manufacturing Industries

The book provides a picture of the increasing significance of Central Europe and especially Poland in global production networks, discussing the underlying economic, social and political factors. The key question it answers is to what extent the growth of production and exports results in industrial upgrading towards the manufacturing of more sophisticated high value-added products, new technologies and the development of non-production functions, especially design and advanced service capabilities.

The book shows that Central European manufacturing no longer exhibits the typical features of production activities in the periphery, in particular low density and diversity, low productivity, narrow specialisation in low value-added activities and poor local linkages, hence limited local value creation and value capture. There is still dependence on foreign-controlled enterprises in several sectors, as well as limited product innovation, which remain major weaknesses. Further, the book assesses the social consequences of the ongoing development of manufacturing capabilities in Poland and its impact on employment conditions including the quality of jobs and level of wages.

The authors provide insight into relationships between globalisation processes, place-specific attributes and current economic policies, and as such the book will be of interest to academics, policy makers and other stakeholders interested in both peripheral economies and core countries and representing various international organisations dealing with economic transition and development.

Bolesław Domański is professor and the head of the Department of Regional Development at the Institute of Geography and Spatial Management, Jagiellonian University, Kraków, Poland.

Grzegorz Micek is an associate professor and the head of the PhD programme in socio-economic geography and spatial management at the Institute of Geography and Spatial Management, Jagiellonian University, Kraków, Poland.

Robert Guzik is a lecturer at the Institute of Geography and Spatial Management, Jagiellonian University, Kraków, Poland.

Krzysztof Gwosdz is an associate professor at the Institute of Geography and Spatial Management, Jagiellonian University, Kraków, Poland.

Arkadiusz Kocaj is a lecturer at the Institute of Geography and Spatial Management, Jagiellonian University, Kraków, Poland.

Routledge Studies in the European Economy

64 The Socioeconomic Impact of COVID-19 on Eastern European Countries
Edited by Paweł Dykas and Rafał Wisła

65 The European Union Digital Single Market
Europe's Digital Transformation
Edited by Łukasz Dawid Dąbrowski and Magdalena Suska

66 Economic Wellbeing and Household Debt
Agnieszka Wałęga, Grzegorz Wałęga and Ryszard Kowalski

67 Transition Economies in Central and Eastern Europe
Austrian Perspectives
Edited by Alicja Sielska

68 The Silver Economy
An Ageing Society in the European Union
Agata Niemczyk, Katarzyna Szalonka, Anna Gardocka-Jałowiec, Wioletta Nowak, Renata Seweryn, Zofia Gródek-Szostak

69 Knowledge Cohesion
Uniting Europe Through Research Networks
İbrahim Semih Akçomak, Umut Yılmaz Çetinkaya, Erkan Erdil and Müge Özman

70 Financial Stability, Economic Growth and Sustainable Development
Edited by Marc Baudry, Sławomir Ireneusz Bukowski and Marzanna Barbara Lament

71 Crisis Era European Integration
Economic, Political and Social Lessons from Croatia
Edited by Jakša Puljiz and Hrvoje Butković

72 The Evolution of European Manufacturing Industries
The Dynamics of Core–Periphery Relationships
Bolesław Doman'ski, Grzegorz Micek, Robert Guzik, Krzysztof Gwosdz and Arkadiusz Kocaj

For more information about this series, please visit www.routledge.com/series/SE0431

The Evolution of European Manufacturing Industries

The Dynamics of Core–Periphery Relationships

Bolesław Domański, Grzegorz Micek, Robert Guzik, Krzysztof Gwosdz and Arkadiusz Kocaj

Routledge
Taylor & Francis Group
LONDON AND NEW YORK

First published 2025
by Routledge
4 Park Square, Milton Park, Abingdon, Oxon OX14 4RN

and by Routledge
605 Third Avenue, New York, NY 10158

Routledge is an imprint of the Taylor & Francis Group, an informa business

British Library Cataloguing-in-Publication Data
A catalogue record for this book is available from the British Library

Library of Congress Cataloging-in-Publication Data
A catalog record has been requested for this book

ISBN: 978-1-032-55322-1 (hbk)
ISBN: 978-1-032-55323-8 (pbk)
ISBN: 978-1-003-43011-7 (ebk)

DOI: 10.4324/9781003430117

Typeset in Sabon
by Taylor & Francis Books

The Open Access version of Chapters 2, 3 and 9 was funded by Jagiellonian University.

Contents

Figures

Tables

Abbreviations

CE	Central Europe
CKD	completely knocked-down
Comecon	Council for Mutual Economic Assistance
CWS	Centralne Warsztaty Samochodowe (Central Automotive Works) in Warsaw
EASA	European Union Aviation Safety Agency
EU	European Union
FDI	foreign direct investment
FSC Lublin	Fabryka Samochodów Ciężarowych w Lublinie (Truck Factory in Lublin)
FSC Star	Fabryka Samochodów Ciężarowych Star (Star Truck Factory) in Starachowice
FSM	Fabryka Samochodów Małolitrażowych (Low-Powered Car Factory) in Bielsko-Biała and Tychy
FSO	Fabryka Samochodów Osobowych (Passenger Car Factory) in Warsaw
FSR	Fabryka Samochodów Rolniczych Polmo (Polmo Agricultural Automotive Factory) in Poznań
GUS	Główny Urząd Statystyczny (Central Statistical Office)
HVAC	heating, ventilation and air conditioning
JZS	Jelczańskie Zakłady Samochodowe (Jelcz Automotive Works) in Jelcz-Laskowice
MDA	major domestic appliance
P&W	Pratt & Whitney
PIZ	Polish Investment Zone
PZInż	Państwowe Zakłady Inżynierii (National Engineering Works) in Warsaw
SDA	small domestic appliance
SEZ	special economic zone
SKD	semi-knocked-down
UAV	unmanned aerial vehicle
VA	value added

WET	home appliance category, including washing machines, dishwashers and tumble dryers
WSK PZL-Kalisz	Wytwórnia Sprzętu Komunikacyjnego PZL-Kalisz (Communication Equipment Factory PZL-Kalisz) in Kalisz
WSK PZL-Mielec	Wytwórnia Sprzętu Komunikacyjnego PZL-Mielec (Communication Equipment Factory PZL-Mielec) in Mielec
WSK PZL-Rzeszów	Wytwórnia Sprzętu Komunikacyjnego PZL-Rzeszów (Communication Equipment Factory PZL-Rzeszów) in Rzeszów
WSK PZL-Świdnik	Wytwórnia Sprzętu Komunikacyjnego PZL-Świdnik (Communication Equipment Factory PZL-Świdnik) in Świdnik
WZL	Wojskowe Zakłady Lotnicze (Military Aircraft Works)
WSM	Wytwórnia Sprzętu Mechanicznego (Mechanical Equipment Factory) in Bielsko-Biała
ZM Nowotki	Zakłady Mechaniczne im. Marcelego Nowotki (Marceli Nowotko Mechanical Works) in Warsaw

Acknowledgements

This book would not have been possible without the invaluable work of many people. The research team included Agnieszka Świgost-Kapocsi, Anna Avdiushchenko and Magdalena Miśkowiec, who were involved in various stages of data collection and analysis. Nearly 200 company managers, trade union leaders, and representatives of industrial associations and clusters gave their time and shared their views with the research team, contributing to a better understanding of upgrading processes in Polish manufacturing, and the underlying factors and barriers. We are very grateful to Maciej Grodzicki for his critical review and stimulating discussion of an earlier version of the text, and to the anonymous reviewers of our book proposal. Of course, the authors take full responsibility for the opinions expressed and any inaccuracies contained. The authors are deeply indebted to Małgorzata Ciemborowicz and Alicja Marciniak-Nowak for their excellent work on the figures. Finally, we would like to thank the editors of the Routledge Studies in the European Economy series, Kristina Abbotts, Senior Editor at Routledge, and Christiana Mandizha, Editorial Assistant, for their support, constructive feedback and hard work.

The research was funded by the Polish National Science Centre as part of the "Paths and Limits to Industrial Upgrading: High or Low Road of Development in Polish Manufacturing" project [grant no. 2017/27/B/HS4/01935]. The publication has been supported by a grant from the Faculty of Geography and Geology under the Strategic Programme Excellence Initiative at Jagiellonian University.

Bolesław Domański, Grzegorz Micek, Robert Guzik,
Krzysztof Gwosdz and Arkadiusz Kocaj
Kraków, 19 January 2024

Introduction

The turn of the 20th and 21st centuries has seen far-reaching changes in the global economic landscape. On one hand, countries and regions have continued to integrate into global production networks. On the other hand, several sudden political and economic shocks have occurred, which have influenced the location of economic activities and their linkages. These include a breakdown of state socialism in Europe since 1989, the Asian crisis of 1997–1998, the global financial crisis of 2008–2009, the COVID-19 pandemic of 2020–2021 and the Russian invasion of Ukraine in 2022. Additionally, there have been changes in political power and international relations, as well as national public policy adjustments in various countries. In the context of growing environmental concern, various measures have been introduced to neutralise negative trends and their effects. Manufacturing production and related supply chain organisation have been particularly affected.

Central Europe (CE) is a region whose economic role has significantly increased in recent decades. Poland stands out as a particularly noteworthy case in the region for attracting massive foreign investment in manufacturing activities, concentrating more and more output and value added, and integrating within global production networks. According to Piątkowski (2018), no Central European country performed better economically and socially than Poland after the end of the socialist system. As the largest economy in CE, Poland's growth trajectory since the 1990s has been remarkable. Over the last three decades, the country has become one of the largest manufacturing centres in the European Union and a major exporter, with an increasing surplus in the trade of manufactured goods with Western Europe. This has led to economic convergence between Poland and Western Europe.

There is a wealth of literature on the post-socialist transformation of Central European countries and their economic development in general (Gorzelak et al., 2010; Kołodko, 2010; Lux & Horváth, 2018). Several books have been written about Poland's economic growth and transformation (Piątkowski, 2018; Churski & Kaczmarek, 2022). However, the reasons behind the improved position of Poland and other Central European economies in the manufacturing industry are surprisingly weakly explained. This is in contrast to various books that analyse industrial upgrading in China, South-East Asian countries (Yu,

DOI: 10.4324/9781003430117-1

2017; Gereffi, 2018; Zhang, 2018; Liu, 2020; Lee et al., 2021; Teipen et al., 2022), Latin America (Andreoni & Tregenna, 2020) and Africa (Kaplan, 2016; Whitfield et al., 2020a, 2020b; Obasaju et al., 2021; Pasquali, 2021). There is a significant body of work on foreign direct investment (FDI), including studies by Makhavikova (2018), Marinova and Marinov (2018), Trąpczyński et al. (2019) and Gál and Lux (2022). However, some books, such as Szent-Iványi (2017), do not have a dedicated chapter on Poland. Several journal papers have focused on the development of individual industries in the region, particularly the automotive sector. Examples include Domański and Gwosdz (2009), Jacobs (2017), Pavlínek (2002, 2016, 2022, 2023), Pavlínek and Žížalová (2016), Pavlínek and Ženka (2016), Adăscăliței and Guga (2020), Molnar et al. (2020), and Szalavetz and Sass (2023). However, few publications provide a thorough and detailed analysis of the manufacturing development in this region (including its historical background), a multi-source-based evolutionary perspective and a discussion of underlying factors and consequences.

Therefore, it is important to examine the increasing significance of CE and Poland in European manufacturing. The book has two main objectives: firstly, to clarify the development of Poland's manufacturing industry and to identify the economic, social and political factors that have contributed to this process in recent decades; secondly, to assess its economic and social impact. The main question addressed in the book is as follows: to what extent does the growth of production and exports lead to industrial upgrading towards the manufacturing of more sophisticated high value-added products, new technologies and the development of non-production functions, particularly research and development (R&D) and advanced service capabilities? The book also presents an assessment of the impact of the development of manufacturing capabilities in Poland on employment conditions, including the number and quality of jobs and the level of wages. Additionally, it provides a comparative analysis of the changing position of six CE countries in the European manufacturing context.

For the in-depth study of industrial development, three medium-high- and high-tech sectors have been selected: the automotive (NACE C29), aircraft (NACE C303) and home appliance industries (NACE C275). These sectors are FDI-driven, export-oriented, fast-growing and globalized. They differ in size and importance in each national economy.

The book presents several novel features. Firstly, it describes the evolution of manufacturing in Poland's historically peripheral economy. Secondly, the case study of Polish manufacturing provides valuable insights into the interplay between globalisation trends, place-specific attributes and economic policies. Thirdly, the book combines various methodological approaches, including evolutionary, relational and institutional ones. The book follows the integrative paradigm advocated in economic geography by Hassink and Gong (2017) by drawing on four large strands of literature: global production networks (GPNs; Yeung, 2015), the core–periphery model (e.g. Friedmann, 1972; Wallerstein, 1979, 2004), industrial upgrading (Humphrey & Schmitz, 2002; Blažek, 2016;

Gereffi, 2019) and the debate on the role of foreign investment in economic development (Gál & Lux, 2022).

Data sources

The authors utilise a range of quantitative and qualitative data sources to achieve their research objectives. These include data from international organisations and national statistical offices at both country and industrial sector levels, in-house datasets based on various dispersed sources, as well as in-depth interviews and focus groups with managers and representatives of business environment institutions and trade unions.

Chapters 2–5 primarily source country-level data on industrial production and its attributes since the 1990s from Eurostat and OECD publications. The analysis of FDI predominantly relies on the United Nations Conference on Trade and Development (UNCTAD) database due to its extensive time series. The UN Comtrade database (denominated in USD) is used to explore countries' standings in total foreign trade and exports of specific categories of industrial goods. Eurostat data are used to provide a detailed view of trade in the three sectors examined in the book, particularly at the HS2-4-6 and CN8 classification levels. Although Eurostat data offer greater detail, they have limitations in terms of data series duration and geographic coverage, mainly focusing on the EU countries.

The book's analysis extends beyond industries narrowly defined by NACE code, using a chain-based approach to cover all significant suppliers. This includes not only enterprises assembling final products and manufacturers of components classified in the same sector but also broad networks of suppliers classified in various industrial sectors. As a result, the analysis encompasses both the "broad sector" and the "narrow sector". The former refers to all companies with at least 25% of their turnover in a specific industry, whereas the latter refers to the statistical classification based on the main activity of the company.

The research would not have been possible without the authors' meticulously constructed unique databases at both the company and plant levels. These databases have been created through a comprehensive and detailed process of data collection, including acquiring data from national statistical offices, national court registers, industry associations and other dispersed sources.

The study identifies 810 automotive industry establishments, 176 aircraft factories and 136 home appliance plants at the plant level. Data are collected from annual company reports, financial statements, press releases and interviews to obtain a range of variables. This section describes the variables used in the analysis of Polish manufacturing industries in Chapters 3–5 and their shifting geographies in Chapter 6. The variables include the year of establishment, primary products, non-production functions such as R&D, ownership types and structures, position in the supply chain, workforce size, export data, certification status and detailed location information. Simultaneously, the annual reports of major companies operating in the studied sectors are analysed in order to identify related enterprises and the scale and direction of intra-corporate trade. Over 600 annual reports have been investigated in this procedure. Data triangulation using various data sources is applied to ensure the quality of the information used in the research and the resulting robustness of results.

To conduct a thorough analysis of the upgrading process at the company level, the authors have created a separate multivariable database that includes the largest enterprises in each of the analysed industries. Detailed financial and non-financial data have been collected for these companies for the years 2007–2008, 2011–2012 and 2018–2019, which are used to construct upgrading indicators. Industry-specific quality measures tailored to each sector are also employed. The study of the automotive industry is supported by the database of IATF 16949 certificate holders, and the study of the aviation sector is supported by the European Union Aviation Safety Agency (EASA) database of Approved Production Organisations. Additionally, data on patent applications and grants from the US Patent Office are utilized.

The reports published by the International Labour Organization (ILO), World Employment Confederation, European Trade Union Institute, the Polish Ministry of Family and Social Policy and national labour surveys are valuable sources of information in the labour market analysis in Chapter 7. Numerous industry reports are also used in the sector-specific Chapters 3–5.

The research is enriched by more than 100 interviews conducted between 2018 and 2023 with company managers, trade union leaders and employment agencies. In addition, in-depth insights are drawn from seven focus group interviews with trade union representatives and two focus group interviews with employment agency managers. Key themes explored in the interviews include:

- the scope of upgrading of domestic companies and foreign affiliates operating in Poland and CE within GPNs and European production networks,
- mechanisms, strategies and barriers of industrial upgrading,
- factors expected to influence upgrading in the near future (the next five to ten years),
- the potential impact of EU and Polish regulations on environmental, social and labour standards,
- the competitive position of other countries,
- the impact of labour market dynamics, such as labour shortages and the use of temporary and foreign workers, on industrial upgrading.

In essence, the breadth and diversity of the sources used allow the complex processes of industrial upgrading to be examined from different perspectives and at various scales, from the European context to the level of individual firms.

The book is divided into four parts. The first section (Chapters 1 and 2) provides an insight into the theoretical debate on the core–periphery model and industrial upgrading, as well as outlining the broader context of the development of European manufacturing industries. The second part (Chapters 3–5) examines changes in three selected industries in Poland and their determinants. The institutional, social and regional dimensions are presented in the third section (Chapters 6–8). The book concludes with a thorough discussion of the determinants and consequences of industrial upgrading.

References

Adăscăliței, D., & Guga, Ș. (2020). Tensions in the periphery: Dependence and the trajectory of a low-cost productive model in the Central and Eastern European automotive industry. *European Urban and Regional Studies*, 27(1), 18–34. doi:10.1177/0969776418795205.

Andreoni, A., & Tregenna, F. (2020). Escaping the middle-income technology trap: A comparative analysis of industrial policies in China, Brazil and South Africa. *Structural Change and Economic Dynamics*, 54, 324–340. doi:10.1016/j.strueco.2020.05.008.

Blažek, J. (2016). Towards a typology of repositioning strategies of GVC/GPN suppliers: The case of functional upgrading and downgrading. *Journal of Economic Geography*, 16(4), 849–869. doi:10.1093/jeg/lbv044.

Churski, P., & Kaczmarek, T. (Eds.). (2022). *Three decades of Polish socio-economic transformations: Geographical perspectives*. Cham: Springer.

Domański, B., & Gwosdz, K. (2009). Toward a more embedded production system? Automotive supply networks and localized capabilities in Poland. *Growth and Change*, 40(3), 452–482.

Friedmann, J. (1972). A general theory of polarized development. In N.M. Hansen (Ed.), *Growth centers in regional economic development* (pp. 82–107). New York: The Free Press.

Gál, Z., & Lux, G. (2022). FDI-based regional development in Central and Eastern Europe: A review and an agenda. *Tér és Társadalom*, 36(3), 68–98. doi:10.17649/TET.36.3.3439.

Gereffi, G. (2018). Development models and industrial upgrading in China and Mexico. In *Global value chains and development: Redefining the contours of 21st-century capitalism* (pp. 205–227). Development trajectories in global value chains. Cambridge: Cambridge University Press.

Gereffi, G. (2019). Economic upgrading in global value chains. In S. Ponte, G. Gereffi, & G. Raj-Reichert (Eds.), *Handbook on global value chains* (pp. 240–254). Cheltenham: Edward Elgar Publishing. doi:10.4337/9781788113779.00022.

Gorzelak, G., Bachtler, J., & Smętkowski, M. (Eds.). (2010). *Regional development in Central and Eastern Europe: Development processes and policy challenges* (1st ed.). Abingdon: Routledge. doi:10.4324/9780203855386.

Hassink, R., & Gong, H. (2017). Sketching the contours of an integrative paradigm of economic geography. *Papers in Innovation Studies, Centre for Innovation, Research and Competence in the Learning Economy (CIRCLE)*, 2017 / 12. doi:10.13140/RG.2.2.32158.64322.

Humphrey, J., & Schmitz, H. (2002). How does insertion in global value chains affect upgrading in industrial clusters? *Regional Studies*, 36(9), 1017–1027.

Jacobs, A.J. (2017). *Automotive FDI in emerging Europe*. Cham: Palgrave Macmillan.

Kaplan, D. (2016). Linkage dynamics and natural resources: Diversification and catch-up. In P.G. Sampath & B. Oyelaran-Oyeyinka (Eds.), *Sustainable industrialization in Africa* (pp. 195–218). London: Palgrave Macmillan. doi:10.1007/978-1-137-56112-1_4.

Kołodko, G.W. (2010). Two decades of great postsocialist transformation – and what next? *Acta Oeconomica*, 60(4), 361–373. http://www.jstor.org/stable/27895933.

Lee, K., Qu, D., & Mao, Z. (2021). Global value chains, industrial policy, and industrial upgrading: Automotive sectors in Malaysia, Thailand, and China in comparison with Korea. *European Journal of Development Research*, 33(2), 275–303. doi:10.1057/s41287-020-00354-0.

Liu, Y. (2020). *Local dynamics of industrial upgrading: The case of the Pearl River Delta in China*. Singapore: Springer Nature.

Lux, G., & Horváth, G. (2018). *The Routledge handbook to regional development in Central and Eastern Europe*. Abingdon: Routledge.

Makhavikova, H. (2018). *Determinants of FDI in Central and Eastern Europe: The effects of integration into the European Union*. Cham: Springer.

Marinova, S.T., & Marinov, M.A. (2018). *Foreign direct investment in Central and Eastern Europe*. Abingdon: Routledge.

Molnar, E., Kozma, G., Meszarosi, M., & Kiss, E. (2020). Upgrading and the geography of the Hungarian automotive industry in the context of the fourth industrial revolution. *Hungarian Geographical Bulletin*, 69(2), 137–155. doi:10.15201/hungeobull.69.2.4.

Obasaju, B.O., Olayiwola, W.K., Okodua, H., Adediran, O.S., & Lawal, A.I. (2021). Regional economic integration and economic upgrading in global value chains: Selected cases in Africa. *Heliyon, 7*(2), E06112. doi:10.1016/j.heliyon.2021.e06112.

Pasquali, G.P. (2021). When value chains go South: Upgrading in the Kenyan leather sector. *Journal of World Business*, 56(2), 101161. doi:10.1016/j.jwb.2020.101161.

Pavlínek, P. (2002). Transformation of the Central and East European passenger car industry: Selective peripheral integration through foreign direct investment. *Environment and Planning A*, 34(9), 1685–1709. doi:10.1068/a34263.

Pavlínek, P. (2016). Whose success? The state–foreign capital nexus and the development of the automotive industry in Slovakia. *European Urban and Regional Studies*, 23(4), 571–593.

Pavlínek, P. (2022). Relative positions of countries in the core-periphery structure of the European automotive industry. *European Urban and Regional Studies*, 29(1), 59–84. doi:10.1177/09697764211021882.

Pavlínek, P. (2023). Transition of the automotive industry towards electric vehicle production in the East European integrated periphery. *Empirica*, 50(1), 35–73. doi:10.1007/s10663-022-09554-9.

Pavlínek, P., & Ženka, J. (2016). Value creation and value capture in the automotive industry: Empirical evidence from Czechia. *Environment and Planning A*, 48(5), 937–959.

Pavlínek, P., & Žížalová, P. (2016). Linkages and spillovers in global production networks: Firm-level analysis of the Czech automotive industry. *Journal of Economic Geography*, 16(2), 331–363.

Piątkowski, M. (2018). *Europe's growth champion: Insights from the economic growth of Poland*. Oxford: Oxford University Press.

Szalavetz, A., & Sass, M. (2023). Disentangling the semi-periphery: Evolutionary trajectories and perspectives of the Austrian and Hungarian automotive industries. *Post-Communist Economies*, 35(3), 211–235. doi:10.1080/14631377.2023.2171179.

Szent-Iványi, B. (2017). *Foreign direct investment in Central and Eastern Europe: Post-crisis perspectives*. Cham: Palgrave Macmillan.

Teipen, Ch., Dünhaupt, P., Herr, H., & Mehl, F. (Eds.). (2022). *Economic and social upgrading in global value chains. Comparative analyses, macroeconomic effects, the role of institutions and strategies for the Global South*. Cham: Palgrave Macmillan.

Trąpczyński, P., Gorynia, M., Nowak, J., & Wolniak, R. (2019). EU countries from Central and Eastern Europe, and the investment development path model: A new assessment. *Argumenta Oeconomica*, 2(43), 385–406.

Wallerstein, I. (1979). *The capitalist world economy*. Cambridge: Cambridge University Press.

Wallerstein, I. (2004). *World-systems analysis: An introduction*. Durham, NC: Duke University Press.

Whitfield, L., Staritz, C., Melese, A.T., & Azizi, S. (2020a). Technological capabilities, upgrading, and value capture in global value chains: Local apparel and floriculture firms in Sub-Saharan Africa. *Economic Geography*, 96(3), 195–218. doi:10.1080/00130095.2020.1748497.

Whitfield, L., Staritz, C., & Morris, M. (2020b). Global value chains, industrial policy and economic upgrading in Ethiopia's apparel sector. *Development and Change*, 51 (4), 1018–1043. doi:10.1111/dech.12590.

Yeung, H.W.-c. (2015), Regional development in the global economy. *Regional Science Policy & Practice*, 7(1), 1–23. doi:10.1111/rsp3.12055.

Yu, H. (2017). *Chinese regions in change: Industrial upgrading and regional development strategies*. Abingdon: Routledge.

Zhang, Q. (2018). *Transforming economic growth and China's industrial upgrading*. Singapore: Springer.

1 Industrial Upgrading in the Context of the Core–Periphery Debate

Economic peripheries

a Four approaches to the economic periphery

The core–periphery dichotomy has been present in the academic literature for decades. From the perspective of political and security studies, peripheries lack political control over power processes, the potential to create norms and standards, and lag behind the centre economically (Rokkan & Urwin, 1983; Pawłuszko, 2023). In economics and economic geography, the core–periphery model is usually approached from four main perspectives. The first original approach of **polarised development**, introduced by Friedmann (1972), views development as a discontinuous process that occurs through a series of radical innovations that gradually coalesce into innovative clusters and eventually into interconnected innovation systems. Core regions are the main centres of change (innovation) and the periphery is defined by its relationship of dependence on the core. The core and periphery are inherently dynamic and represent the second stage in a four-stage sequential model of spatial economic development. It is argued that subsequent stages involve the gradual dispersion of economic activities, leading to the emergence of spatial integration of various interdependent and relatively well-developed territorial units.

The second approach uses a core–periphery dichotomy in **world systems** analysis. According to Wallerstein's (1974) world system theory, there are systematic patterns of uneven development between the core and the periphery of the world. The core is characterised by high income and high-profit economic activity (Wallerstein, 1979, 2004). From this perspective, the core refers to the centre of capital-intensive and high-technology industries. Due to significant barriers to entry, some rapidly growing peripheral regions may find it difficult to join the core. Wallerstein (1974) recognises the need for social change throughout the world system, from capitalism to a post-capitalist system. In this approach, peripheries are characterised by a low level of economic and social development, with class struggle, weaker economies of scale and agglomeration economies. They may be caused by demographic problems, which are the most frequently cited characteristics of peripheries, as identified by Eder (2019b). This often leads

DOI: 10.4324/9781003430117-2

to a lack of human capital, supporting infrastructure and investment. In addition, peripheries are often geographically remote and difficult to access, which further exacerbates their situation. As a result, they are often unable to become the core and remain trapped in their initial positions (Arrighi & Drangel, 1986).

The third perspective on economic peripheries is provided by neo-Marxist **dependency theories**. These theories (for an overview, see Ghosh, 2001) recognise the drivers of development and underdevelopment, mainly in Latin American countries but also in Poland (see Grodzicki & Geodecki, 2016), and acknowledge the significant role of transnational corporations (TNCs) in shaping development and delivering inequalities (Dos Santos, 1970; Peet & Hartwick, 2015). Lampón et al. (2016, p. 597) note that the powerful command areas "decide on how activities and technologies are going to be distributed" due to their power. In addition, the central actors exploit labour in some areas, resulting in large profits. As a result, weaker economies become dependent on demand from the world system and grow only as a reflection of changes in the core countries (Dos Santos, 1970; Peet & Hartwick, 2015). The capacity of the periphery to make strategic decisions is insufficient. In addition, the periphery is seen as having limited dynamism in economic and social terms (Bar-El & Parr, 2003).

TNCs are believed to have a significant impact on public regulations and are considered crucial in the new international division of labour, where some emerging economies become labour-intensive export platforms through foreign investment (Fröbel et al., 1980). Peripheral areas are often dependent on large firms and can become trapped in a cycle of limited or dependent development (Dawley, 2011). In addition, economic peripheries dominated by external investment often experience a leakage of employment multiplier effects and lower economic surpluses, resulting in lower tax revenues (Jones & Munday, 2020). Investment in peripheral areas is frequently perceived as disconnected from the hinterland and may be dominated by foreign-owned plants (Pavlínek, 2018). The low territorial embeddedness of such companies may explain the weak localised knowledge flows, and scarce and fragmented links with local partners and other organisations (Grabher, 1993; Oinas, 1997; Coe & Lee, 2013; Wood et al., 2019).

The fourth approach to peripheries, like Friedmann's concept, is inherently dynamic. Vernon's (1966) **product life-cycle theory** suggests a shift in the manufacture of mature and standardised products from the core to the periphery. Low-cost labour is the driving force behind the search for semi-skilled and unskilled labour in the latter, while the former focuses on introducing new products to maintain its dominant position. However, this concept often introduces three categories of countries: (i) the technological core (with high production costs); (ii) the manufacturing core, which focuses on the production of final products; and (iii) the manufacturing periphery, which relies on low-cost semi-skilled and unskilled labour.

To conclude the discussion of these approaches, it is useful to ask which of the original theoretical concepts of the periphery we are referring to: the original concept of J. Friedmann (1972) or the world system theory of I. Wallerstein (1974)? Several authors refer to the latter, ignoring some basic elements of Wallerstein's theory. Firstly, Wallerstein strongly criticised the idea of individual countries progressing through stages, as the entire world system can undergo social change from the current capitalist system to a post-capitalist one. Secondly, he emphasised that the most salient feature of the semi-periphery is acute class struggle. It is therefore questionable whether Wallerstein's approach provides a valid theoretical perspective for analysing and interpreting contemporary processes of economic and social change in Central European countries. Interestingly, Friedmann's earlier core–periphery model, which depicts a gradual dispersion of economic activities and spatial integration of different territorial units, may be more useful in this context.

The core–periphery dichotomy has been widely used in research on global production networks (GPNs) and global value chains (GVCs). GVCs, as described by Gereffi (1999, 2014), offer a novel outlook on the dynamics of core–periphery relationships and the potential for national/regional economies to upgrade to higher value-added processes. The GPN approach represents an elaboration of this theoretical perspective, moving beyond the linear conceptualisation of production as a stepwise sequence of economic activities (Coe et al., 2008). It provides a comprehensive relational framework for studying the complex relationships between enterprises, non-business institutions and territories (countries/regions). The concept of "**strategic coupling**" between GPNs and regional assets, as described by Yeung (2015), is central in this context. The uneven distribution of power is also a key factor to consider. Strategic coupling refers to the deliberate alignment and coordination of activities between domestic and foreign firms with the aim of leveraging each other's resources, capabilities and market access to achieve mutual benefits and competitive advantage. Through strategic coupling, domestic companies can tap into the global networks and expertise of foreign investors, while foreign investors can gain access to local knowledge, cost advantages and government incentives. This strategic coupling facilitates the seamless integration of domestic and foreign actors, ultimately leading to enhanced competitiveness and the development of local industries in the global market (Coe et al., 2004; Coe & Yeung, 2015; Yeung, 2015; Pavlínek, 2022b).

Zöllner et al. (2023) argue that the traditional core–periphery conceptualisation, based on attributional or point data, is too static to capture the contemporary economic development of regions. What is needed is a relational perspective of networks that encourages us to "understand socio-economic phenomena as intertwined and mutually interdependent processes, putting economic actors [and] their spatial organisation of labour in value chains" (p. 364) at the centre of our conceptual framework.

A growing body of evidence suggests that a variety of endogenous and exogenous factors may determine different development paths for individual regions within a country (Blažek, 2016; Liu, 2017; Pike et al., 2017). This book uses the broader GPN metaphor to discuss the impact of these multi-actor, multilayered economic relationships on industrial upgrading.

Economic peripheries exist at different spatial scales, ranging from global (North–South) to local (Eder, 2019b). Typically, a country or group of countries is recognised as a periphery. This is common in political studies, where Central and Eastern Europe (Cabada, 2020) or the countries of Mercosur and the Visegrad Group (Lehoczki, 2022) are treated as semi-peripheries. This book focuses primarily on peripheries at the country level, with some analysis of inner peripheries (Dubownik et al., 2022).

b Criteria for distinguishing the economic periphery

Peripheries are often identified by their remoteness. According to Pugh and Dubois (2021, p. 269), "macro-remoteness is based on long physical distances and travel times from large agglomerations and dominant economic centres at national and continental scales." It is argued that limited accessibility to global economic centres makes a region or country peripheral. However, the idea that remoteness is an inherent characteristic of every periphery should be questioned. There are cases of countries and regions that are accessible but remain economically peripheral. It is also unclear whether low labour costs (Pavlínek, 2018) should be a criterion for distinguishing periphery from core. In some regions, rising labour costs have led to economic deprivation, which has kept them in the periphery (as in the case of southern Italy – De Vivo & Rinaldi, 2022). If the above proxies do not accurately identify all economic peripheries, what other criteria could be used to distinguish them? Cairó-i-Céspedes and Palacios Cívico (2022, p. 1955) identify seven dimensions of economic peripheries:

> (1) the low degree of financial autonomy or dependency of an economy with regard to the international financial system; (2) the outward-looking position of the modern sector; (3) the large role of the local elites in the process of capital accumulation, in mainly running non-productive activities linked to international trade; (4) the low capacity of a country to export capital mainly through foreign investment; (5) the strong level of transnational capital existing in the national economy; (6) the limited role of the state in the assumption of regulatory and welfare functions; (7) the high degree of income inequality in the population.

Mudambi and Santangelo (2016) summarise peripheries as areas of organisational and institutional "thinness" in the form of a lack of critical mass of innovative firms, low levels of supporting organisations, and weak technological resources and absorptive capacity of local units. Grodzicki and Geodecki (2016) consider weak connectedness to the global economy, illustrated by the sum of inward and outward foreign direct investment (FDI) as a share of gross domestic product (GDP) and the ratio of the sum of imports and exports to GDP, as a proxy for peripherality.

Since the focus of this book is on the manufacturing sector, it can be argued that the main characteristics shared by the peripheral countries are as follows:

- low density of economic activity, including resultingly weak agglomeration economies,
- specialisation in low value-added activities,
- low diversity of products and services offered,
- low territorial embeddedness of foreign companies in local economies,
- weak capacity to generate and absorb innovation (Eder, 2019a),
- resulting power dependence on the core countries that house strategic functions,
- weak economic power.

It is important to measure all these features in relation to other economies in order to gain a comprehensive understanding. In conclusion, the term periphery refers not only to areas that specialise in low value-added industrial segments and occupy a low position in the international division of labour (Grodzicki & Geodecki, 2016), but also to those with low levels of economic development and limited economic power (Barry, 2004). These areas are dependent on lead firms from other countries and/or regions.

Beyond the dual model: exploring other types of peripheries

a Semi-peripheries

An increasing number of authors acknowledge that the core–periphery dichotomy fails to recognise the intermediate position of countries located between the core and the periphery (Cairó-i-Céspedes & Palacios Cívico, 2022). From a general economic perspective, such states are increasingly classified as semi-peripheries. Wallerstein (1974) introduced the term semi-periphery to describe developing countries that occupy a middle structural position in the world economy (Cairó-i-Céspedes & Palacios Cívico, 2022). The emergence of semi-peripheries can be attributed to countries that, to some extent, move up the GPNs but do not reach the core position, as they still host both low and high value-added activities. For example, semi-peripheries may contain special economic zones, financial centres or tourist resorts that are integrated to some extent with the global economy, but partially disconnected from their local environment (Sidaway, 2012).

The question of what distinguishes semi-peripheries from peripheries needs to be addressed. Semi-peripheries are still seen as FDI-driven economies (Pavlínek, 2018; Mordue & Sweeney, 2020), trapped in their dependence on foreign capital. They are often seen as having an ambiguous source of competitive advantage (Mordue & Sweeney, 2020), with limited R&D capacity. Income inequalities persist despite the rise of the middle class (Cairó-i-Céspedes & Palacios Cívico, 2022). The two main differences with traditional peripheries are the stronger presence of domestic firms and the ability to host global headquarters of TNCs. Firstly, semi-peripheries experience a relatively stronger development of domestic enterprises, which is a characteristic of lower and upper semi-peripheries (see Szalavetz & Sass, 2023). However, Pavlínek (2018) questions whether indigenous coupling, understood as large-scale value capture and upgrading triggered by the global expansion of domestic firms (Coe & Yeung, 2015), can emerge there. Secondly, semi-peripheral countries, such as Austria, Belgium, Finland and Sweden in the case of the automotive industry, may have relatively high production costs and host global headquarters of large transnational suppliers, which distinguishes them from classical peripheries (Mordue & Sweeney, 2020). In summary, many authors argue that semi-peripheries represent a fragile intermediate status in a core–periphery model, given their limited differences from classical peripheries.

b Integrated peripheries

Another type of periphery can be distinguished in the automotive industry, which may also apply to other sectors. Integrated peripheries emerged in the 1980s and 1990s in Mexico, Spain and Portugal (Humphrey et al., 2000; Layan, 2000; Carrillo, 2004), followed by Türkiye and Central and Eastern Europe (Humphrey et al., 2000; Pavlínek, 2002). More recently, Serbia and Morocco have been claimed to be integrated into the European production system (Pavlínek, 2018). In the context of the automotive industry, only a few distinctive features of integrated peripheries are usually distinguished (Pavlínek, 2018, 2020, 2023). These relatively small differences include their proximity to large core markets, which reduces transport costs, as well as higher economic and labour market dynamics compared to classical peripheries. The remaining characteristics of integrated peripheries are similar to those of classical peripheries. These are foreign control of industries through FDI, which is associated with weak linkages between foreign firms and the host economy, resulting in low value capture in integrated peripheries. In addition, low-cost industrial production is based on low labour costs and there is an international orientation of production with limited value added. Finally, standardised final products and/or components are produced. Integrated peripheries, like typical peripheries, suffer from a relatively weak position of domestic industry due to the dominance of FDI. Based on his previous research (Pavlínek & Žížalová, 2016; Pavlínek, 2018), Pavlínek (2023) argues that indigenous companies in integrated peripheries mainly serve as low-cost suppliers of niche products and simple components.

The negative perception of integrated peripheries is strongly influenced by their low comparative position. Pavlínek (2018) sees integrated peripheries as dependent on foreign capital for both production and strategic functions. Non-productive competences are weaker than productive ones. Such an understanding is often accompanied by a pessimistic view of the future prospects for local industries. As Pavlínek (2018, p. 161) summarises, "the quantity and quality of supplier linkages are likely to remain low."

In summary, integrated peripheries are integrated into the macro-regional production network due to their proximity to core countries. FDI and increased trade are believed to facilitate the integration of peripheries within GPNs (Pavlínek, 2022a, 2022b). However, other characteristics of integrated peripheries are similar to those of classical peripheries.

As shown, there are different versions of the core–periphery model. According to the literature review, in particular the recent paper by Szalavetz and Sass (2023), three categories of countries can be identified based on their position in GVCs: peripheries (divided into unintegrated and integrated), semi-peripheries (of lower and upper levels) and core economies. However, the core–periphery model can be further extended by distinguishing five or more different levels. Pavlínek (2022a) identified a stable upper-order core in Germany, a stable lower-order core in France and Italy, and an unstable lower-order core in Sweden and the UK. There are also semi-peripheries, including Austria, the Netherlands, Spain, Belgium and Finland, which are stable, and Denmark, Czechia and Slovenia, which are unstable. Finally, there are peripheries, including Poland, Portugal, Romania, Estonia and Lithuania, which are stable, and Ireland, Hungary, Latvia and Slovakia, which are unstable (Pavlínek, 2022a).

In addition to its industrial dimension, peripherality can also be analysed through the lens of a **fragile labour market** (see Chapter 7), characterised by low wages and weak working conditions, such as the presence of temporary workers. Labour market peripherality is said to contribute to a "race to the bottom" in these areas (Drahokoupil, 2009; Pavlínek, 2016). This is typically characterised by unstable employment conditions, temporary contracts, declining wages and growing income inequalities, including the gender pay gap.

Towards a summary of peripherality

All in all, the book recognises two interrelated dimensions of peripherality: the economic and the social. The economic dimension is shaped by the characteristics of the economic system, which includes both foreign and domestic enterprises. The social dimension is shaped by the labour market situation and institutional context.

Based on a literature review, the authors find that the peripheries share several common characteristics. These include a low density of firms, specialisation in simple activities, a low diversity of products and services offered, and a weak capacity to generate and absorb innovation. Peripheries are often dependent on lead firms from core countries and regions, which can lead to economic backwardness.

Overall, there is a multidimensional continuum of core–periphery relations that can lead to different country classifications. It is important to note that the characteristics of peripherality can vary even within the same country. For example, there may be significant foreign control over production and strategic functions, while at the same time there may be domestic firms that are globally expanding and highly integrated into GPNs, as is evident in the case of outward FDI by some Polish automotive firms (Micek et al., 2021).

The book adopts a country-level approach, focusing on Poland as a historical periphery. According to the common Wallersteinian understanding of periphery, peripheral countries are seen as inherently weak and trapped in their historically determined inferior position. However, the claim that peripheries are unable to translate their current economic dynamics into higher levels of socio-economic development (Cairó-i-Céspedes & Palacios Cívico, 2022) is debatable. Such a perspective would suggest that both peripheries and semi-peripheries cannot change their competitive position in a global economy. In fact, peripheries change over time and an economic growth or creativity-based (Hautala, 2015) shift can occur there, attracting new workers in advanced industries due to their unique assets. The authors adopt an evolutionary perspective on the periphery, following the recommendations of Eder (2019a) and Pugh and Dubois (2021). This means that countries that have historically represented the periphery can change their situation. The book addresses the question of how and why peripheries can move to more favourable positions.

The core–periphery concept is attractive because of its simplicity and its ability to categorise countries on a single scale. However, there are significant limitations to this conceptualisation. Firstly, the criteria for this categorisation are necessarily arbitrary and open to debate. The use of dichotomies or a three-tier model, such as core–semi-periphery–periphery, oversimplifies economic and social power dynamics. Secondly, the core–periphery concept focuses on hierarchical relations rather than complex network relations, including horizontal ones and the increasing interdependence of different actors. Contemporary economic development is driven by networks (Coe & Yeung, 2015), with large corporations constituting the nodes of economic networks. Zöllner et al. (2023, p. 364) argue that "peripheralisation and centralisation are relational processes with dynamic, overlapping and trans-scalar networks, challenging the traditional perspective of a nested core-periphery pattern as the organising principle of space." Thirdly, many analyses of the periphery focus on narrow sectors as defined by NACE, ignoring the broader context, including changes in the whole system, such as labour and tax regulations, policies and the business environment. Fourthly, there is the question of whether nation states are appropriate territorial units for analysing power and dependency relations. Some scholars suggest taking a regional or even local perspective when discussing core–periphery relations. Fifthly, the model under discussion often fails to acknowledge a dynamic interpretation that captures changes and their mechanisms (Bar-El & Parr, 2003; Zöllner et al., 2023). Despite profound changes in their characteristics and relations with the core, emerging economies are often still perceived as trapped in a peripheral position (Pavlínek, 2022a). Sixthly, the main fallacy of the core–periphery perspective is that it suggests that development is a process of imitating the characteristics and trajectories of the areas defined as the core. This excludes the catching-up of territories with different characteristics and development regimes (peripheries), since they cannot copy the model of the core, and it ignores the existence of different development paths, which also vary between the areas classified as the core. Moreover, development should not be seen as an approach to a predefined state, as this is a teleological explanation. Finally, the concept of core and periphery alone does not provide sufficient explanatory power, despite numerous attempts to explain the dominant role of the core and the dependent position of the periphery.

In summary, the traditional core–periphery concept is moderately adequate for explaining development processes that naturally change over time. However, we believe that the broader GPN paradigm, as outlined by Coe and Yeung (2015), has far greater explanatory power in interpreting contemporary production processes such as strategic coupling, territorial embeddedness and the network economy. Therefore, we have chosen to integrate the GPN perspective with certain aspects of the core–periphery model, particularly its dependency dimension.

Introducing industrial upgrading

According to some scholars, industrial upgrading can be a source of resilience, leading to a shift towards the core. This view of development is dynamic (Kurikka & Grillitsch, 2021). Micek et al. (2021, pp. 1–2) argue that "the evolutionary resilience perspective provides an interesting point of departure for analysing cases of companies (business enterprises) that have used crisis and economic shocks and/or structural changes in their industries for their development and an escape from the path-dependent lock-in." Conversely, limited resilience can lead to downgrading and trajectories of decline (Blažek et al., 2020). To understand the dynamic resilience perspective, it is important to first become familiar with the concept of industrial upgrading.

Industrial upgrading refers to the shift towards higher value-added products, processes and functions based on improvements in technology, knowledge and skills. In other words, upgrading leads to increased benefits and profits from participation in GPNs (Barrientos et al., 2011). The concept of industrial upgrading has been subject to serious misunderstandings and shortcomings (Ponte & Ewert, 2009; Blažek, 2016; Kumar & Beerepoot, 2021). A more nuanced perspective is needed when studying upgrading, which requires a focus on the specific perspectives of firms and inter-firm networks (Glückler & Panitz, 2016). We adopt a relational understanding of upgrading (Glückler & Panitz, 2016), which encompasses the upgrading of both companies and relational positions in GPNs. It is argued that industrial upgrading, like innovation, requires diversity and inclusion (Solheim, 2022) in both enterprises and networks.

a Types and dimensions of industrial upgrading

Industrial upgrading typically has two interrelated dimensions: **economic and social**. There is an interdependence between economic and social upgrading within the GPN, as noted by Barrientos et al. (2011). The high and low paths of development are associated with different employment conditions and labour market dynamics, including the role of long-term versus temporary workers, skills, remuneration and automation trends (Barrientos et al., 2011; Jürgens & Krzywdzinski, 2016). Social upgrading refers to the improvement of workers' entitlements as social actors, which enhances the quality of their employment (Barrientos et al., 2011). Improvements in the areas of adequate job creation, social protection, rights at work, social dialogue and gender equality can also be considered as social upgrading (Dünhaupt et al., 2022).

There are different claims about the relationship between economic and social upgrading. According to Barrientos et al. (2011), economic upgrading can lead to better job opportunities, such as the development of GPNs that facilitate changes in job characteristics. On the other hand, it is often argued that FDI-based development in the form of export platforms does not generate social benefits and does not improve the quality of life, as shown by the impact of the North American Free Trade Agreement (NAFTA) on the downgrading of labour and wage freezes in the Mexican automotive industry (Covarrubias, 2020). There is no social upgrading in the periphery if only local elites benefit. Teipen et al. (2022) show significant national differences in upgrading processes across countries in the Global South and find that economic upgrading does not always lead to social upgrading. Dünhaupt et al. (2022, p. 21) argue that "social upgrading in a national economy is only possible to a limited extent if it is not linked with economic upgrading."

The literature review identifies five dimensions of industrial (economic) upgrading, depending on the subject of upgrading processes, and six elements of social upgrading (Figure 1.1).

There are two ways to upgrade the entire value chain. Firstly, **GPNs can be upgraded** through innovation systems and trade policies. This can also be achieved by occupying higher value niches in GVCs (Humphrey & Schmitz, 2002; Gereffi, 2019) and GPNs. Using the example of Škoda under VW control, Blažek (2016) argues that there can be a gradual shift of the entire GPN towards more demanding market segments. Secondly, the entire **industrial structure** can be upgraded. Research has extensively documented the situation in Chinese cities (Dai et al., 2022; Guan et al., 2022; Qiu et al., 2023). For example, Guan et al. (2022) use an industrial structure hierarchy coefficient based on the share of a given industry in a region in regional GDP. They also use a weighted value of the product of the proportional relationship between industries and the labour productivity of each industry. Industrial structure upgrading refers to the improvement of industrial structures in specific territories, such as the country in this case. The **path upgrading** of a particular industry at the national level can also be studied, as discussed by Grillitsch et al. (2018) and Blažek et al. (2020) in their discussion of path upgrading and downgrading processes. It is important to note that this dimension of upgrading is not simply the sum of the upgrading processes of individual firms. Fourthly, it is not only enterprises and GPNs that can be upgraded. **Clusters** can also be

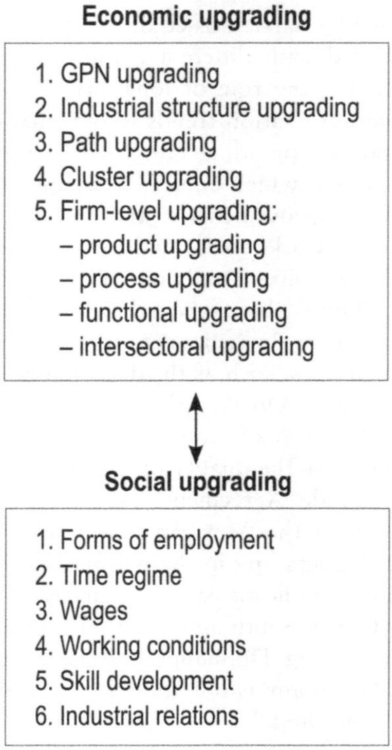

Figure 1.1 Types and dimensions of economic and social upgrading
Source: authors' elaboration.

upgraded with the support of knowledge institutions and entire regional and national innovation systems (Naqvi & Memon, 2018). Fifthly, GPNs, industrial structures, specific industries and clusters undergo upgrading when individual companies make significant advances in their products, processes and functions. Discussions of **firm-level upgrading** often focus on the automotive industry, as seen in Adăscăliței and Guga's (2020) discussion of Renault's strategy in Romania. However, there are also papers on the aviation sector, such as the contribution by Blažek et al. (2021). This book examines upgrading from the perspective of both individual companies and industrial structures.

Studies of firm upgrading typically distinguish four types of upgrading (Humphrey & Schmitz, 2002; Gibbon & Ponte, 2005): product, process, functional and intersectoral upgrading. **Product upgrading** involves the creation of more advanced and higher-quality products. **Process upgrading** implies the adoption of improved production systems, new technologies and/or modern management practices (Pickles et al., 2006; Kumar & Beerepoot, 2021). The case of the Renault factory in Romania highlights the significant impact of investments in technology and machinery that simultaneously reduce production costs and improve product quality (Jipa-Muşat & Prevezer, 2023). In modern management, Industry 4.0 is seen as an opportunity for industrial upgrading (Lee et al., 2020). The most studied types of upgrading are product upgrading and process upgrading (Blažek, 2016).

The prevalence of **functional upgrading**, understood as the acquisition of new functions, such as R&D, or tasks to increase the overall skill content of activities (see Humphrey & Schmitz, 2002), is debatable (Blažek, 2016). This type of upgrading can be hindered by "buyers eager to protect their core competence as well as by resource requirements and associated risks" (Blažek 2016, p. 853; Humphrey & Schmitz, 2004). However, Blažek (2016, p. 865) identifies five subtypes of functional upgrading:

> (i) penetration among existing higher-tier suppliers; (ii) abandoning some lower value-added activities; (iii) voluntary transfer of some higher-level functions from a higher-tier supplier; (iv) development of a new product that creates a new market; and (v) upgrading through the acquisition of a technological firm or a higher-tier supplier.

The authors of the book adopt a narrower interpretation of the functional upgrading of foreign companies, as outlined by Jipa-Muşat and Prevezer (2023), which involves the establishment of R&D units and shared service centres.

The fourth type of industrial upgrading is **intersectoral upgrading**. This occurs when a firm diversifies or moves to a new sector within a given value chain, either horizontally or vertically, based on its technological or product competencies. This concept is discussed in the case of Taiwanese manufacturing in the 1990s by Humphrey and Schmitz (2002), and further explained by Pickles et al. (2016). Intersectoral upgrading happens when a firm changes its GPN and decides to manufacture for another sector, or even to make final products. It is assumed that all four types of upgrading should allow firms to capture higher value. However, it is important to note that these types of upgrading can sometimes be difficult to distinguish. For example, process and product upgrading may be interlinked, as new processes may generate new products (Ponte & Ewert, 2009; Blažek, 2016).

In certain research contexts, industrial upgrading can have a narrow interpretation, particularly in discussions of structural transformation processes such as reindustrialisation. Capello and Cerisola (2023, p. 2) state that "reindustrialisation takes place by reinforcing the pre-existing specialised industrial structure through an upgrading strategy, as firms adapt to new conditions based on their established practices." Industrial upgrading is also viewed differently by some economists, who distinguish four dimensions: learning, quality upgrading, technology adoption and product innovation (Verhoogen, 2023).

Blažek (2016) identifies additional types of upgrading, the most prominent of which is interchain upgrading, which represents a shift of suppliers to another GPN serving an upmarket segment. Instead of (or in addition to) offering low-value supplies to buyers specialising in serving lower market segments, "the producer might succeed in supplying the other GPN that enjoys a more favourable position in the market" (Blažek, 2016, p. 854). This phenomenon occurs in the automotive industry, as described by Glogar (2013) and cited by Blažek (2016), when the supplier expands its supplies to various high-end car manufacturers.

b Determinants of industrial upgrading

Industrial upgrading, particularly at the firm level, is influenced by various factors such as the specialisation, size and ownership of the enterprise, as well as its network centrality in GPNs and the specific characteristics of the region. The authors suggest that these determinants can be divided into three groups: firm-level, network-related and territorial factors (see Table 1.1). The book focuses primarily on the firm-level dimension, with Chapter 6 dealing with territorial

Table 1.1 Determinants of industrial upgrading of enterprises

Determinant of industrial upgrading	*References*
Firm-level dimension	
Tier (lead firms, Tier-1, -2, -3 etc., firms outside GPNs)	Molnar et al. (2020); Blažek et al. (2021); Blažek & Lypianin (2022); Blažek & Holická (2022)
Specialisation	Blažek & Lypianin (2022)
Size of company based on employment/ revenues/value added	Éltető et al. (2015); Molnar et al. (2020); Blažek et al. (2021); Blažek & Lypianin (2022); Blažek & Holická (2022)
Ownership/owner strategy	Éltető et al. (2015); Blažek et al. (2021)
Chain diversification	Blažek et al. (2021)
Access to end market	Blažek & Holická (2022)
Network dimension	
Knowledge spillovers	Humphrey & Schmitz (2002); Grodzicki (2018)
Rising quality standards	Blomström & Kokko (1998)
Thickness of regional and national innovation systems	Szalavetz (2017); Naqvi & Memon (2018)
Density of network structures	Naqvi & Memon (2018)
Regional capabilities	
Localised capabilities (tangible and intangible regional assets)	Fortwengel (2011); Liu (2017); Pipkin & Fuentes (2017)
Institutional factors (e.g. policy framework)	Pipkin & Fuentes (2017); Molnar et al. (2020); Jipa-Muşat & Prevezer (2023)
Support of knowledge institutions	Naqvi & Memon (2018)

Source: authors' elaboration.

characteristics. Economists identify three groups of drivers of upgrading: output-side drivers (the impact of exporting and local TNC demand on upgrading outcomes; the impact of competition in output markets), input-side drivers (the role of imported inputs and other factors that influence the prices and availability of domestic inputs), and know-how drivers (in particular, the motivation of entrepreneurs that influences (or not) their efforts to maximise profits) (Verhoogen, 2023).

Blažek and Lypianin (2022) investigated the determinants of upgrading Czech electro-engineering suppliers in GPNs at the **firm level**. They tested whether tier, ownership, size, specialisation and regional capabilities influenced the economic performance of companies. The key determinants appear to be ownership and tier. Blažek and Holická (2022) also tested similar variables for over 250 Czech companies. The study revealed that domestic firms tend to capture a larger share of value as compared to foreign enterprises. This is due to their increased spending on capital investments and R&D.

Blažek et al. (2021) attempted to combine upgrading with the notions of **value creation** and **value capture** (Coe & Yeung, 2015). The study confirmed that both value creation and value capture tend to be lower for foreign-owned firms in the Czech aerospace industry. Foreign subsidiaries may receive financial support from their parent companies, as explained by Blažek et al. (2021). This applies to both original equipment manufacturers (OEMs) and Tier-1 suppliers. Blažek et al. (2021) also highlighted the importance of the intensity of involvement in different GPNs. Chain diversification can lead to higher value capture, while firms that are predominantly focused on a single sector may be less able to create and capture value, as confirmed by Blažek and Holická's (2022) findings in the automotive sector.

There are also **network-related** determinants of industrial upgrading. Naqvi and Memon (2018) argue that the thickness of the regional innovation system and the density of the network structure in which the firm is involved affect the level of upgrading. Various territorial characteristics have been identified as factors that either facilitate or hinder upgrading processes (Table 1.1). These determinants differ not only between countries but also between regions. Old industrial regions and towns are of particular interest in this context, as they are often seen as destined for economic decline due to deindustrialisation and a lock-in with traditional economic activities. Much has been written on the limited prospects for their upgrading, diversification into technologically related industries and/or creation of new development paths based on the Western European experience. However, there is much less literature on this topic in Central Europe, where the situation may be different.

The authors argue that there are localised capabilities, which are formed by tangible and intangible assets embedded in a particular territory (Domański & Gwosdz, 2009). These capabilities include local skills, industrial culture, reliability of suppliers and local authorities, which can influence economic upgrading (Pipkin & Fuentes, 2017; Molnar et al., 2020; Jipa-Muşat & Prevezer, 2023).

They can be divided into generic and specialised capabilities (Ceci & Masini, 2011).

The prevailing outlook on economic upgrading opportunities in Central European countries is generally pessimistic. The contribution of TNCs to economic upgrading and innovation generation is often presented as minimal, especially in the case of Hungary (Éltető et al., 2015; Gál & Lux, 2022; Otsuka et al., 2023). According to Otsuka et al. (2023), Hungarian GPNs do not significantly facilitate knowledge spillovers due to TNCs' strategy of locating low-cost production there, limited R&D-related activities (focused on R&D support rather than R&D itself) and unwillingness to share knowledge outside the GPNs. Furthermore, Szalavetz (2017) argues that the upgrading of TNCs' manufacturing subsidiaries does not lead to additional value capture for the upgraded actors. Pavlínek and Ženka (2011) share similar views on the dominance of foreign firms and the selective nature of upgrading in the Czech automotive industry. The relationship between foreign subsidiaries and domestic firms remains highly asymmetric, with weak and dependent supplier linkages. This raises questions about the long-term positive effects of large-scale automotive FDI in Czechia (Pavlínek, 2018). Central Europe is often seen as an integrated periphery, characterised by weak linkages between foreign firms and the national economy, resulting in lower value capture. What is perceived as a strategy in response to rising labour costs is the relocation of large foreign investors out of the country (see the case of the Dacia/Renault plant discussed by Adăscăliței & Guga, 2020).

c Measures of industrial upgrading

There are few widely accepted measures of upgrading at the enterprise level. Some variables, particularly those related to social upgrading, are less easy to quantify, such as freedom of association, collective bargaining rights, voice and empowerment (Barrientos et al., 2011). Furthermore, Blažek et al. (2021) stress that distinguishing between indicators that include value creation and those that include value capture is a difficult task (Shin et al., 2012; Pavlínek & Ženka, 2016), as some variables may fall into both categories. Smith (2016) uses measures that reveal the potential to create applied value as a proxy for "value created", whereas variables that demonstrate the ability to acquire value that can be exchanged are used as a proxy for "value capture". Blažek et al. (2021, p. 2104) provide the simplest definition of "value capture" as the value retained by firms or their units located in a given territory. This value is retained within a given country.

Table 1.2 provides an overview of the indicators of firm-level industrial upgrading used by different authors. In addition, Grodzicki and Geodecki (2016) and Lee et al. (2021) have proposed measures of upgrading at the country level: the share of domestic or foreign value added in exports, export orientation (re-exported intermediate imports) and the international competitiveness of intermediate inputs (domestic value added embodied in foreign exports).

Table 1.2 Measures of firm-level industrial upgrading

Proxy of industrial upgrading	*References*
Value created	
Turnover per employee	Pavlínek & Ženka (2011)
Profitability (return on assets; ROA)	Blažek et al. (2021)
Monthly wages and salaries per employee	Pavlínek & Ženka (2011); Molnar et al. (2020); Blažek & Lypianin (2022)
Share of value added in total revenues	Pavlínek & Ženka (2011); Blažek et al. (2021); Blažek & Lypianin (2022)
Capital productivity (share of value added in tangible assets)	Pavlínek & Ženka (2011)
R&D intensity (share of total R&D expenditures in value added; share of R&D employment in total employment)	Pavlínek & Ženka (2011)
Increase of value and change in the structure of exports towards higher value-added products	Pavlínek et al. (2009); Pavlínek & Ženka (2011); Tian et al. (2019)
Change in employment of manual and non-manual workers	Molnar et al. (2020)
Skill intensity of employment (the share of high-skilled labour (measured in hours worked) in total employment)	Tian et al. (2019)
Average gross earnings relative to the national industry and local economy average	Molnar et al. (2020)
Share of temporary workers	Barrientos et al. (2011)
Share of female supervisors	Barrientos et al. (2011)
Share of trade union members in the workforce	Barrientos et al. (2011)
Automation and robotisation level	Adăscăliței & Guga (2020)
Value capture	
Labour intensity (personnel cost : turnover ratio; **share of wages and salaries in total revenues**)	Blažek et al. (2021); Blažek & Lypianin (2022)
Profit : turnover ratio (return on revenue; ROR)	Blažek & Lypianin (2022)
Labour productivity (gross value added per employee)	Pavlínek & Ženka (2011); Tian et al. (2019); Adăscăliței & Guga (2020); Blažek & Lypianin (2022)
Factor productivity (average value added per employee; value added per unit of tangible assets)	Pavlínek & Ženka (2011)
Capital intensity of production (**depreciation in relation to total revenues**)	Pavlínek & Ženka (2016); Blažek et al. (2021)

Proxy of industrial upgrading	*References*
Capital intensity (tangible assets per employee)	Pavlínek & Ženka (2011)

Source: authors' elaboration.

Note: variables used in the book are shown **in bold.**

Pavlínek and Ženka (2016) and Blažek et al. (2021) provide a comprehensive overview of indicators of firm performance, while linking them to upgrading activities. They treat the annual growth rate of total revenues, value added in relation to total revenues, and return on assets (ROA) as proxies for the value created in industrial upgrading. Wages and depreciation as a percentage of total revenues were considered as measures of value capture. Among these variables, Blažek et al. (2021) found that ROA had insignificant correlations. Moreover, the explanatory power of ROA may be questionable, as in the case of the Czech aerospace industry, where third-tier domestic suppliers surprisingly turned out to be the most profitable companies.

A summary of indicators of industrial upgrading is presented by Pavlínek and Ženka (2011). They distinguish five primary indicators of industrial upgrading: revenues per employee, average gross value added per employee and gross value added per unit of tangible assets, wages and salaries per employee and R&D expenditure as a share of total value added; and five secondary indicators: tangible assets per employee, value added as a share of revenues, gross value added per employee, gross value added divided by tangible assets and R&D employment as a share of total employment.

The limited acceptance of proxies for upgrading stems from different approaches to the issue. Tian et al. (2019) provide an interesting perspective on industrial upgrading at multiple levels (country, GPN and industry) by examining a range of indicators, including labour productivity growth (value added per unit of labour) and the increase in the skill intensity of employment (the share of hours worked by high-skilled workers in total employment). Özatağan (2011) conducted interviews with representatives of automotive suppliers in Bursa, Türkiye, to investigate the extent to which firms (i) introduce process improvements that increase production speed, reduce cost-price ratio, improve delivery speed and improve product quality; (ii) innovate work systems; and (iii) introduce human resource management/organisational systems and new technologies. She also analysed product upgrading – the extent to which firms develop or modify new products and introduce new designs – and functional upgrading – the intensity of marketing and branding activities.

The authors of the book have selected three main indicators of economic upgrading to be used in the statistical descriptive analysis. Firstly, the share of value added in total revenues is used as a proxy for value creation and knowledge intensity. This variable reflects the position of the company within GPNs. Secondly, the share of wages and salaries in total revenues serves as a measure of labour intensity and reflects the degree of value capture. Thirdly, depreciation as a percentage of total revenues is used as a measure of the capital intensity of production, illustrating the level of investment.

Conclusions

Our aim is not to provide a comprehensive review of the literature on economic and social peripheries, as has recently been done by Pugh and Dubois (2021) and Eder (2019b). Rather than extending the notion of peripheries to all peripheral, mountainous, rural, border (Kühn, 2015) or suburban and backward places (Rodríguez-Pose, 2018), we aim to focus on economic peripheries at the country level. We understand them as countries with a low level of economic development, low density of firms, limited diversity of products and services, and specialisation in low value-added activities, with a consequent dependence on core countries, weak economic power and low territorial embeddedness of dominant foreign companies. The integrated peripheries have the above characteristics of classical peripheries and are close to the end markets.

It is argued that there is a need to go beyond the simple core–periphery duality in explaining the changing position of countries and regions in GPNs. Dichotomies tend to reflect economic differences between countries, but peripheral status may differ for specific industries. Even a tripartite distinction between core, semi-periphery and integrated periphery (Mordue & Sweeney, 2020) does not reflect the real complexities. The authors of this book therefore argue for a dynamic core–periphery continuum.

The authors distinguish five dimensions of economic (industrial) upgrading, namely GPN, industrial structure, cluster, pathway and firm-level upgrading. Upgrading at the firm level focuses on four of its types, namely product, process, functional and intersectoral upgrading (Humphrey & Schmitz, 2002). There is also social upgrading, with six elements examined: the development of more stable forms of employment and socially acceptable working time arrangements, the pursuit of higher wages and better working conditions, skills development and improved industrial relations. The literature review has shown that upgrading is shaped by the firm's position in supply chains (tier) and ownership, although in some cases domestic companies may capture more value than foreign enterprises. Value creation is proxied by the share of value added in total sales, whereas value capture is proxied by the share of wages in total revenues and the amount of depreciation in relation to total revenues.

References

Adăscăliței, D., & Guga, Ş. (2020). Tensions in the periphery: Dependence and the trajectory of a low-cost productive model in the Central and Eastern European automotive industry. *European Urban and Regional Studies*, 27(1), 18–34. doi:10.1177/0969776418795205.

Arrighi, G., & Drangel, J. (1986). The stratification of the world-economy: An exploration of the semiperipheral zone. *Review (Fernand Braudel Center)*, 10(1), 9–74. https://www.jstor.org/stable/40241047.

Bar-El, R., & Parr, J.B. (2003). Overreliance on the core–periphery model? The case of Israel. *Environment and Planning C: Government and Policy*, 21(3), 353–369.

Barrientos, S., Gereffi, G., & Rossi, A. (2011). Economic and social upgrading in global production networks: A new paradigm for a changing world. *International Labour Review*, 150(3–4), 319–340.

Barry, F. (2004). Enlargement and the EU periphery: Introduction. *The World Economy*, 27(6), 753–759. doi:10.1111/twec.2004.27.issue-6.

Blažek, J. (2016). Towards a typology of repositioning strategies of GVC/GPN suppliers: The case of functional upgrading and downgrading. *Journal of Economic Geography*, 16(4), 849–869. doi:10.1093/jeg/lbv044.

Blažek, J., Bělohradský, A., & Holická, Z. (2021). The role of tier, ownership, and size of companies in value creation and capture. *European Planning Studies*, 29(11), 2101–2120. doi:10.1080/09654313.2021.1889991.

Blažek, J., & Holická, Z. (2022). Value capture by companies of different ownership, tier, size, and distance to market: A cross-sectoral analysis. *Area*, 54(4), 655–665. doi:10.1111/area.12819.

Blažek, J., Květoň, V., Baumgartinger-Seiringer, S., & Trippl, M. (2020). The dark side of regional industrial path development: Towards a typology of trajectories of decline. *European Planning Studies*, 28(8), 1455–1473. doi:10.1080/09654313.2019.1685466.

Blažek, J., & Lypianin, A. (2022). What drives the economic performance of suppliers in global value chains/global production networks – tier, ownership, size, specialization, or region? *Norsk Geografisk Tidsskrift - Norwegian Journal of Geography*, 76(5), 255–269. doi:10.1080/00291951.2022.2150303.

Blomström, M., & Kokko, A. (1998). Multinational corporations and spillovers. *Journal of Economic Surveys*, 12(2), 1–31.

Cabada, L. (2020). Central Europe between the West and East: Independent region, the bridge, buffer zone, or 'eternal' semi-periphery? *Politics in Central Europe*, 16(2), 419–432. doi:10.2478/pce-2020-0018.

Cairó-i-Céspedes, G., & Palacios Cívico, J.C. (2022). Beyond core and periphery: The role of the semi-periphery in global capitalism. *Third World Quarterly*, 43(8), 1950–1969. doi:10.1080/01436597.2022.2079488.

Capello, R., & Cerisola, S. (2023). Regional reindustrialization patterns and productivity growth in Europe. *Regional Studies*, 57(1), 1–12. doi:10.1080/00343404.2022.2050894.

Carrillo, J. (2004). Transnational strategies and regional development: The case of GM and Delphi in Mexico. *Industry and Innovation*, 11(1–2), 127–153. doi:10.1080/1366271042000200484.

Ceci, F., & Masini, A. (2011). Balancing specialized and generic capabilities in the provision of integrated solutions. *Industrial and Corporate Change*, 20(1), 91–131. doi:10.1093/icc/dtq069.

Coe, N.M., Dicken, P., & Hess, M. (2008). Global production networks: Realizing the potential. *Journal of Economic Geography*, 8(3), 271–295.

Coe, N.M., Hess, M., Yeung, H.W.-c., Dicken, P., & Henderson, J. (2004). Globalizing regional development: A global production networks perspective. *Transactions of the Institute of British Geographers*, 29(4), 468–484.

Coe, N.M., & Lee, Y.-S. (2013). 'We've learnt how to be local': The deepening territorial embeddedness of Samsung–Tesco in South Korea. *Journal of Economic Geography*, 13(2), 327–356. doi:10.1093/jeg/lbs057.

Coe, N.M., & Yeung, H.W.-c. (2015). *Global production networks: Theorizing economic development in an interconnected world*. Oxford: Oxford University Press.

Covarrubias, A. (2020). The boom of the Mexican automotive industry: From NAFTA to USMCA. In A. Covarrubias & S. Ramirez (Eds.), *New frontiers of the automobile industry. Exploring geographies, technology, and institutional challenges* (pp. 323–348). Cham: Palgrave Macmillan.

Dai, S., Zhang, W., Wang, Y., & Wang, G. (2022). Examining the impact of regional development policy on industrial structure upgrading: Quasi-experimental evidence from China. *International Journal of Environmental Research and Public Health*, 19 (9), 5042. doi:10.3390/ijerph19095042.

Dawley, S. (2011). Transnational corporations and local and regional development. In A. Pike, A. Rodríguez-Pose, & J. Tomaney (Eds.), *Handbook of local and regional development* (pp. 394–412). Abingdon and New York: Routledge.

De Vivo, P., & Rinaldi, C. (2022). Reacting to the 2008 crisis: Competitiveness performances of Southern Italy and CEE regions. *Cambridge Journal of Regions, Economy and Society*, 15(1), 117–139. doi:10.1093/cjres/rsab035.

Domański, B., & Gwosdz, K. (2009). Toward a more embedded production system? Automotive supply networks and localized capabilities in Poland. *Growth and Change*, 40(3), 452–482.

Dos Santos, T. (1970). The structure of dependence. *The American Economic Review*, 60 (2), 231–236.

Drahokoupil, J. (2009). *Globalization and the state in Central and Eastern Europe: The politics of foreign direct investment*. London: Routledge.

Dubownik, A., Churski, P., Adamiak, C., & Szyda, B. (2022). Cohesion policy in the struggle against the marginalization of the inner peripheries: Polish experience and recommendations. In P.K. Pradhan & W. Leimgruber (Eds.), *Nature, society, and marginality. Perspectives on geographical marginality*, vol. 8 (pp. 271–290). Cham: Springer. doi:10.1007/978-3-031-21325-0_18.

Dünhaupt, P., Herr, H., Mehl, F., & Teipen, Ch. (2022). Introduction: Governance, rent-seeking and upgrading in global value chains. In Ch. Teipe, P. Dünhaupt, H. Herr, & F. Mehl (Eds.), *Economic and social upgrading in global value chains. Comparative analyses, macroeconomic effects, the role of institutions and strategies for the Global South* (pp. 1–31). Cham: Palgrave Macmillan.

Eder, J. (2019a). Innovation in the periphery: A critical survey and research agenda. *International Regional Science Review*, 42(2), 119–146. doi:10.1177/0160017618764279.

Eder, J. (2019b). Peripheralization and knowledge bases in Austria: Towards a new regional typology. *European Planning Studies*, 27(1), 42–67. doi:10.1080/09654313.2018.1541966.

Éltető, A., Magasházi, A., Szalavetz, A., & Túry, G. (2015). Upgrading of Hungarian subsidiaries in machinery and automotive global value chains. IWE Working Paper 217. Budapest: Institute of World Economics – Centre for Economic and Regional Studies.

Fortwengel, J. (2011). Upgrading through integration? The case of the Central Eastern European automotive industry. *Transcience Journal*, 2(1), 1–25.

Friedmann, J. (1972). A general theory of polarized development. In N.M. Hansen (Ed.), *Growth centers in regional economic development* (pp. 82–107). New York: The Free Press.

Fröbel, F., Heinrichs, J., & Kreye, O. (1980). *The new international division of labor*. New York: Cambridge University Press.

Gál, Z., & Lux, G. (2022). FDI-based regional development in Central and Eastern Europe: A review and an agenda. *Tér és Társadalom*, 36(3), 68–98. doi:10.17649/TET.36.3.3439.

Gereffi, G. (1999). International trade and industrial upgrading in the apparel commodity chain. *Journal of International Economics*, 48(1), 37–70.

Gereffi, G. (2014). The governance of global value chains. *Review of International Political Economy*, 12(1), 78–104.

Gereffi, G. (2019). Economic upgrading in global value chains. In S. Ponte, G. Gereffi, & G. Raj-Reichert (Eds.), *Handbook on global value chains* (pp. 240–254). Cheltenham: Edward Elgar Publishing. doi:10.4337/9781788113779.00022.

Ghosh, B.N. (2001). *Dependency theory revisited*. Routledge Revivals. London: Routledge. doi:10.4324/9781315187389.

Gibbon, P., & Ponte, S. (2005). *Trading down: Africa, value chains, and the global economy*. Philadelphia, PA: Temple University Press.

Glogar, L. (2013). *Position of Czech automotive firms in global value chains*. Presentation at the workshop "Global Production Networks: Theory and Practice", South Moravian Innovation Centre, Brno, June 2013.

Glückler, J., & Panitz, R. (2016). Relational upgrading in global value networks. *Journal of Economic Geography*, 16(6), 1161–1185.

Grabher, G. (1993). Rediscovering the social in the economics of interfirm relations. In G. Grabher (Ed.), *The embedded firm* (pp. 1–31). London: Routledge.

Grillitsch, M., Asheim, B., & Trippl, M. (2018). Unrelated knowledge combinations: The unexplored potential for regional industrial path development. *Cambridge Journal of Regions, Economy and Society*, 11(2), 257–274. doi:10.1093/cjres/rsy012.

Grodzicki, M. (2018). *Konwergencja w warunkach integracji gospodarczej. Grupa Wyszehradzka w globalnych łańcuchach wartości*. Kraków: Wydawnictwo Uniwersytetu Jagiellońskiego.

Grodzicki, M., & Geodecki, T. (2016). New dimensions of core-periphery relations in an economically integrated Europe: The role of global value chains. *Eastern European Economics*, 54(5), 377–404. doi:10.1080/00128775.2016.1201426.

Guan, H., Guo, B., & Zhang, J. (2022). Study on the impact of the digital economy on the upgrading of industrial structures. Empirical analysis based on cities in China. *Sustainability*, 14(18), 11378. doi:10.3390/su141811378.

Hautala, J. (2015). Interaction in the artistic knowledge creation process: The case of artists in Finnish Lapland. *Geoforum*, 65, 351–362.

Humphrey, J., Lecler, Y., & Salerno, M.S. (2000). Introduction. In J. Humphrey, Y. Lecler, & M.S. Salerno (Eds.), *Global strategies and local realities: The auto industry in emerging markets* (pp. 1–15). London: Palgrave Macmillan. doi:10.1057/9780333977712_6.

Humphrey, J., & Schmitz, H. (2002). How does insertion in global value chains affect upgrading in industrial clusters? *Regional Studies*, 36(9), 1017–1027.

Humphrey, J., & Schmitz, H. (2004). Chain governance and upgrading: Taking stock. In H. Schmitz (Ed.), *Local enterprises in the global economy: Issues of governance and upgrading* (pp. 349–381). Cheltenham: Edward Elgar.

Jipa-Muşat, I., & Prevezer, M. (2023). Trajectories of value capture, strategic coupling and labour regime reconfiguration: Coal mining, automotives and business services in post-socialist Romania. *European Urban and Regional Studies*, 30(4), 465–484. doi:10.1177/09697764231165200.

Jones, C., & Munday, M. (2020). Capital ownership, innovation and regional development policy in the economic periphery: An energy industry case. *Local Economy*, 35 (6), 545–565.

Jürgens, U., & Krzywdzinski, M. (2016). *New worlds of work: Varieties of work in car factories in the BRIC countries*. Oxford: Oxford University Press.

Kühn, M. (2015). Peripheralization: Theoretical concepts explaining socio-spatial inequalities. *European Planning Studies*, 23(2), 367–378. doi:10.1080/09654313.2013.862518.

Kumar, R., & Beerepoot, N. (2021). Matching global service standards—the role of intermediaries in economic upgrading of support-service firms in global production networks. *Journal of Economic Geography*, 21(6), 899–923. doi:10.1093/jeg/lbaa039.

Kurikka, H., & Grillitsch, M. (2021). Resilience in the periphery: What an agency perspective can bring to the table. In R. Wink (Ed.), *Economic resilience in regions and organizations* (pp. 147–171). Wiesbaden: Springer.

Lampón, J.F., Lago-Peñas, S., & Cabanelas, P. (2016). Can the periphery achieve core? The case of the automobile components industry in Spain. *Papers in Regional Science*, 95(3), 595–612. doi:10.1111/pirs.12146.

Layan, J.B. (2000). The integration of peripheral markets: A comparison of Spain and Mexico. In J. Humphrey, Y. Lecler, & M.S. Salerno (Eds.), *Global strategies and local realities: The auto industry in emerging markets* (pp. 122–148). London: Palgrave Macmillan. doi:10.1057/9780333977712_6.

Lee, K., Malerba, F., & Primi, A. (2020). The fourth industrial revolution, changing global value chains and industrial upgrading in emerging economies. *Journal of Economic Policy Reform*, 23(4), 359–370. doi:10.1080/17487870.2020.1735386.

Lee, K., Qu, D., & Mao, Z. (2021). Global value chains, industrial policy, and industrial upgrading: Automotive sectors in Malaysia, Thailand, and China in comparison with Korea. *The European Journal of Development Research*, 33(2), 275–303. doi:10.1057/s41287-020-00354-0.

Lehoczki, B. (2022). Semi-periphery regionalisms in a changing world order: The case of Mercosur and Visegrad Group. *Third World Quarterly*, 43(4), 779–796. doi:10.1080/01436597.2021.2024757.

Liu, Y. (2017). The dynamics of local upgrading in globalizing latecomer regions: A geographical analysis. *Regional Studies*, 51(6), 880–893.

Micek, G., Guzik, R., Gwosdz, K., & Domański, B. (2021). Newcomers from the periphery: The international expansion of Polish automotive companies. *Energies*, 14(9), 2617. doi:10.3390/en14092617.

Molnar, E., Kozma, G., Meszarosi, M., & Kiss, E. (2020). Upgrading and the geography of the Hungarian automotive industry in the context of the fourth industrial revolution. *Hungarian Geographical Bulletin*, 69(2), 137–155. doi:10.15201/hungeobull.69.2.4.

Mordue, G., & Sweeney, B. (2020). Neither core nor periphery: The search for competitive advantage in the automotive semi-periphery. *Growth and Change*, 51(1), 34–57. doi:10.1111/grow.12354.

Mudambi, R., & Santangelo, G. (2016). From shallow resource pools to emerging clusters: The role of multinational enterprise subsidiaries in peripheral areas. *Regional Studies*, 50(12), 1965–1979. doi:10.1080/00343404.2014.985199.

Naqvi, I.B., & Memon, Z.A. (2018). Upgrading of developing countries industrial clusters' firms: Conceptual-theoretical framework. *International Journal of Knowledge-Based Development*, 9(4), 420–440.

Oinas, P. (1997). On the socio-spatial embeddedness of business firms. *Erdkunde*, 51(1), 23–32.

Otsuka, K., Natsuda, K., & Csonka, L. (2023). Global value chains and knowledge spillover to local economy in Visegrad 4 countries. *Society and Economy*, 45(3), 293–312. doi:10.1556/204.2023.00010.

Özatağan, G. (2011). Shifts in value chain governance and upgrading in the European periphery of automotive production: Evidence from Bursa, Turkey. *Environment and Planning A: Economy and Space*, 43(4), 885–903. doi:10.1068/a43428.

Pavlínek, P. (2002). Transformation of the Central and East European passenger car industry: Selective peripheral integration through foreign direct investment. *Environment and Planning A*, 34(9), 1685–1709. doi:10.1068/a34263.

Pavlínek, P. (2016). Whose success? The state–foreign capital nexus and the development of the automotive industry in Slovakia. *European Urban and Regional Studies*, 23(4), 571–593. doi:10.1177/0969776414557965.

Pavlínek, P. (2018). Global production networks, foreign direct investment, and supplier linkages in the integrated peripheries of the automotive industry. *Economic Geography*, 94(2), 141–165. doi:10.1080/00130095.2017.1393313.

Pavlínek, P. (2020). Restructuring and internationalization of the European automotive industry. *Journal of Economic Geography*, 20(2), 509–541.

Pavlínek, P. (2022a). Relative positions of countries in the core-periphery structure of the European automotive industry. *European Urban and Regional Studies*, 29(1), 59–84. doi:10.1177/09697764211021882.

Pavlínek, P. (2022b). Revisiting economic geography and foreign direct investment in less developed regions. *Geography Compass*, 16(4), e12617. doi:10.1111/gec3.12617.

Pavlínek, P. (2023). Transition of the automotive industry towards electric vehicle production in the East European integrated periphery. *Empirica*, 50(1), 35–73. doi:10.1007/s10663-022-09554-9.

Pavlínek, P., Domański, B., & Guzik, R. (2009). Industrial upgrading through foreign direct investment in Central European automotive manufacturing. *European Urban and Regional Studies*, 16(1), 43–63. doi:10.1177/0969776408098932.

Pavlínek, P., & Ženka, J. (2011). Upgrading in the automotive industry: Firm-level evidence from Central Europe. *Journal of Economic Geography*, 11(3), 559–586. doi:10.1093/jeg/lbq023.

Pavlínek, P., & Ženka, J. (2016). Value creation and value capture in the automotive industry: Empirical evidence from Czechia. *Environment and Planning A*, 48(5), 937–959.

Pavlínek, P., & Žížalová, P. (2016). Linkages and spillovers in global production networks: Firm-level analysis of the Czech automotive industry. *Journal of Economic Geography*, 16(2), 331–363.

Pawłuszko, T. (2023). Peripherality of the CEE region. In R. Zięba (Ed.), *Politics and security of Central and Eastern Europe. Contemporary challenges* (pp. 11–32). Cham: Springer.

Peet, R., & Hartwick, E. (2015). *Theories of development: Contentions, arguments, alternatives*. New York: Guilford Publications.

Pickles, J., Smith, A., Begg, R., Buček, M., & Roukova, P. (2016). *Articulations of capital: Global production networks and regional transformations*. Chichester: John Wiley & Sons.

Pickles, J., Smith, A., Bucek, M., Roukova, P., & Begg, R. (2006). Upgrading, changing competitive pressures, and diverse practices in the East and Central European apparel industry. *Environment and Planning A*, 38(12), 2305–2324.

Pike, A., Rodríguez-Pose, A., & Tomaney, J. (2017). Shifting horizons in local and regional development. *Regional Studies*, 51(1), 46–57.

Pipkin, S., & Fuentes, A. (2017). Spurred to upgrade: A review of triggers and consequences of industrial upgrading in the global value chain literature. *World Development*, 98, 536–554.

Ponte, S., & Ewert, J. (2009). Which way is "up" in upgrading? Trajectories of change in the value chain for South African wine. *World Development*, 37(10), 1637–1650.

Pugh, R., & Dubois, A. (2021). Peripheries within economic geography: Four "problems" and the road ahead of us. *Journal of Rural Studies*, 87, 267–275. doi:10.1016/j.jrurstud.2021.09.007.

Qiu, Y., Wang, H., & Wu, J. (2023). Impact of industrial structure upgrading on green innovation: Evidence from Chinese cities. *Environmental Science and Pollution Research*, 30(2), 3887–3900. doi:10.1007/s11356-022-22162-1.

Rodríguez-Pose, A. (2018). The revenge of the places that don't matter. *Cambridge Journal of Regions, Economy and Society*, 11(1), 189–209. doi:10.1093/cjres/rsx024.

Rokkan, S., & Urwin, D. (1983). *Economy, territory, identity: Politics of West European peripheries*. London: Sage.

Shin, N., Kraemer, K., & Dedrick, L. (2012). Value capture in the global electronics industry: Empirical evidence for the "smiling curve" concept. *Industry and Innovation*, 19(2), 89–107.

Sidaway, J.D. (2012). Geographies of development: New maps, new visions? *The Professional Geographer*, 64(1), 49–62. doi:10.1080/00330124.2011.586878.

Smith, J. (2016). *Imperialism in the 21st century: Globalization, super-exploitation, and capitalism's final crisis*. New York: NYU Press.

Solheim, M.W.C. (2022). Diversity and inclusion is a must to make innovation work for all. *Nature*, 612, S11. doi:10.1038/d41586-022-04205-2.

Szalavetz, A. (2017). Upgrading and value capture in global value chains in Hungary: More complex than what the smile curve suggests. In B. Szent-Iványi (Ed.), *Foreign direct investment in Central and Eastern Europe* (pp. 127–150). Cham: Palgrave Macmillan.

Szalavetz, A., & Sass, M. (2023). Disentangling the semi-periphery: Evolutionary trajectories and perspectives of the Austrian and Hungarian automotive industries. *Post-Communist Economies*, 35(3), 211–235. doi:10.1080/14631377.2023.2171179.

Teipen, Ch., Dünhaupt, P., Herr, H., & Mehl, F. (Eds.). (2022). *Economic and social upgrading in global value chains. Comparative analyses, macroeconomic effects, the role of institutions and strategies for the Global South*. Cham: Palgrave Macmillan.

Tian, K., Dietzenbacher, E., & Jong-A-Pin, R. (2019). Measuring industrial upgrading: Applying factor analysis in a global value chain framework. *Economic Systems Research*, 31(4), 642–664. doi:10.1080/09535314.2019.1610728.

Vernon, R. (1966). International investment and international trade in the product cycle. *Quarterly Journal of Economics*, 80(2), 190–207.

Verhoogen, E. (2023). Firm-level upgrading in developing countries. *Journal of Economic Literature*, 61(4), 1410–1464. doi:10.1257/jel.20221633.

Wallerstein, I. (1974). *The modern world system*. New York: Academic Press.

Wallerstein, I. (1979). *The capitalist world economy*. Cambridge: Cambridge University Press.

Wallerstein, I. (2004). *World-systems analysis: An introduction*. Durham, NC: Duke University Press.

Wood, S., Coe, N.M., Watson, I., & Teller, Ch. (2019). Dynamic processes of territorial embeddedness in international online fashion retailing. *Economic Geography*, 95(5), 467–493. doi:10.1080/00130095.2019.1592672.

Yeung, H.W.-c. (2015), Regional development in the global economy. *Regional Science Policy & Practice*, 7(1), 1–23. doi:10.1111/rsp3.12055.

Zöllner, S., Heidinger, M., Sager, S., Lüthi, S., & Thierstein, A. (2023). Advanced producer services in Germany: A relational perspective on spatial core–periphery structures, 2009–19. *Regional Studies, Regional Science*, 10(1), 347–368. doi:10.1080/21681376.2023.2185536.

2 The Transformation of Central European Manufacturing in the European Context

This chapter examines the evolving role of Central Europe (CE) in the manufacturing industry of the European Union (EU). It compares the position of the Central European countries with other economies and analyses various aspects of manufacturing activity, such as employment, production value, investment, profitability, research and development (R&D) and trade linkages. The chapter pays particular attention to three manufacturing sectors: automotive, domestic appliances and aircraft. The analysis of the current role and trends in CE covers both the region as a whole and its six countries: Poland, Romania, Czechia, Hungary, Slovakia and Slovenia, which are the main manufacturing producers. The analysis is preceded by a historical overview, with particular emphasis on the post-socialist transformation.

Historical overview of Central European industrialisation up to the end of the 20th century

a Industrial development from the Industrial Revolution up to 1945

In order to understand the current state of manufacturing in CE, it is essential to provide a historical overview. The historical context is crucial because contemporary industrial development and its operations are evolutionarily embedded in production traditions, spatial arrangements, linkages, skills and other resources that have developed over a long period of time in a specific location. During the 19th-century industrialisation and the period of the first globalisation (1850–1914), none of the countries in what is now CE operated as independent states. Most of them were part of the Habsburg Monarchy, which included the south-eastern region of Poland (Galicia). The remaining parts of contemporary Poland were under the control of the Prussian and Russian empires. These lands shared the fate and development of the great powers of which they were an integral part until the end of the First World War. The region's location between East and West allowed influences and patterns to permeate, creating specific conditions for development. Economic impulses, including industrialisation, came mostly from the West. As a result, the region was highly diverse (Klein et al., 2017). The western part of the region developed

DOI: 10.4324/9781003430117-3

more rapidly as a result of these influences, such as Czechia, while the eastern part, which was on the periphery of Western Europe and bordered historically hostile areas such as Russia and the Ottoman Empire, often faced adversity and developed more slowly (see Table 2.1). The rapid economic development and industrialisation of the second half of the 19th century only served to accentuate these differences (Pollard, 1986).

In addition to its location in Europe, the availability of natural resources conducive to industrial growth was an important factor. The coal deposits in Upper Silesia were instrumental in the region's development into one of Germany's major industrial areas. The capital generated was reinvested in industries beyond the coal and metallurgical complex. The development of the railways also contributed to industrialisation. By the end of the 19th century, the railway network in Czechia and Silesia was among the most developed in Europe, but it was very poor in the eastern part of the region due to lack of capital, low demand and military considerations. Industrial development in the western part of the Habsburg Empire and in Silesia, which belonged to Prussia, was based mainly on the textile and metallurgical industries, accompanied by mechanical engineering. In the Hungarian part of the Habsburg Monarchy, the leading sector was the processing of agricultural products (Good, 1984). In the part of Poland under Russian rule, industrial concentrations also emerged, such as Łódź, which became the largest textile centre in this part of Europe. The Habsburg Monarchy was also very diverse in terms of human capital resources. The prevalence and duration of education were high in the western part of the region, similar to Prussia, but significantly lower in the Hungarian part, especially in the peripheral regions in the east and south (Schulze & Fernandes,

Table 2.1 Gross domestic product (GDP) per capita in CE and selected countries, 1870–1989, in 1990 dollars

Country/Province	*1870*	*1910*	*Country*	*1937*	*1989*
Austrian provinces	1,953	2,802	Austria	3,156	16,360
Czech provinces	1,638	2,545	Czechoslovakia	2,882	8,768
Upper Hungary (Slovakia)	1,018	1,650			
Greater Hungary	987	1,683	Hungary	2,543	6,903
Poland (1921 borders)	946	1,690	Poland (1921 borders)	1,915	
			Poland (1945 borders)		5,684
Yugoslavia	599	1,057	Yugoslavia	1,273	6,193
Romania	931	1,660	Romania	1,130	3,941
United Kingdom	3,190	4,611	United Kingdom	6,218	16,414
Germany	1,839	3,348	Germany	4,685	16,558
Italy	1,499	2,332	Italy	3,319	15,969

Source: Maddison (2010) and Klein et al. (2017).

2009). This corresponded to the low level of human capital development in the eastern parts of Poland, which belonged to Russia. The second half of the 19th century saw the emergence of large diversified industrial conglomerates, some of which are still in operation today. The Czech company Škoda Auto, for example, is a car manufacturer with a long history dating back to 1895.[1] It is one of the oldest continuously operating car producers in Europe, second only to Tatra, a commercial vehicle manufacturer also based in Czechia.

The disintegration of the Austro-Hungarian monarchy after the First World War marked the beginning of a new era. Hungary's territory shrank considerably, while Romania expanded. Czechoslovakia and Yugoslavia were born, and an independent Poland was reborn. Tsarist Russia also collapsed. The political changes and increasingly protectionist trade policies led to a rupture with previous markets and restricted access to resources, hindering the flow of innovation (Klein et al., 2017). In order to maintain competitiveness and further growth while enduring the Great Depression, inflation and trade barriers, manufacturing companies had to expand internationally. An interesting example is the Czech conglomerate Bata, founded in 1894, which was the largest shoe manufacturer in Europe and was also active in other industries. By 1938, the Bata Group employed 65,000 people and had factories in many countries, including Czechoslovakia, Poland, Germany, Switzerland, Slovenia and Belgium, as well as Brazil and India. The group also had a network of 4,000 shops in Europe, 1,000 in Asia and 300 in North America.

b Socialist economy and industry of the CE countries, 1945–1989

The socialist system that emerged in CE after the Second World War was characterised by centralised power aimed at controlling all aspects of political, economic and social activity. This was reflected in state ownership of the means of production, the administrative allocation of goods and the fixing of prices to replace market relations between enterprises. Economic growth was limited by supply rather than demand, due to a constant investment drive by central decision-makers. This drive was not restrained by rigid budgetary constraints or the threat of bankruptcy. The unrestrained expansion of state organisations created an excessive and virtually insatiable demand for inputs. This justified the continued pursuit of greater production and investment, thus creating an economy of chronic shortages (Kornai, 1992). The prioritisation of economic growth was based on an ideology of industrialisation as a means of progress and the belief that it was the foundation of the military strength of the state and the socialist bloc, as well as the political power of the ruling elite. This led to the distorted structure of socialist economies, which became relatively over-industrialised with underdeveloped services. In 1988, the share of employment in manufacturing and mining was 38% in Czechoslovakia, 35% in Romania, 31% in Hungary and 28% in Poland. This contrasted with the United Kingdom and France, where the share was only 21%. Services accounted for between 36%

(Poland) and 41% (Hungary) of the economically active population, while agriculture represented 21% (Hungary) and 28% (Poland and Romania).

Industrial growth was pursued primarily through investment in expanding production capacity and increasing employment, rather than through improved efficiency. The focus was on increasing output, with no incentives to innovate, improve product quality, increase productivity or reduce costs. The strategy of "extensive development" resulted in a growing gap in productivity and technological progress between socialist industry and its Western European counterpart. The forced military-oriented industrialisation was reflected in the mining and manufacturing structure of the socialist countries, which relied heavily on the extraction of mineral resources, especially fuels, and prioritised the production of capital goods such as iron and steel, basic chemicals and heavy machinery. The production of consumer goods largely lagged behind. This kind of energy-intensive growth inevitably had serious environmental consequences. The industrial structure was also unbalanced in terms of the size of enterprises, with a strong dominance of large, often monopolistic, state-owned organisations and relatively few medium-sized and small producers.

The autarkic tendencies of the socialist economies were reinforced by domestic shortages, resulting in limited foreign trade. Central European countries traded mainly with the Soviet Union and with each other through the Council for Mutual Economic Assistance (Comecon). Comecon attempted to impose specialisation in some industrial sectors, such as Czechoslovakia's manufacturing of cars and Hungary's production of buses. There were weak links with the capitalist world. In 1985 the latter accounted for 16% of Czechoslovakia's trade, 21% of Poland's and 34% of Hungary's. Exports to Western Europe consisted mainly of natural resources and simple products; the share of machinery and transport equipment was somewhat higher in the case of Czechoslovakia.

Overall, post-war economic growth in the socialist economies was much slower than in Western Europe. As a result, by 1988 even Czechia was lagging behind historically less developed countries in Southern Europe, such as Spain and Greece, in terms of GDP per capita.

c Post-socialist transformation since 1989

The fundamental political, economic and social changes in the CE countries began in 1989. The post-socialist transition was a process of multiple transformations, including the (re)introduction of parliamentary democracy, local and regional self-government and market economy institutions. This marked the end of the command economy, dominated by central decision-makers, and the return to independently functioning enterprises, market relations and private ownership. The growth of the latter was a gradual process that took different forms in individual countries. It involved the restitution of private property, the privatisation of state-owned enterprises through their sale to domestic and foreign investors, and the emergence of millions of new firms. This was

accompanied by a rapid and radical shift in international trade linkages. Opening up to Western Europe led to an influx of imported goods, while at once creating new export markets. At the same time, trade with the Soviet Union collapsed.

From a macroeconomic perspective, two distinct periods of post-socialist transformation can be identified. The first period, known as the shock phase, was characterised by a rapid transition from a centrally planned system to a market economy, resulting in a significant decline in GDP and industrial production. In Romania, for example, GDP fell by 25% in three years, while in Slovakia and Hungary it fell by 25% in four years. Polish GDP fell by 18% in two years and Czech GDP by 13% in three years. Between 1989 and 1992, the decline in value added in mining and manufacturing was even more pronounced, falling by around one-third. For several decades, companies had operated without autonomy, as buyers sought out suppliers rather than the other way around. However, with the sudden opening of the CE economies, most trade barriers were removed and enterprises had to learn quickly how to find customers and compete with other producers and imported goods. The decline in production resulting from the high level of industrial employment inherited from the socialist era led employers to shed workers and, as a result, unemployment rose. In 1993, the unemployment rate reached 16.4% in Poland, 14.4% in Slovakia and Slovenia, 12.1% in Hungary and 10.2% in Romania. In Czechia the unemployment rate was much lower. In addition, hyperinflation in Poland reached 586% in 1990. Poland and Hungary had accumulated huge foreign debts, having borrowed heavily from the West since the 1970s.

The adjustment of firms to a new institutional framework, local entrepreneurship, growing domestic consumption and exports to Western Europe led to economic growth and an increase in industrial production. This growth began in Poland in 1992, in Czechia, Slovenia and Romania in 1993, and in Hungary and Slovakia in 1994. Economic growth was accompanied by structural changes in the economy, including an increasing share of services and radical restructuring of manufacturing and mining. CE's share of world exports rose, especially for manufactured goods exported to Western Europe. The internationalisation of the CE economies was also reflected in the steady growth of foreign direct investment (FDI). Initially, this investment was directed towards domestic markets, leading to import substitution. However, it gradually shifted towards export-oriented investment, taking advantage of lower costs and facilitating integration into European supply chains.

The successful post-socialist transformation of Czechia, Hungary, Poland, Romania, Slovenia and Slovakia has been attributed to rapid institutional reforms and the expansion of the private sector (Kornai, 1997; Kołodko, 2000; Koźmiński, 2008), with the share of the private sector in GDP and employment reaching between 60% and 70% in all countries by 1995. This led to a radical de-monopolisation of national economies without the emergence of oligarchic structures. The growth of private entrepreneurship was significant in the 1990s, while the privatisation of state-owned enterprises took place in various forms and at different speeds in the CE economies (Williams & Baláž, 1999; Jeffries, 2002). The establishment of transparent democratic and market institutions was facilitated by the historical roots of Western European culture in these countries, in contrast to Eastern European and Balkan societies, which have a longer tradition of autocratic regimes, patrimonial relations and higher levels of corruption (Turnock, 2003; Van Zon, 2008). Past migration and subsequent personal connections also facilitated the development of closer ties with the West. During the socialist era, Hungary, Poland and Yugoslavia were among the most open societies, while Czechoslovakia had a more strict and rigid regime.

Macroeconomic trends in CE in the European context since the end of the 20th century

a Economic performance and quality of life

Since the early 1990s, economic growth in the six CE countries has been faster than in other post-socialist countries and among the most dynamic in the world. In Poland, GDP in real terms (constant prices) almost tripled, while in Slovakia it more than doubled. In Romania, Slovenia and Czechia, it has increased by 80%–90%, and in Hungary by 70% since 1989 (Figure 2.1). This growth was significantly higher than in Western Europe, helping to bridge the gap. In 2022, the GDP at purchasing power parity (PPP) of Czechia and Slovenia reached 89%–91% of the average GDP per capita of the EU, which was close to that of Italy. Meanwhile, Poland's GDP was 80% of the EU average

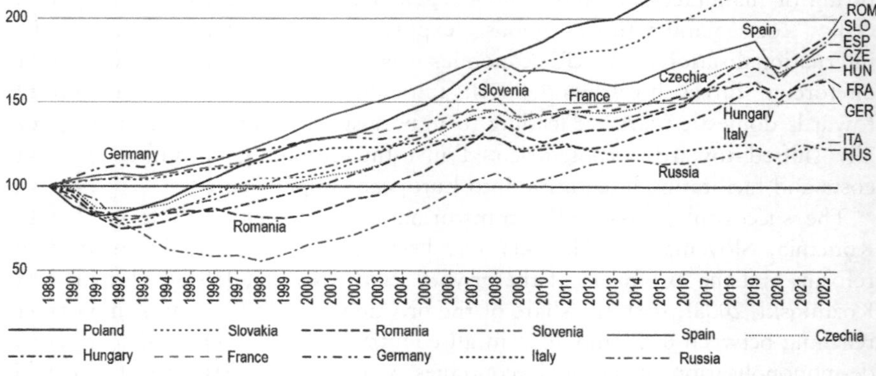

Figure 2.1 GDP growth of selected European countries 1989–2022 (1989 = 100)
Source: authors' calculations based on World Bank data (2022).

and Hungary and Romania's were 77%, just below Spain's. Slovakia's GDP level was 67% of the EU average. It is worth noting that in 1990, Poland's GDP was only 26% of the EU27 average, while Czechia's was about 58%. The catching up was especially spectacular in historically less developed countries – Poland and Slovakia. All six CE countries are classified as high-income economies by the World Bank now.

Aspirations for closer integration with Western Europe and eventual membership of the EU were important. They stimulated and guided institutional reforms in Central European countries. The accession of new post-socialist members to the EU was strongly supported by Western European companies, which saw the benefits of new markets. Growing trade links and FDI in CE from the early 1990s on show that economic integration preceded formal accession to the EU.

There have been many effects of the entry of CE countries into the EU. The main focus is often on the impact of EU funds. From 2007 to 2020, the six countries discussed in this text received approximately €370 billion in European funds, which amounts to more than €4,130 per inhabitant over a 14-year period. This funding was crucial in financing investments in infrastructure modernisation, environmental improvements and human capital development. The EU funds have been estimated to have a net effect of 0.3–0.8 percentage points on the annual GDP growth of individual CE countries (Orłowski, 2020), or even higher when considering aggregate fiscal effects (Durand & Espinoza, 2021). However, it is widely agreed that the consequences of these funds went beyond their direct impact. The effective use of these funds required a general improvement in the quality of public administration. Membership in the EU has provided a stable framework for economic development and safe investment for both domestic and foreign companies (Becker et al., 2010; Bachtler et al., 2014; Piątkowski, 2021).

The lack of barriers within the European single market, combined with cost advantages and the quality of the labour force, has encouraged the relocation of manufacturing production to CE. This was accompanied by productivity gains, technological modernisation and organisational changes. Many domestic brand manufacturers emerged, including national champions, some of which were successful on international markets.

In the post-socialist era, CE countries have experienced good economic performance, as reflected in GDP growth and their higher position in the World Bank's Ease of Doing Business index. Importantly, this economic growth has been accompanied by a general improvement in the quality of life. Unemployment rates are at record lows (Figure 2.2), the proportion of people living in poverty has fallen and income inequality remains below the EU average. CE countries score well on health indicators such as infant mortality and life expectancy, and on educational opportunities and achievement. The significant improvement in the quality of human capital due to the boom in higher education has been an important factor in economic development. The environmental situation is much better than under socialism. However, air quality

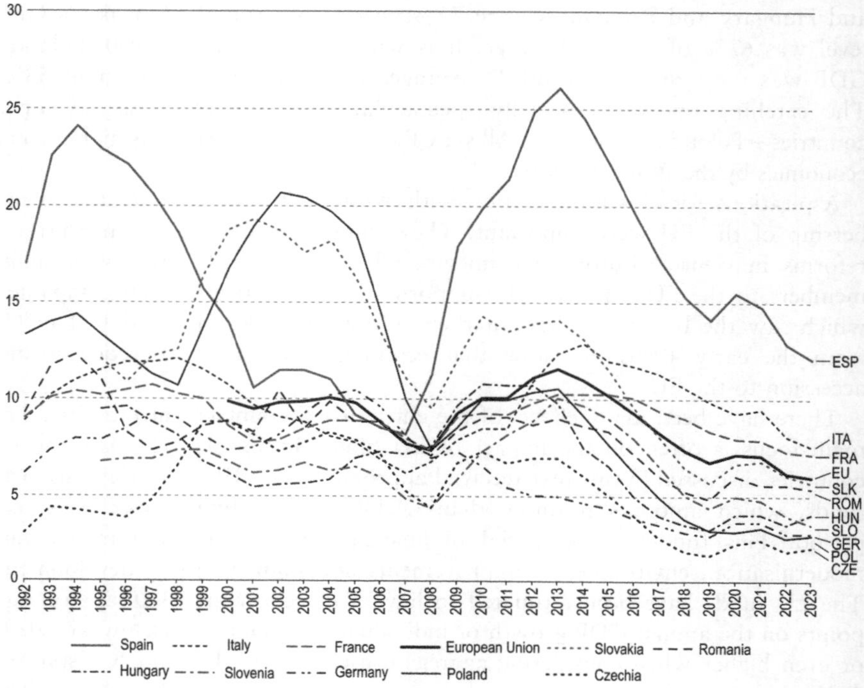

Figure 2.2 Unemployment rate in selected European countries, 1992–2023
Source: authors' calculations based on Eurostat.

remains a problem due to the widespread use of fossil fuels for local heating. Non-material aspects of social well-being have generally improved more than material ones. CE countries tend to have higher positions in international rankings such as the UN Human Development Index and the Boston Consulting Group's Sustainable Economic Development Assessment than in terms of GDP per capita (Table 2.2). The proportion of people reporting satisfaction with their lives is comparable to that of France and the United Kingdom (EBRD, 2016). Meanwhile, the fifth survey on the quality of life in European cities shows that satisfaction with life tends to be higher in Slovenian, Czech, Slovakian and Polish urban areas than in most French, Italian and Spanish cities, with Hungarian cities in the middle of the rankings (European Commission, 2020; Castelli et al., 2023). The evidence suggests that many parts of CE societies have benefited from the development of their economies. Poland is considered the country with the most inclusive nature of economic growth and also has low social inequalities (Piątkowski, 2018).

This is not to say that these processes did not have social costs. They were particularly high in the early stages of the post-socialist transformation, when the labour market was difficult and many people lost their jobs. There are still areas of social exclusion, especially in the peripheral non-metropolitan regions

Table 2.2 Position of selected European countries in world rankings*

Country	GDP per capita PPP		Human Development Index		Sustainable Economic Development Assessment	
	1990	2021	1990	2021	2008	2020
France	20	21	17	26	20	20
Italy	16	27	20	28	23	29
Czechia	28	28	27	30	27	24
Slovenia	30	30	25*	21	22	22
Spain	25	35	24	25	21	25
Poland	53	36	41	32	38	28
Hungary	41	38	39	43	29	37
Romania	59	39	44	49	51	46
Portugal	31	40	46	36	25	26
Slovakia	48	43	47	42	36	33

Source: authors' elaboration based on data from the World Bank, the United Nations and the Boston Consulting Group.
*Note: excluding Andorra, Hong Kong, Liechtenstein, Monaco and San Marino; Human Development Index for Slovenia in 1995.

and at local level. In addition, the effectiveness of health services is unsatisfactory in several countries, and political tensions and conflicts are evident.

Large-scale migration to Western Europe, particularly the United Kingdom, occurred due to open borders and the search for better job opportunities and living conditions. It is estimated that about 2.8 million Romanians and 2.3 million Poles left their countries, and about 300,000 people migrated from Hungary and Czechia (Fihel, 2011; United Nations Population Division, 2020). Although the emigration of young people may have temporarily eased the difficult labour market conditions at the beginning of the 21st century, it generally had negative long-term consequences due to the loss of human capital and the deterioration of the demographic situation in ageing CE societies. Some return migration, estimated at 300,000 people in Poland in 2018–2020, has occurred in the aftermath of Brexit. The gap in the labour market has subsequently been filled by migrants from Eastern Europe, mainly from Ukraine (see Chapter 7).

b FDI

The economic transformation and growth of CE countries have been accelerated by massive inflows of FDI, mostly from developed core countries and made by large transnational corporations (TNCs) (Jacobs, 2017; Pavlinek, 2017). FDI, together with trade linkages discussed below, are the key elements that connect less developed countries to international production networks (Coe & Yeung,

2015). They create linkages and relationships between the firms, countries and regions involved and, over time, can lead to the integration of local suppliers into these networks through a process of strategic coupling. This is particularly evident in the automotive industry, which is not only recognised as the most globalised industrial sector (Dicken, 2015), but also stands out for having the most extensive supply chains. FDI inflows in CE since the 1990s are discussed here in the broader context of selected Western European countries, as well as Türkiye and Mexico.

Poland, as the largest economy in CE, stood out with the highest FDI inflows for almost the whole period from 1990 to 2021. Whereas most countries in the region experienced their highest inflows after joining the EU between 2005 and 2009, Poland and Romania maintained high levels of FDI after 2010 (see Figure 2.3). In 2021, Poland received a record $24.8 billion of FDI, accounting for 18% of the EU's total inflows. In that year, Germany led the way with $31.3 billion. Poland is one of the world's top 20 host economies for FDI, with a total inflow of $299 billion from 1990 to 2021. This compares with $163 billion for Czechia, $790 billion for Spain and $710 billion for Mexico. The differences are smaller in the last decade, 2012–2021, when Poland received $138 billion and all six CE countries $311 billion, while Spain received $249 billion and Mexico $329 billion.

The size of a country is an important factor to consider when looking at FDI. Inflows per capita give a clearer picture of the magnitude of FDI and show that Czechia and Slovenia have caught up with Spain and Germany, while Poland

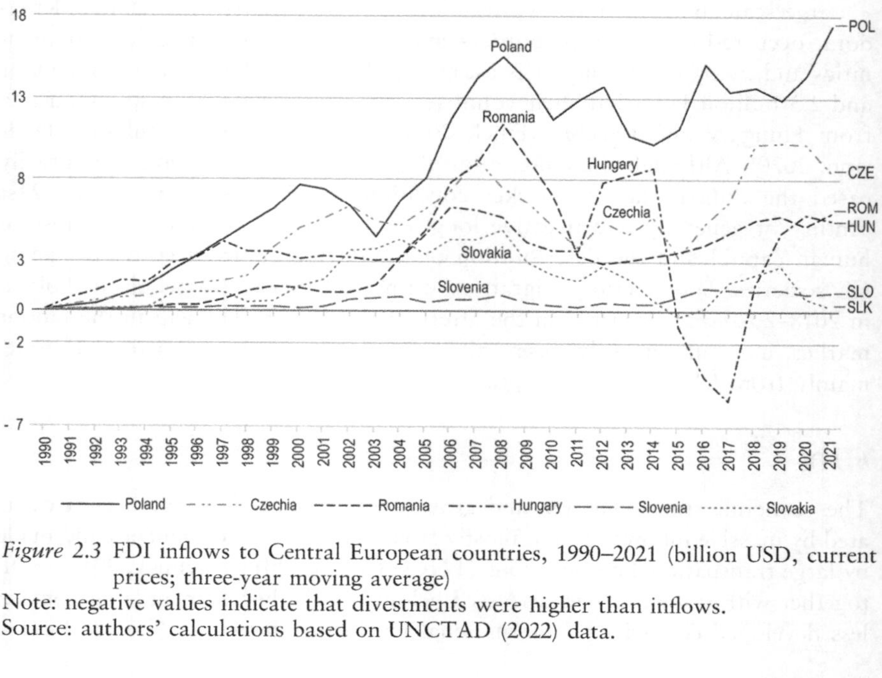

Figure 2.3 FDI inflows to Central European countries, 1990–2021 (billion USD, current prices; three-year moving average)

Note: negative values indicate that divestments were higher than inflows.

Source: authors' calculations based on UNCTAD (2022) data.

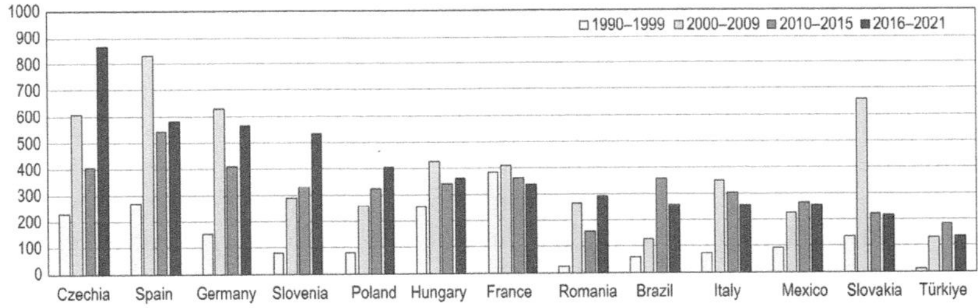

Figure 2.4 Average annual FDI inflows per capita to selected countries (USD, current prices)
Source: authors' calculations based on UNCTAD (2022) data.

and Hungary have equalled or surpassed France and Italy in recent years (Figure 2.4). Poland and Slovenia are the only countries to have experienced growth in per capita inflows over the whole period. Due to its size, Mexico has a lower FDI per capita than the Central European countries, but it still has a higher FDI per capita than Türkiye. FDI as a percentage of GDP was very high in Slovakia between 2000 and 2009, reaching 9%, but has fallen to 1.2% since 2010, while it has remained around 4% in Czechia, 3.5% in Hungary and Romania and 3% in Poland over the last two decades. This is higher than the EU average and the index for Mexico and Türkiye.

FDI statistics can be influenced by various financial operations, transfers of ownership and the intermediary role played by certain countries offering favourable tax and regulatory conditions. It is important to note that these factors can affect the accuracy of the statistics. For example, we observe very high FDI rates in tax havens and other specialised locations for such transactions (Lane & Milesi-Ferretti, 2018; Damgaard et al., 2019). CE countries remain outside the main channels of these flows, so it is worth examining the statistics published by UNCTAD on greenfield projects, which better reflect investment attractiveness. fDimarkets.com, a platform owned by the *Financial Times*, has been collecting data on greenfield projects since 2003. These projects represent between 40% and 55% of total investment in different years, with between 10,000 and 18,000 projects covered each year. Of the 281,900 greenfield projects recorded between 2003 and 2021, 47% are industrial investments. The automotive industry has the largest share in terms of both number of projects (6.5%) and value (8.2%).

Europe has attracted a significant number of greenfield projects, with one-quarter of the world total located on the continent. Since 2003, the six CE countries have accounted for more than one-fifth (21.8%) of the total number of greenfield projects in the EU27, despite having a smaller share of EU GDP. The value of greenfield projects in the region is even higher at 28.3% ($718 billion), indicating that larger projects are located in CE compared to Western Europe. Poland has attracted 6,400 projects worth $282 billion, the third highest in the EU after Germany ($332 billion) and Spain ($297 billion). This is more than France and Italy, but less than Mexico. Among the CE countries, Romania ranks second with $180 billion, while Czechia lags behind with $76 billion. In recent years (2017–2021), Poland has held a dominant position in greenfield investment in the region, with $104 billion invested, compared to $26 billion in Hungary and $15 billion in Czechia.

FDI analysis is available for the automotive and aircraft industries for the period 2014–2021. The USA is the largest net recipient of automotive FDI among Organisation for Economic Co-operation and Development (OECD) countries, followed by France and Sweden. Poland ranks fourth with $8.7 billion, while Czechia ranks sixth with $4.3 billion, overtaking both Germany and Spain during this period. It is important to note that these results reflect the balance of investment inflows and disinvestments.

Investment in the aircraft industry is much lower. In addition, data on this sector are incomplete due to the confidentiality of information on defence production. According to the available data, the USA has the highest net investment of $5.3 billion between 2014 and 2021, followed by Poland ($909 million) and South Korea ($546 million). Over the same period, France records a cumulative disinvestment of $5 billion and Germany a disinvestment of $0.6 billion.

The massive inflow of FDI into CE was made possible by trade liberalisation and, since 2004, EU membership. This was part of a broader trend towards globalisation, with the geographical reorganisation of production by TNCs in search of new markets, lower costs and labour resources. Geographical proximity, especially to Germany, and improved transport links between these countries and Western Europe, as well as investment incentives, have also played a role (Jacobs, 2017; Becker & Cieślik, 2020).

Finally, it is worth noting that CE countries have also become a source of FDI in recent years, especially Czechia and Poland, with outflows of $40.7 billion and $29.4 billion, respectively, between 2011 and 2021. This reflects the growing maturity of these economies. However, the level of outward FDI is still several times lower than in Western European countries.

The size, characteristics and trends of manufacturing in Poland and Central European countries in the European context

a The changing share of CE in EU manufacturing

There are 664,799 manufacturing enterprises in the six Central European countries, representing almost one-third of all firms in this sector in the EU (31.4%). Poland has the second-largest number of manufacturing companies in the EU after Italy (359,238) and more than Germany and France (Table 2.3). The number of manufacturing producers in Czechia (181,296) is particularly impressive, significantly higher than in the United Kingdom. In addition, the number of firms has increased by one-third in Poland and by one-fifth in Czechia since 2005. This contrasts with a fall of one-quarter in Italy and one-fifth

Table 2.3 Share of selected countries in the number of enterprises, employment and output of EU manufacturing in 2005 and 2021 (%)

Country	*Number of enterprises*		*Employment*		*Output*	
	2005	*2021*	*2005*	*2021*	*2005*	*2021*
Germany	10.4	9.7	23.6	27.9	28.3	29.3
Italy	24.8	17.0	13.0	12.0	16.3	14.5
France	11.9	10.8	12.1	10.8	17.2	12.1
Spain	11.2	8.2	8.5	7.2	9.0	7.6
Poland	9.3	11.5	7.4	9.6	3.0	4.9
Netherlands	2.2	3.7	2.4	2.5	4.4	4.6
Belgium	1.8	1.8	1.9	1.7	4.0	3.8
Sweden	2.8	2.3	2.5	2.1	3.3	2.9
Austria	1.4	1.5	2.0	2.4	2.4	2.8
Czechia	7.6	8.6	4.1	4.0	1.9	2.6
Hungary	3.1	2.8	2.5	2.6	1.4	1.6
Romania	2.8	3.6	5.5	4.0	0.8	1.4
Slovakia	0.4*	3.9	1.5*	1.5	0.6*	1.1
Slovenia	0.8	1.0	0.8	0.7	0.4	0.4
CE	24.1	31.4	21.9	22.4	8.1	12.0
EU27	100.0	100.0	100.0	100.0	100.0	100.0

Source: authors' calculations based on Eurostat data.
*Note: number of enterprises and output in Slovakia in 2006 and employment in Slovakia in 2008.

in Spain, and a slightly smaller decline in Sweden. Hungary was the only CE economy where their number has decreased. At the same time, it has remained stable in Germany and France, while it has grown significantly in the Netherlands.

CE accounts for 22.4% of EU manufacturing employment, with 6.3 million people working in the sector. Of these, 2.7 million are in Poland (more than in the United Kingdom), 1.1 million each in Czechia and Romania and 0.7 million in Hungary. Poland is the fourth-largest employer in manufacturing in the EU, after Germany, Italy and France, while Czechia and Romania are sixth and seventh, respectively, after Spain. Notably, Poland has seen the highest growth in manufacturing employment since 2005 (25%). The only other EU countries where employment in the sector rose during this period were Germany and Austria, with an increase of 14%. Employment in the sector peaked in Czechia in 2008 and then fell by 10%. In 2018, employment was at its highest in Hungary and Slovakia, followed by a decline of around 5%. It is interesting to note that the number of persons employed in manufacturing fell significantly in Romania after 2005. Since then, it has decreased in most Western European countries, including France and Italy (by 11%–14%), and much more in Spain (by 18%) and Sweden (by 21%).

The CE countries' contribution to the value of EU manufacturing output is much smaller than their share of employment, reflecting lower productivity, which is discussed in more detail below. CE accounts for 12.0% of EU manufacturing output (up from 8.1% in 2005) and 10.4% of gross value added. Since 2005, Poland's share of value added has increased to 4.4%, Czechia's to 2.1%, Hungary's to 1.3% and Romania's to 1.2%. Germany represents more than one-third of EU manufacturing value added, with Italy and France each contributing around 12% and Spain another 6%.

CE has achieved the most prominent position in the manufacture of tobacco products, accounting for 28.2% of EU production. It also has substantial market shares in electrical equipment (19.1%), automotive (18.7%), furniture (18.7%), rubber and plastic products (18.4%) and computer, electronic and optical products (16.1%) (Figure 2.5).

The electrical equipment sector includes the manufacture of domestic appliances, where CE accounts for 24.8%. However, using a three-digit industrial classification, the region's most prominent role is in the production of automotive parts and accessories, with a share of 33.4% (compared to 16.0% in 2008). Significant increases in the share of CE have also occurred in the other industries mentioned above, except for tobacco products, and in printing and reproduction of recorded media (now 13.4%). Interestingly, the share is more limited in basic metals (11.5%), which is one of the key sectors of socialist industry, as well as in food products (11.0%) and labour-intensive industries such as wearing apparel (8.3%) and leather products (6.0%).

Poland has the highest shares for tobacco products (25.7%), domestic appliances (12.9%), furniture (12.5%) and rubber and plastic products (8.3%). Compared to the other CE countries, its share is lower in the manufacture of computer, electronic and optical products (3.4%) and in the automotive sector (4.0%). However, Poland's share is twice as high in the manufacture of automotive parts and accessories (8.4%).

It should be emphasised that the actual role of CE in EU manufacturing output and value added is larger than the data presented indicate. Firstly, this is due to the undervaluation of output in CE resulting from the lower prices of products manufactured there compared to those made in Western Europe, reflecting official exchange rates. Therefore, PPP valuation may provide a more accurate approximation of the real value. Secondly, a significant part of production is exported, often through TNCs. Thus, the value of products may be influenced by the transfer pricing of intra-company trade between subsidiaries of the same corporation located in different countries. Despite strict regulations on transfer pricing, products may be exported below their market value in importing countries, leading to an understatement of official figures. There are indications that this is the case, for example, in the household appliance industry, as shown by the large discrepancy between the share of CE in the number of products

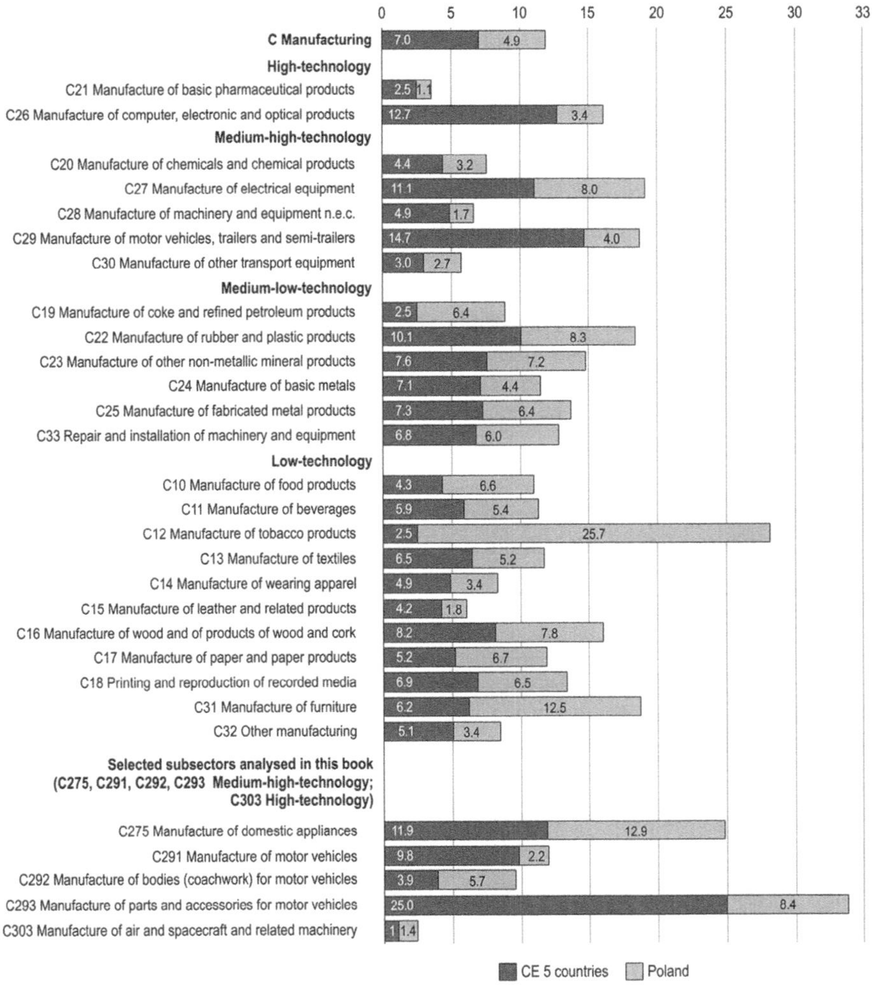

Figure 2.5 Shares of CE and Poland in the value of output of selected manufacturing sectors by technological intensity in 2021 (%)

Note: the five CE countries include Czechia, Romania, Hungary, Slovakia and Slovenia.

Source: authors' calculation based on Eurostat data.

manufactured and exported, on the one hand, and their value, on the other, and as confirmed by interviews with company managers.

b CE and Poland in the automotive, aircraft and home appliance industries

The production of motor vehicles and their components is one of the most important manufacturing sectors in CE. Since 2005, CE's share of EU employment in the automotive industry has increased from 23.4% to 30.4%.

This growth is also reflected in the value of output, which has risen to 18.8%, and in gross value added, which has increased to 14.2%. This increase occurred in all six CE countries. The highest growth in value added was in Romania, Slovakia and Poland, while the highest rise in employment was in Poland. In terms of employment, the automotive sector in Poland accounts for 8.6% of the EU workforce, making it the third largest in Europe. It is only slightly less than the number of people employed in the sector in France. Czechia ranks fourth (7.1%), employing more people than the automotive industries of Italy and Spain (Table 2.4). Romania and Czechia now employ similar numbers of people, while Hungary accounts for 4.0% of EU employment and small Slovakia for 3.2%. The German automotive sector has seen an increase in employment, while employment in France and Italy has remained stable since the financial crisis in 2009. These three countries, which form the Western European core, account for more than half of EU employment in the sector.

Table 2.4 Employment in the automotive, aircraft and home appliance industries in selected European countries, 2008 and 2021

Country	*Automotive industry*		*Aircraft and spacecraft industry*		*Domestic appliance industry*	
	2008	*2021*	*2008*	*2021*	*2008*	*2021*
Germany	796,347	877,362	65,677	82,631	52,527	62,848
France	259,467	225,084	91,530	131,503	17,198	22,332
Poland	151,326	210,064	14,790	16,667	27,412	30,640
Czechia	157,645	172,601	5,783*	7,266	7,973	6,303
Romania	113,167	167,141	3,053	5,064	10,595	16,259
Italy	180,415	166,264	33,026	48,099	49,608	26,543
Spain	163,162	156,526	16,693	23,131	16,549	10,306
Hungary	77,065	96,534	198	1,299	10,698	13,426
Sweden	77,382	83,210	NA	12,433	4,996	617
Slovakia	57,386	76,944	325	286	3,258	2,832
Austria	33,211	37,657	928	1,644	4,882	3,859
Belgium	42,003	29,123	5,211	4,899	1,345	604*
Netherlands	23,497	22,562	2,994	3,351	3,092	3,682
Slovenia	14,804	16,194	96	297*	10,055	7,634
CE	571,393	739,438	24,245	30,879	69,991	77,094
EU27	2,227,612	2,429,936	256,679	342,638	237,211	222,125*

Source: Eurostat.

*Note: aircraft in Czechia in 2009; aircraft in Slovenia and domestic appliances in Belgium in 2020; domestic appliances in EU27 excluding Ireland in 2021.

The Czech automotive industry has grown more slowly than those in other CE countries, but remains the largest in the region in terms of value of output (5.6%), ahead of Poland (4.0%). The two countries' share of value added in the EU is similar, with Poland at 4.0% and Czechia at 3.9%. Hungary, Romania and Slovakia account for 2.1%, 2.0% and 1.9%, respectively. Despite a relative decrease in Western Europe, it still accounts for the vast majority of production. Germany represents 54% of value added, followed by France with 8.7%, Italy with 6.8% and Spain with 5.4%.

The Central European countries produce 12.9% of motor vehicles and engines, with Czechia leading the way with 4.1% and Slovakia making a strong showing with 3.2%. Although Poland has experienced a decline in car production over the last decade, it remains an important engine manufacturer. The CE region plays the most prominent role in the manufacture of automotive parts and accessories, accounting for 46.8% of EU employment, 33.8% of output and 26.1% of value added. Poland, Romania and Czechia rank second, third and fourth in terms of employment in the EU, with 13.0%, 12.2% and 10.3%, respectively. They are ahead of France and Italy, with 7.5% and 7.6%, respectively. Poland is the fourth-largest producer of automotive parts in the EU, contributing 7.9% of total value added, after Germany (37.0%), France and Italy (10.0%–10.4%). Meanwhile, Czechia is the sixth-largest producer with a contribution of 5.9%, after Spain; Romania and Hungary rank seventh and eighth with 5.2% and 3.5%, respectively. Slovakia's share (2.9%) is higher than that of Sweden and Austria (Table 2.5). In addition, Poland is an important producer of bodies, trailers and semi-trailers, being the third-largest employer in the EU (9.6%) after Germany and France, but much smaller in terms of value added (5.9%). The six CE countries account for 17.9% of employment and 10.3% of value added.

Several CE countries have developed a strong dependence on the automotive sector. The sector accounts for 36.5% of manufacturing output in Slovakia, 25.6% in Czechia, 22.3% in Hungary and 19.7% in Romania. This is also reflected in the dominance of automotive products in exports, which will be discussed later. In Slovenia (10.9%) and Poland (9.7%), the contribution of the automotive industry is lower than in Germany (19.1%) and similar to that of Spain (10.7%) and France (8.8%). The share of total employment in manufacturing is highest in Slovakia and Romania, at 15.9% and 14.7%, respectively. It is also significant in Czechia and Hungary, at 13.7% and 12.6%, respectively. In Slovenia and Poland, it is similar to that of Spain and France, between 7.2% and 7.4%.

The role of CE in the production of home appliances is even greater than in the automotive sector, accounting for 34.7% of employment and 24.8% of output, although only 15.8% of value added. This suggests that the region is primarily a location for the assembly of final products, with a less significant role in the manufacture of components. In particular, there is a significant difference in the geographical distribution of this sector compared to the

Table 2.5 Size of the automotive component industry in selected European countries, 2008 and 2021

Country	Number of enterprises		Employment		Value added (mln euro)	
	2008	2021	2008	2021	2008	2021
Germany	1,232	1,228	268,507	260,784	17,556	22,904
France	702	533	81,584	89,540	4,591	6,413
Italy	1,626	1,594	95,861	88,942	4,418	6,178
Poland	1,180	1,113	106,136	153,839	2,490	4,878
Spain	1,063	871	79,448	77,102	3,852	4,497
Czechia	897	887	117,892	121,139	2,859	3,666
Romania	404	341	92,416	143,631	1,002	3,246
Hungary	354	317	60,937	70,975	1,672	2,173
Slovakia	97	238	41,082	52,578	555	1,791
Sweden	625	490	18,299*	15,972	1,434	1,499
Austria	83	60	13,874	13,884	962	1,347
Belgium	321	122	10,676	6,816	639	529
Netherlands	142	195	5,438*	4,562*	311*	429*
Slovenia	101	137	9,908	10,303	249	418
CE	3,033	3,033	428,371	552,465	8,826	16,173
EU27	10,003	9,443	1,035,762	1,181,700	43,535	61,870

Source: Eurostat.

*Note: employment in Sweden in 2009; employment and value added in the Netherlands in 2009 and 2020.

automotive industry. The latter has become very important in all six CE countries. However, more than half of the production of domestic appliances in CE is concentrated in Poland alone. Poland accounts for 12.9% of EU output, the third-highest share after Germany and Italy. It also accounts for 7.4% of EU value added, the fourth highest, and 13.8% of employment, the second highest. Romania and Hungary are significant producers of household appliances, accounting for 7.3% and 6.0% of EU employment and 2.2%–2.5% of value added, respectively. Slovenia also contributes to production with 2.4% of EU value added. Since 2009, production has increased particularly in Poland and Hungary, with spectacular growth in Romania. Slovenia has traditionally been an important producer of household appliances, with the Gorenje brand, founded in 1950 and acquired by China's Hisense in 2019. In contrast, the sector is much smaller in Czechia, accounting for only 2.8% of EU employment and 1.3% of value added, and even smaller in Slovakia, where it contributes only 0.6% of EU value added. Moreover, in neither of these countries has there been any significant growth in the sector in recent years (see Table 2.4). Slovenia has the highest share of the sector in total manufacturing, accounting for 5.3% of output and 3.5% of employment. In Poland and Romania, the sector accounts for 1.9%–2.0% of manufacturing output and 1.1%–1.4% of employment.

At the same time, Germany has significantly increased its share in the production of domestic appliances at the expense of Italy. A decade ago, the value of production in Italy was similar to that in Germany, but now Italy's share of EU value added has fallen from 22.1% to 14.2%. Germany alone now accounts for 43% of the sector's value added, with France representing 11%. The latter has seen an increase in production since 2016. Spain's domestic appliance industry has shrunk by half in a decade to 4.2%, and the sector has almost disappeared in Sweden. Meanwhile, the Netherlands has seen growth.

The aircraft industry in the EU is about twice the size of the domestic appliance sector and about five times smaller than the automotive industry, in terms of both value added and employment. The role of CE in aircraft manufacturing is much more limited than in the previous two sectors, accounting for only 9.0% of EU employment and 3.3% of value added. Production is almost entirely concentrated in Poland, Czechia and Romania (see Table 2.4). The former accounts for 4.9% of EU employment and 2.0% of value added, Czechia for 2.1% and 0.7% and Romania for 1.5% and 0.4%, respectively. It is worth noting that the share of these three CE countries in EU value added is higher than in the output value. Although the sector has grown in these countries since 2008, the same is true for Western European economies. France (45% of EU value added) and Germany (26%) are the main aircraft manufacturers, followed by Italy (14%) and Spain (6%). The sector accounts for 0.5%–0.6% of total manufacturing output and employment in Poland and 0.6% of employment in Czechia.

c Foreign control

Foreign-controlled enterprises play a prominent role in CE manufacturing, due to the immense FDI inflows. Their share reaches 69% of value added in Slovakia, 66% in Hungary and Romania and 59% in Czechia. The highest dominance of foreign affiliates is found in Ireland (91%), with a significant presence also in Luxembourg (58%) and Belgium (49%). The proportion of foreign enterprises in Poland (43%) and Slovenia (38%) is similar to that in Sweden and the Netherlands (40%–41%). This compares with 33% in Austria and Spain, 26% in France and Germany and the lowest figure of 20% in Italy (see Table 2.6).

More people are employed in foreign-controlled manufacturing enterprises than in nationally owned firms only in Slovakia (52%) and Luxembourg (51%); in Ireland, Romania and Hungary the proportion is 50%, while in Czechia the share of foreign-owned companies is 45%. They account for around one-third of employment or slightly less in Sweden (37%), Slovenia (34%), Poland, Belgium and the Netherlands (32%) and Austria (30%). Their share tends to be lower in Spain, France and Germany (21%–23%).

Table 2.6 Share of foreign-controlled enterprises in manufacturing and total business economy in selected countries, 2020 (%)

Country	*Manufacturing*		*Total business economy except financial and insurance activities*	
	Value added	*Persons employed*	*Value added*	*Persons employed*
Ireland	90.6	50.3	73.5	29.5
Slovakia	69.4	52.3	45.8	28.2
Hungary	66.3	49.9	46.5	24.8
Romania	66.0	50.0	42.5	28.9
Czechia	59.4	44.9	42.3	28.5
Lux-embourg	58.4	50.9	44.8	41.3
Belgium	49.4	31.9	25.4	15.3
Poland	43.4	32.5	30.9	20.1
Sweden	41.2	37.3	26.2	23.0
Netherlands	40.4	32.0	28.5	17.5
Slovenia	37.9	34.3	27.8	23.4
Austria	33.4	29.6	26.0	21.0
Spain	32.9	22.9	23.7	14.6
Portugal	30.9	20.3	26.9	15.6
France	26.0	22.3	NA	NA
Germany	26.0	20.8	19.1	12.9
Italy	20.4	13.5	17.1	9.4

Source: authors' calculations based on Eurostat data.

Figures on foreign control may be overstated as they indicate the country where the controlling enterprise is registered. It is common for many European holdings to be registered in Luxembourg, Cyprus and the Netherlands, even though the majority shareholders are from other countries. This is also the case for some large Polish-owned producers.

The share of foreign-controlled enterprises in the total business economy (excluding financial and insurance activities) is more limited than in manufacturing. Apart from Ireland, where it reaches 73% of value added, it is highest in Hungary, Slovakia and Luxembourg (45%–47%), Romania and Czechia (42%), i.e. in four CE economies. It is between one-quarter and one-third in Poland (31%), the Netherlands and Slovenia (28%) and Sweden, Austria and Belgium (25%–26%). In terms of employment, the share is 28% in Romania, Czechia and Slovakia, 24%–25% in Hungary, Slovenia and Sweden and 20%–21% in Austria and Poland.

The degree of dependence on foreign capital varies considerably between industrial sectors (Table 2.7). The automotive industry is one of the most dominated by foreign-owned producers. In Slovakia and Hungary, foreign producers account for 96%–97% of value added and 91%–94% of employment, while in Czechia and Poland the figures are 92% and 86%, and 87% and 82%, respectively. In Belgium and Spain, the shares are between 80% and 90%, the exceptions being Germany, France and Italy in 2020. Other two-digit NACE sectors in which foreign-controlled enterprises predominate in the CE countries are the manufacture of computers, electronic and optical products, electrical equipment (including domestic appliances), other transport equipment, tobacco products, beverages and paper. However, Poland has the highest share of domestic manufacturers among the CE economies in most industries. For example, they account for almost 30% of value added in electrical machinery, 40% in other transport equipment and around 45% in computers and electronics (compared with 26% in Czechia and 10%–12% in Hungary and Romania). Two-thirds or more of the value added in Poland's manufacturing is generated by domestically owned firms in the production of coke and refined petroleum products, furniture, fabricated metal products, food products, wearing apparel, leather, textiles, printing and reproduced media. In addition, more than half of the value added in the production of pharmaceuticals, rubber and plastic products, chemicals, wood products, basic metals, machinery and equipment comes from domestically owned enterprises.

The larger size of the economy and domestic market in Poland compared to other CE countries is the principal reason for the broader segment of domestic manufacturers and their higher share. Examples of successful Polish companies that have expanded internationally with their brand name products include Maspex, Black Red White, Synthos and Fakro. Founded in 1990, Maspex has become a leading producer of juices, beverages, water, jams, pasta, instant products and, more recently, vodka in Central and Eastern Europe. The company has grown through acquisitions in Poland, Czechia, Slovakia, Romania, Hungary, Bulgaria, Lithuania and Latvia. Maspex operates 17 production plants and generates revenues in excess of €3 billion. Black Red White began manufacturing furniture in 1991 and currently has 19 factories in Poland and 6 other countries, as well as numerous retail outlets throughout Europe, Japan, the USA, Canada and Mexico. Fakro, founded in 1991, is another private company that has achieved market success beyond the borders of Poland. It is currently the world's second-largest manufacturer of roof windows, after Denmark's Velux, with a 15% share of the global market. Fakro opened its first factory in Ukraine in 1998 and now has three factories there, one of which was destroyed by Russian bombing. It launched production in China in 2003, and later in the USA, and has a sales network covering 60 countries. Synthos was one of the largest chemical factories in Poland before 1989, producing synthetic rubber and various types of plastic. After privatisation, the company expanded both domestically and by acquiring competing plants in Czechia, the Netherlands, France and Germany. In 2021, Synthos made Poland's largest foreign

Table 2.7 Share of foreign-controlled enterprises in selected manufacturing sectors in Central European countries in 2020 (%)

Sector	*Value added*					*Persons employed*				
	Poland	*Czechia*	*Hungary*	*Romania*	*Slovakia*	*Poland*	*Czechia*	*Hungary*	*Romania*	*Slovakia*
automotive industry	87.4	92.2	95.9	88.8	97.2	82.4	85.7	90.8	89.6	94.4
electrical equipment	71.2	73.3	78.8	83.3	78.9	60.4	65.8	64.6	78.5	73.6
paper and paper products	61.5	74.9	83.5	63.8	71.5	43.0	50.5	42.8	40.4	50.5
other transport equipment	60.3	42.5	82.2	63.8	NA	54.0	43.7	71.2	54.7	NA
computer, electronic and optical products	55.5	73.8	90.2	88.3	77.1	51.5	60.7	82.1	84.6	69.2
other non-metallic mineral products	54.3	70.6	73.4	62.6	68.6	35.8	51.6	53.5	38.9	46.3
basic metals	48.4	47.3	77.1	85.6	83.2	41.8	46.0	67.8	81.0	70.7
pharmaceuticals	46.5	81.2	53.0	64.8	NA	40.2	77.1	51.8	54.4	NA
rubber and plastic products	44.8	66.0	71.7	63.7	80.6	39.3	53.8	58.7	51.5	66.7
machinery and equipment	43.5	58.6	69.4	78.1	76.7	35.1	50.5	64.1	68.9	71.9
chemicals and chemical products	37.4	45.6	78.0	80.3	81.3	34.5	46.0	60.6	58.5	66.8
wood and wood products	34.0	36.1	41.6	54.4	26.6	15.7	12.6	19.8	30.7	9.3
textiles	33.3	36.7	62.5	59.9	63.1	32.9	39.3	42.6	57.3	37.8
food products	28.7	29.3	36.4	37.3	39.2	21.2	17.8	21.0	19.6	24.0
furniture	26.0	18.9	44.4	30.6	43.5	20.6	NA	32.5	24.0	38.3
printing and reproduction of recorded media	25.0	16.6	21.6	27.1	6.6	19.9	11.3	10.0	21.2	6.8
fabricated metal products	23.7	34.8	32.7	38.0	36.0	19.8	26.3	24.6	31.3	23.1
leather and leather products	21.0	28.0	78.7	54.7	74.1	14.2	20.3	65.7	50.4	67.0

Sector	*Value added*					*Persons employed*				
	Poland	*Czechia*	*Hungary*	*Romania*	*Slovakia*	*Poland*	*Czechia*	*Hungary*	*Romania*	*Slovakia*
repair and installation of machinery	16.6	24.4	50.1	16.7	26.2	10.5	14.1	25.4	10.4	17.1
wearing apparel	7.9	NA	31.4	34.3	30.6	6.0	12.9	17.3	31.6	25.5
total manufacturing	43.4	59.4	66.3	66.0	69.4	32.5	44.9	49.9	50.0	52.3

Source: authors' calculations based on Eurostat data.

manufacturing investment when it bought a rubber plant from Trinseo in Germany for $460 million. Synthos is now the largest producer of styrene rubber in Europe and the main supplier to Michelin, Continental, Bridgestone, Goodyear and Pirelli. It is also the world's third-largest manufacturer of expanded polystyrene (EPS) and the leading producer in Europe. Synthos has acquired R&D centres in addition to its factories in Germany and the Netherlands. The company is part of Michał Sołowow's group, which also includes Cersanit (a manufacturer of ceramic sanitary ware and ceramic tiles) and Barlinek (a producer of wooden flooring) with plants in various countries. The group operates 18 factories in 9 countries.

d Labour productivity

As a legacy of the socialist era, there was a huge gap in manufacturing labour productivity between the economies of Central and Western Europe, the former of which was between three and five times lower. However, radical restructuring, including changes in ownership, organisation and technology, led to a rapid improvement. Productivity more than doubled between 1992 and 2002 in Poland and Hungary (around a 150% increase in real terms), and grew by 75% in Slovakia and by 55% in Czechia, compared to 33% growth in the EU15 during the same period. It continued to grow faster than in the core Western European economies, reaching 82% of the EU average in Slovenia, 76%–78% in Hungary and Poland, 69%–70% in Czechia and Slovakia and 58% in Romania in 2021 (value added at PPP per employee). Although the productivity gap has narrowed considerably, it is still 10–20 percentage points lower than in Spain (90% of the EU average) and 20–30 percentage points below the level in Italy and France (100%–106% of the EU average) (Figure 2.6). It is worth noting that the actual gap may be somewhat smaller, as value added in CE is to some extent understated by the transfer pricing mechanism mentioned above. According to Grodzicki (2018), the narrowing of the gap is mainly due to intra-sectoral changes rather than the transformation of industrial structures.

The difference in productivity is more significant when measured in terms of value added per hour worked, as people in CE tend to work longer hours. In 2021, productivity in Poland, Slovenia, Hungary, Czechia and Slovakia was 68%–69% of the Italian level. Romania's productivity was much lower, at only 48% of the Italian level.

In the CE automotive industry, Hungary has the highest productivity, with 80% of the EU average value added at PPP per person employed in 2021. It is closely followed by Poland, Slovakia and Czechia with 72%–77%. This is not much different from the productivity of the sector in France and Spain (87%–90% of the EU average). Romania's productivity is significantly lower at 56%. Germany is the clear leader with 135%, followed by the Netherlands, Austria and Sweden. The productivity gap, measured as value added per hour worked, between Czechia, Hungary, Poland and Slovakia on the one hand and Italy on the other, ranges from 23 to 30 percentage points.

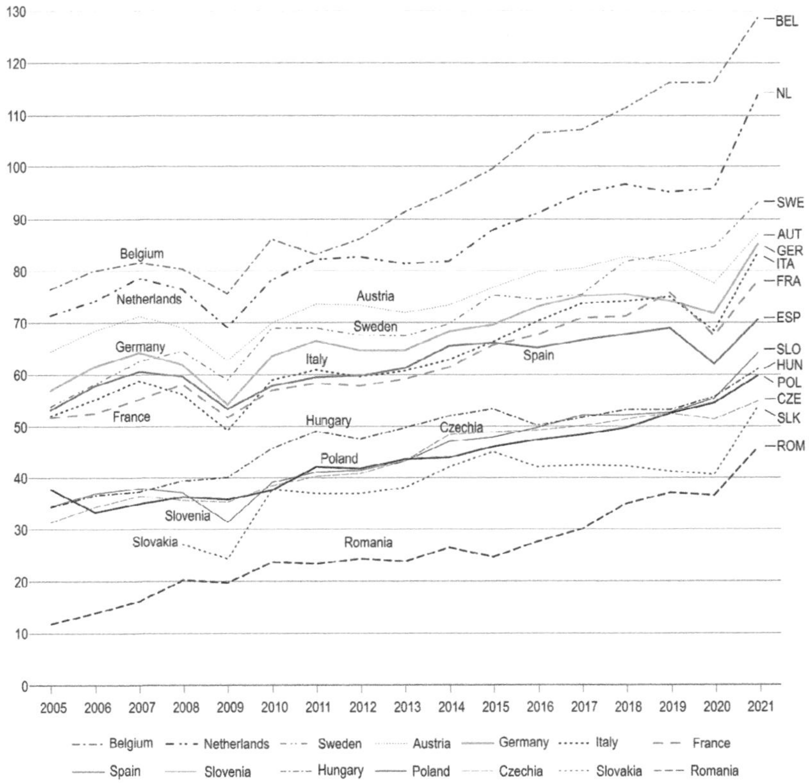

Figure 2.6 Labour productivity per employee in manufacturing (PPP) in selected European countries, 2005–2021 (thousand euro)
Source: authors' calculations based on Eurostat data.

Poland and Slovenia have significantly better productivity levels (90% and 81% of the EU average, respectively, in 2021) than other CE countries (56%–65%) in the manufacture of household appliances. Germany and the Netherlands show the highest productivity rates in this sector in the EU, followed by Italy and France. The largest productivity gap between the CE economies and Germany, France, Italy and Spain is in the aircraft industry. Again, productivity in this sector is relatively highest in Poland (71% of the EU average).

e Investment

The growth of CE manufacturing in recent decades has been the result of massive investment in tangible goods. Its value has more than doubled between 2005 and 2021 in Poland and Hungary, almost doubled in Romania and risen by 40% in Czechia, 25% in Slovenia but only 11% in Slovakia. Meanwhile, Germany and France have seen an increase of around 60%, as opposed to 9% in

Spain. Germany, France and Italy still account for 56% of manufacturing investment in the EU, with Germany alone contributing 24%. The six CE countries now represent 16%. The value of manufacturing investment in Poland is similar to that in Spain, while in Hungary and Czechia it is similar to that in Sweden, Austria and the Netherlands (Figure 2.7).

The difference between manufacturing in Central and Western Europe is particularly evident in the investment rate as a percentage of value added. In the decade 2011–2021, Romania had an average investment rate of 36%, Hungary and Slovakia 27%–28% and Poland and Czechia 21%–22%. This compares with 15% in Spain and France, 14% in Italy and Sweden and 12% in Germany. The EU27 average was 12.7%. This shows that a large part of the profits generated by TNCs in CE countries are continuously reinvested there.

The automotive industry had a particularly high investment rate, with an EU average of 17.6%. It reached 46% in Romania, 39% in Hungary, 35% in Slovakia, 28% in Slovenia and Poland and 25% in Czechia during 2011–2021. Spain and Italy had investment rates of 21%–23%, France 19% and Germany 16%. In recent years, the six CE countries have consumed 23.2% of EU investment in this sector, including 6.0% in Poland and 5.3% in Czechia. In absolute terms, Germany accounts for 43% of EU investment, followed by France (8.8%), Italy (7.1%) and Spain (6.9%). Since 2005, investment has grown rapidly in Poland and Romania, but relatively slowly in Czechia. There has also been a significant increase in Germany, a moderate rise in Spain and a more or less stable level of investment in France and Italy.

The investment rate in EU home appliance production is lower than in the automotive industry, but very high in some CE economies. For example, Romania reached a record level of 42% during 2011–2021, while Poland achieved 27% and Slovenia and Hungary 19%. In contrast, France, Spain, Italy and Germany remained at a level of 11%–12%. Overall, 35.5% of all investment in tangible goods in the EU household appliances sector between 2016 and 2021 was located in CE, with Poland alone accounting for 19.2%. Germany's share of EU investment in this sector is the highest at 36%, with Italy and France each accounting for 13%–16%. In contrast to the manufacture of motor vehicles, the level of investment in the production of domestic appliances remained more or less stable over the decade 2011–2021.

In the aircraft industry, the investment rate in the CE countries was also significantly higher than in Western Europe during 2011–2021, reaching 29% in Romania, 21% in Poland and 16% in Czechia, compared to 9%–11% in Spain, France and Germany. However, the CE region's role in this sector is much smaller than in the other two industries discussed, as evidenced by its low share of EU investment at 6.7%, including 4.2% in Poland. This contrasts with France's share of 62% and Germany's of 28% between 2016 and 2021.

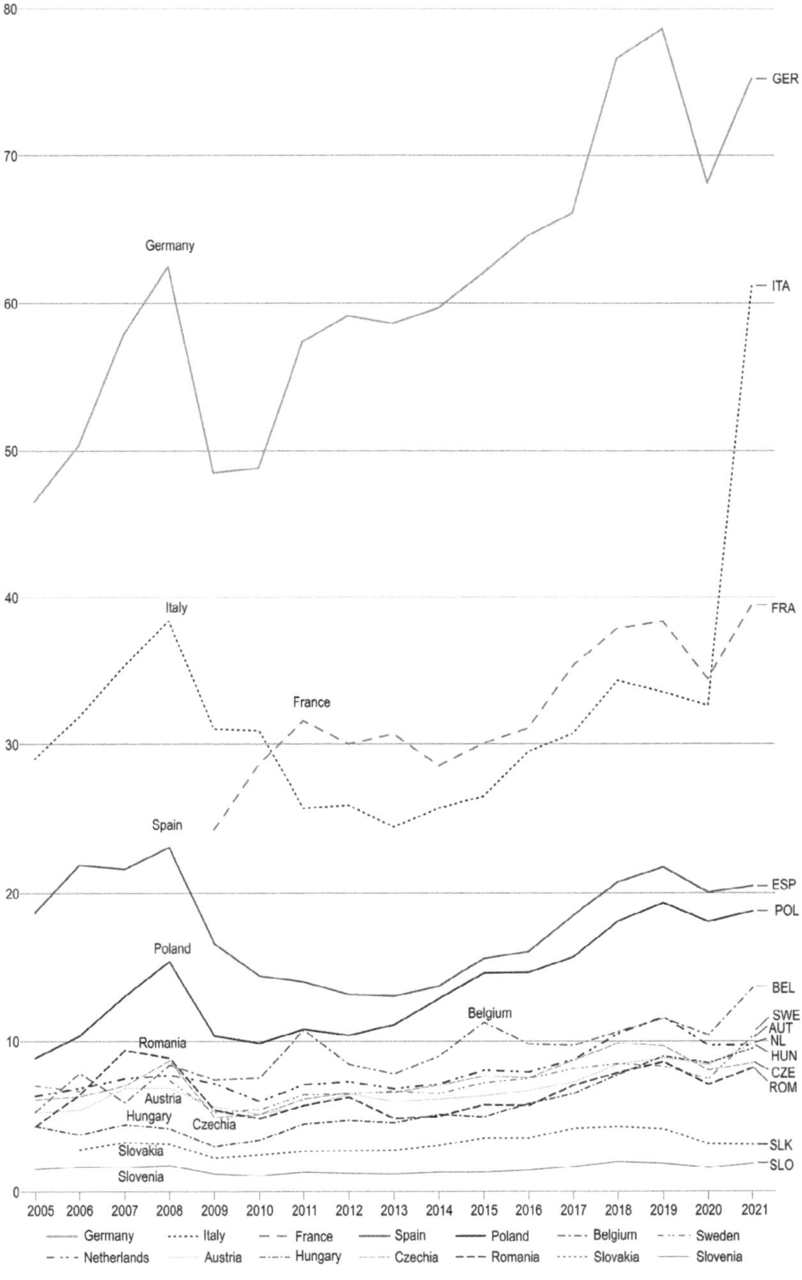

Figure 2.7 Investment in tangible goods in manufacturing, selected countries, 2005–2021 (billion euro)

Source: authors' calculations based on Eurostat data.

f R&D expenditure and employment

The R&D sector in CE is not as developed as in Western Europe. This is reflected in the performance of the innovation systems of the EU Member States. According to the European Innovation Scoreboard (2023), Poland, Slovakia and Hungary are the fourth-, fifth- and sixth-worst performers in the EU, while Romania is the worst. However, Slovenia and Czechia are already close to the EU average and perform better than Spain and Italy. Between 2016 and 2023, the performance indicator has increased by more than 20 percentage points in Czechia. It has also improved significantly in Poland, at a faster rate than in Germany, France and Spain. Progress has been more moderate in Slovakia and Hungary, but almost non-existent in Romania and Slovenia. However, Poland remains one of the three EU countries with the lowest number of small and medium-sized enterprises (SMEs) innovating in products and business processes. It performs better in terms of R&D expenditure in the business sector and is relatively high in terms of "digitalisation", "use of IT technologies" and "intellectual assets".

Business enterprise expenditure on research and development (BERD) in manufacturing has increased significantly in the six CE countries, from €1.4 billion in 2005 to €2.3 billion in 2011 and €5.8 billion in 2021. However, taken together they still represent only about half of BERD in Italy and one-quarter of BERD in France. Total R&D expenditure in CE manufacturing is comparable to that of Belgium, Austria and Sweden. Although CE's share of EU R&D expenditure almost doubled between 2007 and 2021, from 2.3% to 4.2%, it is still much smaller than its position in manufacturing output. Germany accounts for almost half of the EU's manufacturing R&D (45%), while France and Italy contribute around 16% and 8%, respectively. In Poland, BERD expenditure amounts to €2.1 billion, while in Czechia it is €1.5 billion, which is only 19% and 14%, respectively, of similar spending in Italy. The gap is smaller when comparing the CE countries with Spain, with Poland and Czechia accounting for 48% and 35%, respectively, of Spanish BERD in 2021. Slovenia has the highest share of BERD in value added in CE, at 5.3%, surpassing Italy's level of 4.0%. Meanwhile, BERD in Hungary and Czechia (3.8% and 3.3%, respectively) is higher than in Spain (3.2%), while it is lower in Poland (2.1%) and the lowest in Slovakia and Romania (1.4% and 1.1%, respectively). The highest level of R&D expenditures in the EU is shown by Sweden (10.0%), France and Germany (8.5%–8.7%).

There was a sevenfold increase in BERD expenditure in the CE automotive industry, from €220 million in 2005 to €401 million in 2011 and €1,526 million in 2021. This corresponds to around 75% of BERD expenditure in the sector in Italy and 40% in France. The combined expenditures in Czechia (€464 million) and Poland (€407 million) were similar to the Spanish level in 2021, while those in Hungary (€324 million) were slightly lower. Their growth is reflected in a much higher share of BERD in value added, which reached 7.7% in Hungary, 5.9%–6.0% in Slovenia and Czechia and 5.0%–5.2% in Romania and Poland. In Slovakia, however, it was only 1.9%. The largest increase occurred in Poland, from

0.7% in 2007 to 5.0% in 2021, and in Romania, from 1.9% to 5.2% (Table 2.8). This is comparable to the level of 7.8% in Spain. However, it is still significantly lower than in Italy (14.4%), not to mention Germany and France (22.2%–23.7%). Germany accounts for 71% of total EU automotive BERD.

The gap is even wider in the aircraft industry. Poland's spending is about one-tenth of Italy's BERD. France and Germany account for more than two-thirds of EU spending.

The number of researchers in the business enterprise sector (full-time equivalent) in the CE economies more than doubled between 2011 and 2021, reaching 53,773 people. This figure exceeds the number of researchers in Italy's manufacturing sector and is around half the level in France. Poland has the highest number of researchers in CE with 24,419, ahead of Spain, Czechia (10,862) and Hungary (9,661). However, Slovakia and Romania employ significantly fewer researchers (2,250–2,380). Together, the six CE countries account for 9.3% of the researchers in the EU's manufacturing in 2021, while Germany represents 37%.

In the automotive sector, Poland already employs 5,370 researchers, slightly more than Italy, while Hungary (3,329) and Czechia (2,333) have more researchers than Spain. The share of the six CE countries in the number of

Table 2.8 Business R&D expenditure as a percentage of value added and number of R&D personnel as a percentage of employment in the automotive industry in selected countries, 2007 and 2021

Country	*Business R&D expenditure as percentage of value added*		*R&D personnel as percentage of employment (full-time equivalent)*	
	2007	*2021*	*2007*	*2021*
Germany	20.2	23.7	10.9	16.2
France	10.1	22.2	5.9	12.6
Austria	12.6	18.1	8.3	11.2
Italy	10.0	14.4	5.1	11.0
Spain	3.3*	7.8	1.9*	3.9
Hungary	1.8	7.7	1.2	4.5
Slovenia	7.5*	6.0	2.4*	4.5
Czechia	3.0	5.9	2.2	2.9
Romania	1.9*	5.2	0.9*	2.1
Poland	0.7	5.0	0.7	3.4
Belgium	3.1*	3.2	1.5*	3.2
Slovakia	1.8*	1.9	0.1*	1.4

Source: authors' calculations based on Eurostat data.

*Note: Spain, Romania, Slovenia and Belgium in 2008, Slovakia in 2009.

researchers in the EU's automotive industry reached 10.4% in 2021, compared to 5.3% in 2007. Germany has two-thirds of the EU's researchers in this sector, followed by France with 14%. The situation is different in the aircraft industry, where the number of researchers in Poland is less than half of that in Spain and one-quarter of that in Italy. France accounts for more than half of the researchers in this sector.

g Profitability

The profitability of manufacturing activity, measured by the gross operating rate (gross operating surplus as a percentage of turnover), is higher in most CE countries than in Western Europe, despite transfer pricing. For example, it reached 11.5%–11.7% in Poland, Slovenia and Hungary and 10.0% in Czechia during 2016–2021. However, it was lower in Romania (9.4%) and especially in Slovakia (7.8%). Compared to the EU average, Belgium (11.0%), Sweden and Italy (10.1%–10.3%) had higher rates, while Germany and France showed lower ones (8.0% and 6.2%, respectively).

The automotive industry is characterised by a generally lower gross operating rate in the EU (6.2% on average during 2016–2021), but Poland (9.6%), Hungary (8.8%), Czechia, Romania and Slovenia (7.8%–8.0%) have relatively high rates, while Slovakia (5.3%) lags behind. In Germany and Italy, profitability is similar to the EU average, while in France it is lower at 3.3%. CE countries also show above-average profitability in the household appliance sector, with Romania and Hungary at 8.7%–8.8% and Poland at 7.9%. The highest profitability is found in the Netherlands with 13.3%. The operating rate is high in the Polish and Romanian aircraft industry at 16.8%–19.1%. It is also relatively high in Italy (13.7%) and Spain (10.2%).

Strengthening linkages and cooperation: foreign trade in manufactured goods

a Total exports and imports

The size and trends in foreign trade linkages reflect the position of an economy, its degree of internationalisation and its integration into global production networks.

The economic growth of the CE countries and the influx of foreign investment have been accompanied by a huge expansion of trade linkages. In 1999, the combined value of exports from the six CE countries was €100 billion, or 5.1% of the EU27 total. By 2022, this figure had increased tenfold to €978 billion, equivalent to 14.4% of the EU total. Currently, only Germany (23.2%) exports more than CE, whereas in 1999 CE exported less than France, Italy, the Netherlands and Belgium.

Poland's export growth was faster than that of other CE countries and its share in the EU has increased to 5.0%. In 1990, Polish exports totalled $14.4 billion, which rose to $52.7 billion in 2003. Following Poland's accession to the EU in

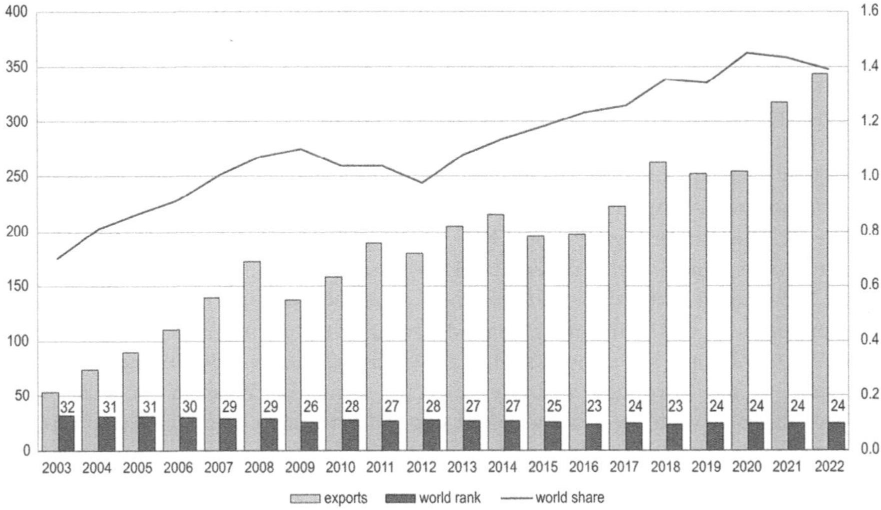

Figure 2.8 Poland's exports of goods, 2003–2022 (billion USD at current prices; % share of world exports, right-hand axis)
Source: authors' calculations based on UN Comtrade database.

2004, export growth accelerated, tripling to $171 billion in 2008. After a slight dip during the financial crisis in 2009, growth continued to exceed $340 billion by 2022. As a result, Poland has become the 7th-largest exporter in the EU and the 24th largest in the world. This is a significant improvement on its rankings in 2003 of 11th and 32nd, respectively (Figure 2.8). However, Poland has a lower share of exports in GDP (62%) than smaller CE economies such as Slovakia (99%), Slovenia and Hungary (90%) and Czechia (75%). This reflects a lesser dependence on exports and a greater role for the domestic market in Poland.

The rising exports were accompanied by an increase in imports, which exceeded Polish exports by 15%–20% until 2012. Since then, the size of exports and imports has been very similar, with a small surplus or deficit in some years. The trade balance has been affected by the changing nature of FDI in the country. In the early post-socialist period, FDI was directed towards the domestic market, but later became mainly export-oriented. There have also been exports of business services. Oil and natural gas remain substantial imports, while Poland has had an increasing trade surplus in manufactured goods with Western Europe since 2003. It is important to note that the country's current account is also affected by inflows of FDI, EU structural funds – of which Poland is a major beneficiary – and remittances from many Polish citizens working in Western Europe.

b Trade in the automotive industry

The analysis of trade in automotive products can be approached in two ways: either narrowly, focusing only on motor vehicles and their parts classified under the automotive industry (NACE 29), or broadly, including other automotive products such as tyres, glass, air conditioning, batteries, lamps and lighting, electrical wiring and seats. For the purposes of this chapter, the broader approach has been taken, with only minor exceptions noted in the text.

It is worth noting that the European automotive industry is largely dominated by German manufacturers. Between 1999 and 2022, Germany's share of EU27 automotive exports was consistently several times higher than that of any other EU country, ranging from 34% to 40%. In 1999, CE exports were only one-tenth of those of the other 20 EU countries (excluding Germany), but by 2022 they had reached two-thirds of their export level (Figure 2.9). The value of CE exports, at €201 billion, is around four times that of France and accounts for 25.5% of total EU exports. This shows a significant shift in the "centre of gravity" of the European automotive sector from the West to the East. Germany, together with the closely linked Central European countries, accounts for a remarkable 61% of the EU's total automotive exports.

In recent years, Czechia and Poland have overtaken Italy and Belgium in terms of automotive exports. Their exports were comparable to those of France and Spain, as of 2022. Slovakia and Hungary have surpassed the Netherlands and Sweden, while Romania is steadily approaching the latter. Figure 2.10 also shows that the CE countries, and Poland in particular, were more resilient to the effects of both the 2009 financial crisis and the COVID-19 pandemic, resulting in a smaller decline in exports than in Western Europe. This can be attributed to the structure of the sector, which is less reliant on passenger car

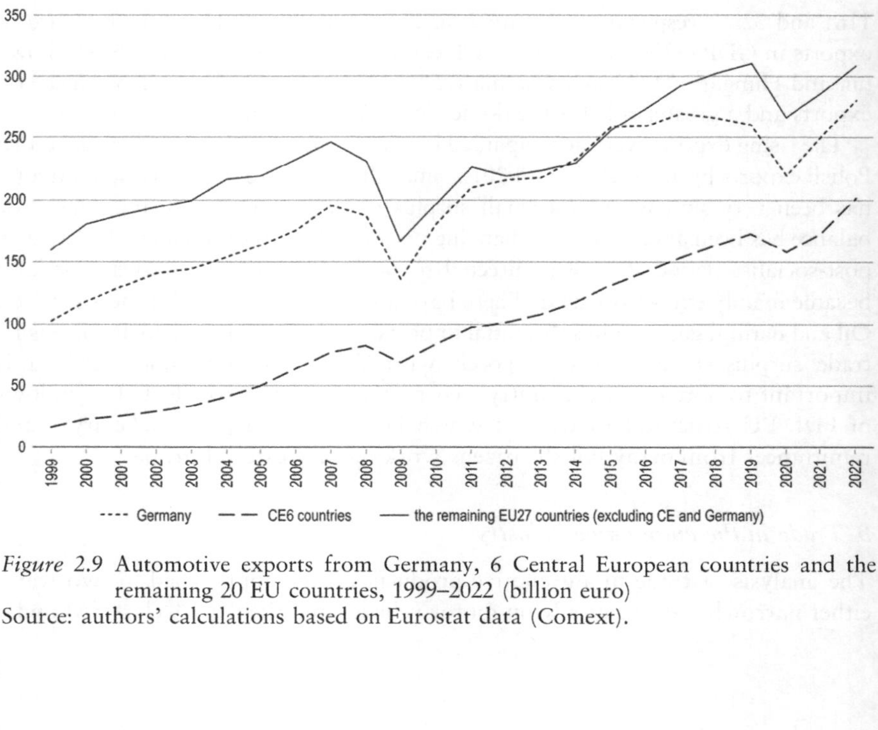

Figure 2.9 Automotive exports from Germany, 6 Central European countries and the remaining 20 EU countries, 1999–2022 (billion euro)

Source: authors' calculations based on Eurostat data (Comext).

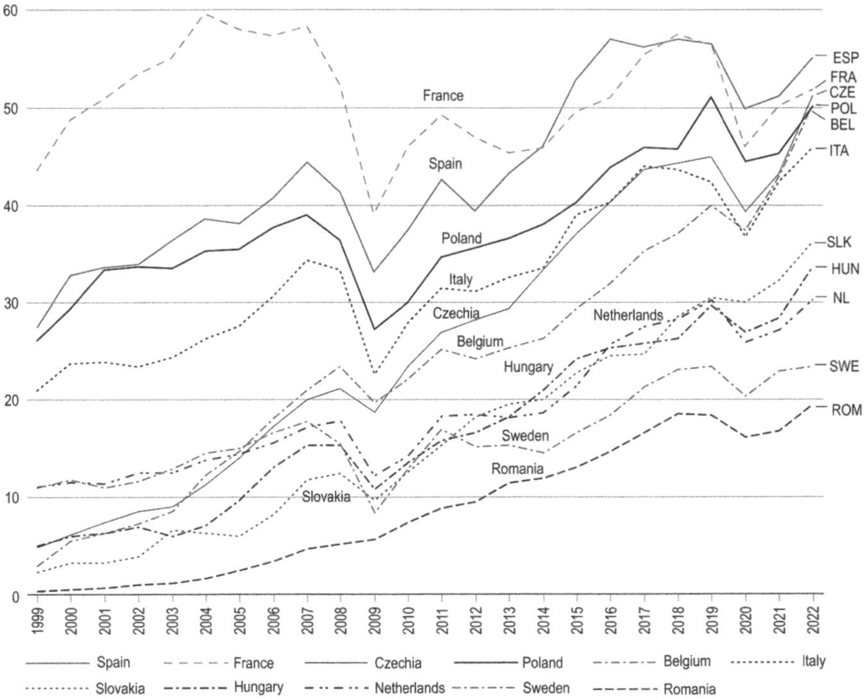

Figure 2.10 Automotive exports of the 11 largest EU exporters (excluding Germany), 1999–2022 (billion euro)

Source: authors' calculations based on Eurostat data (Comext).

assembly, a segment that is more vulnerable to potential crises. From a broader perspective, the Spanish automotive industry has been relatively successful, becoming the second-largest EU exporter since 2014.

The growing importance of the CE countries is even more evident when we look at the trade balance for automotive products. While most Western European economies, with the exception of Germany and Spain, are experiencing a decline or trade deficit, all the CE countries have a growing trade surplus. In 2000, the combined surplus of the six CE countries was €5 billion, only half the size of France's surplus at the time. In 2022, however, the CE countries achieved a surplus of €73 billion, compared with a deficit of €25 billion in France. In the same year, Germany generated a surplus of €113 billion and Spain €6 billion. Germany excepted, Czechia, Poland, Hungary and Slovakia currently have the highest surpluses in Europe (see Figure 2.11).

In 2022, Polish exports in the broad automotive industry totalled €50.3 billion, slightly less than Czechia (€51.2 billion) and France (€51.8 billion) and lower than Spain (€55.0 billion). This placed Poland 5th in the EU and 11th in the world. However, if the narrowly defined NACE29 sector is taken into

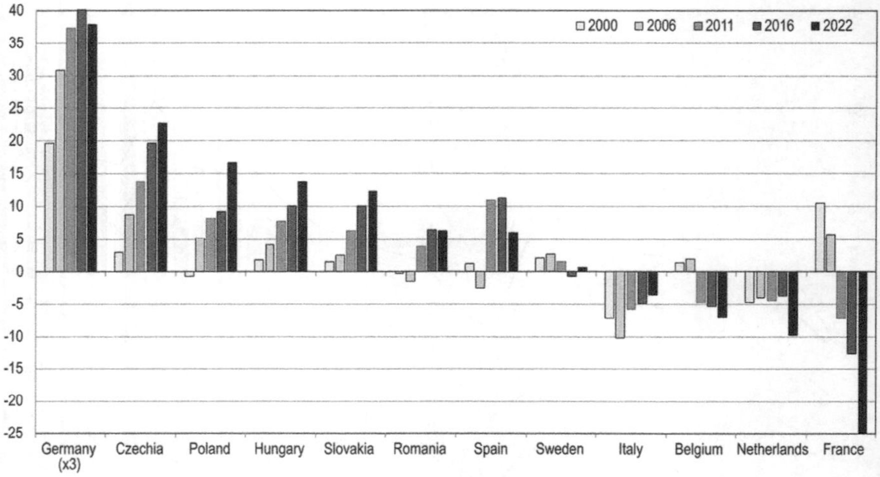

Figure 2.11 Balance of foreign trade in automotive products, 2000–2022 (billion euro)
Source: authors' calculations based on Eurostat data (Comext).

account, the figure falls to €35.1 billion according to Eurostat. This is because Poland is a major exporter of lithium-ion batteries (€8.2 billion), tyres (€2.5 billion) and automotive glass (see Chapter 3).

What distinguishes Poland's automotive exports from those of many other countries is the limited significance of exported passenger cars. For example, Czechia and Slovakia are important assemblers of cars, whereas Poland's high global position is mainly due to exports of automotive parts and accessories, ranking seventh in the world and second in Europe (Figure 2.12). In addition, Poland is the leading European exporter of batteries for electric vehicles and ranks seventh in the world for exports of car engines and their parts. The country also plays a significant role in the global export of buses, ranking fourth in the world and first in Europe. Similarly, it ranks fifth in the world and second in Europe after Germany in the export of trailers and semi-trailers. It is also a substantial exporter of commercial vehicles.

In terms of exports of the products discussed, other CE countries also occupy prominent positions. Czechia is the fourth-largest exporter of automotive components in Europe, behind Italy and ahead of France, the second-biggest exporter of buses in Europe and the fifth largest in the world, while Hungary is the tenth-largest world exporter of engines. In addition, Slovakia is among the world's top 15 exporters of passenger cars, and Romania's role is growing. Due to their smaller size, Czechia, Hungary and Slovakia are among the world leaders in automotive exports per capita.

The structure of Polish automotive exports has changed over time (see Figure 2.13). The share of passenger car exports has fallen significantly from 35.4% in 2009 to only 10.8% in 2022. The role of engines has also declined

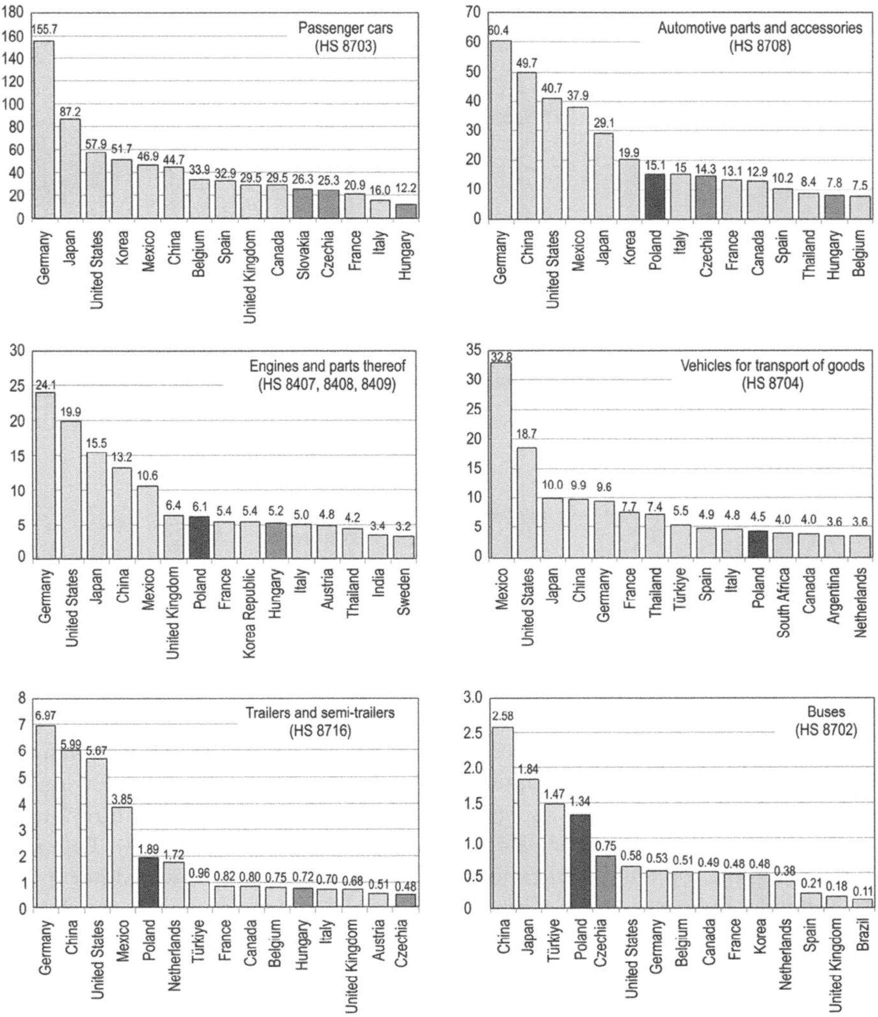

Figure 2.12 Top 15 world exporters of motor vehicles, parts and accessories in 2022 (billion USD)

Source: authors' calculations based on UN Comtrade database.

from a record high of 28.6% in 2001 to 13.0% currently. The share of commercial vehicles has remained stable at around 10%. Meanwhile, exports of automotive parts and accessories have grown rapidly. A particularly impressive example of this trend is the development of batteries for electric vehicles. It is interesting to note that the share of certain labour-intensive products, such as wire harnesses, has fallen significantly (from 8.9% in 1999 to 2.2% in 2022).

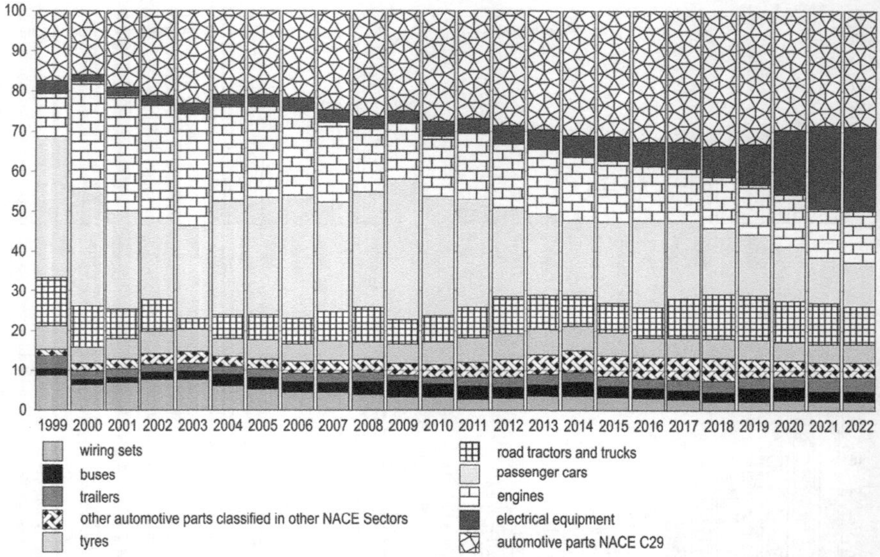

Figure 2.13 Structure of Polish automotive exports, 1999–2022
Source: authors' calculations based on Eurostat data (Comext).

c *Trade in the domestic appliance industry*

The household appliance industry has experienced huge FDI-driven export growth in the CE countries over the last two decades. Although Poland is slightly behind Czechia in automotive exports, it is the absolute leader among the CE countries in home appliance exports and has been the third-largest exporter in the EU since 2013, after Germany and Italy (Figure 2.14). Poland is also among the top ten global exporters. It ranks second in the world in exports of washing machines after China, fourth in dishwashers, sixth in electro-mechanical appliances (e.g. food grinders and mixers), eighth in vacuum cleaners and ninth in refrigerators and freezers (Figure 2.15). In the case of washing machines, Poland accounts for 37.4% and CE as a whole for 55.6% of EU exports. For dishwashers and refrigerators, Poland is the third-largest EU exporter after Germany and Italy. The six CE countries together account for 26.9% of EU exports of domestic appliances, similar to their share in the automotive industry (Table 2.9). Poland's official share of EU exports is 11.9% (€8.9 billion), which is less than its share of mainly export-oriented production and lower than its high world position in exports of major domestic appliances. Unfortunately, the picture is significantly distorted by the re-export within the EU of products manufactured in Poland or imported from China, especially by Sweden and Belgium, which have limited domestic appliance production, as well as by the Netherlands and Austria.

Czechia and Slovakia are among the top ten EU exporters of domestic appliances, with exports rising steadily to €3.1 billion and €2.4 billion,

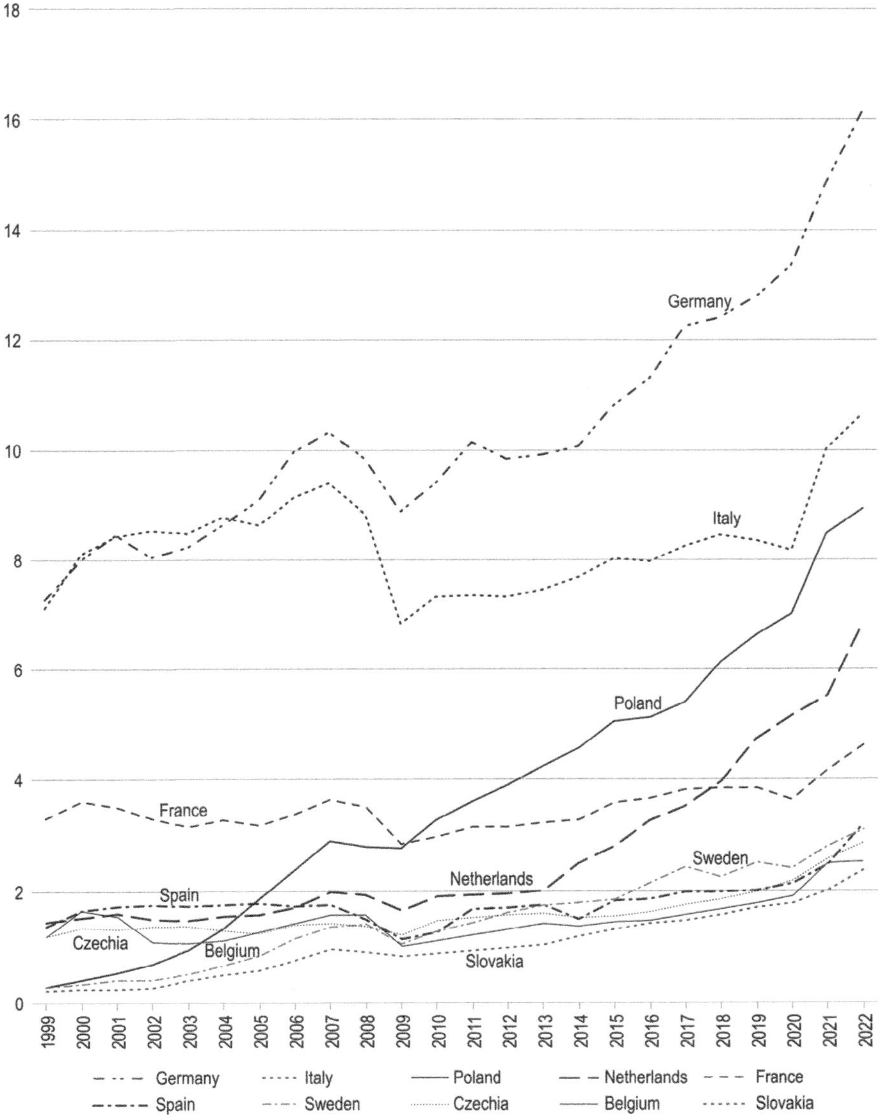

Figure 2.14 Top ten EU exporters of home appliances, 1999–2022 (billion euro)
Source: authors' calculations based on Eurostat data (Comext).

respectively. In recent years, they have overtaken Hungary (€2.26 billion, 11th place in 2022) and previously Slovenia (€1.44 billion), pushing them out of the top ten European exporters. Romania's exports are also growing rapidly (€2.10 billion, 12th) and are now approaching Hungary's level. Hungary is the world's fifth-largest exporter of electromechanical appliances, overtaking Poland.

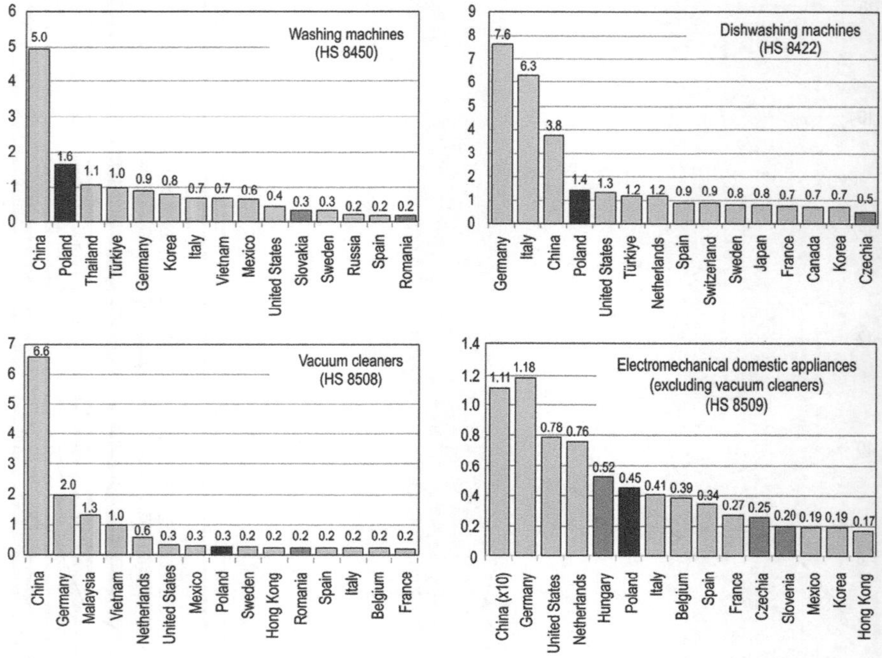

Figure 2.15 Top 15 global exporters of selected home appliances in 2022 (billion USD)
Source: authors' calculations based on UN Comtrade database.

In 2022, Poland had become the country with the largest surplus in trade in home appliances in Europe, narrowly overtaking Italy, which had held the top position since the 1990s. Until 2010, Germany was the country with the second-highest positive balance, but Poland overtook it in 2011. Despite being the largest exporter, Germany has a larger domestic market. Moreover, while Germany's trade surplus is declining, Italy's remains at a similar level. At present, Italy is the only Western European country with a positive trade balance, while the rest are showing increasing trade deficits. In contrast, CE is characterised by higher exports than imports: the surplus has reached €3.7 billion in Poland and is still growing, as is the case in Slovakia, Czechia (Figure 2.16) and Romania, but not in Slovenia and Hungary.

d Trade in the aircraft industry

Poland and other CE countries are not among the main exporters of products classified as aircraft (Figure 2.17). European exports are strongly dominated by France and Germany, where passenger aircraft plants are located, followed by Spain and the Netherlands. However, Poland's exports have recently risen to €4.6 billion, placing it fifth in the EU in 2022, ahead of Italy, while Czechia ranks ninth, followed by Sweden. It should be noted

Table 2.9 Share of CE in the EU27 in the automotive and domestic appliance industries (%)

Country	*Automotive industry*						*Domestic appliance industry*					
	Employment		*Output*		*Exports*		*Employment*		*Output*		*Exports*	
	2005	2021	2005	2021	2005	2022	2008	2021	2008	2021	2005	2022
Germany	37.9	35.8	43.4	47.6	37.9	35.5	22.1	28.3	25.2	30.7	25.4	21.5
Spain	8.3	6.4	9.2	6.9	8.8	7.0	7.0	4.6	8.0	4.6	5.0	4.3
France	14.1	9.3	19.2	9.1	13.4	6.6	7.3	10.1	8.4	10.9	8.9	6.1
Czechia	6.6	7.1	2.9	5.6	3.2	6.5	3.4	2.8	1.6	1.6	2.4	4.1
Poland	5.8	8.6	2.7	4.0	3.4	6.4	11.6	13.8	10.5	12.9	5.2	11.9
Belgium	2.1	1.2	2.9	1.6	8.2	6.3	0.6	0.3	0.8	0.3	3.5	3.4
Italy	8.4	6.8	7.9	7.3	6.4	5.8	20.9	11.9	26.6	18.4	24.1	14.2
Slovakia	2.6*	3.2	1.2*	3.4	1.4	4.6	1.4	1.3	1.0	0.9	1.6	3.2
Hungary	2.9	4.0	1.9	2.9	2.2	4.3	4.5	6.0	2.3	2.1	2.7	3.0
Netherlands	1.0	0.9	1.1*	1.2	3.4	3.8	1.3	1.7	3.5	4.9	4.4	9.1
Sweden	3.8	3.4	4.7	3.7	3.5	2.9	2.1	0.3	2.1	0.2	3.5	3.8
Austria	1.6	1.5	2.5	1.9	3.6	2.6	2.1	1.7	2.8	1.7	2.7	4.5
Romania	4.9	6.9	0.6	2.3	0.6	2.5	4.5	7.3	1.3	4.0	1.1	2.8
Slovenia	0.5	0.7	0.4	0.4	0.7	1.3	4.2	3.4	2.7	3.2	2.5	1.9
CE	23.4	30.4	9.7	18.8	11.5	25.5	29.5	34.7	19.5	24.8	15.5	26.9

Source: authors' calculations based on Eurostat data.

*Note: Slovakia automotive output 2006 and employment 2008; Netherlands automotive output 2009.

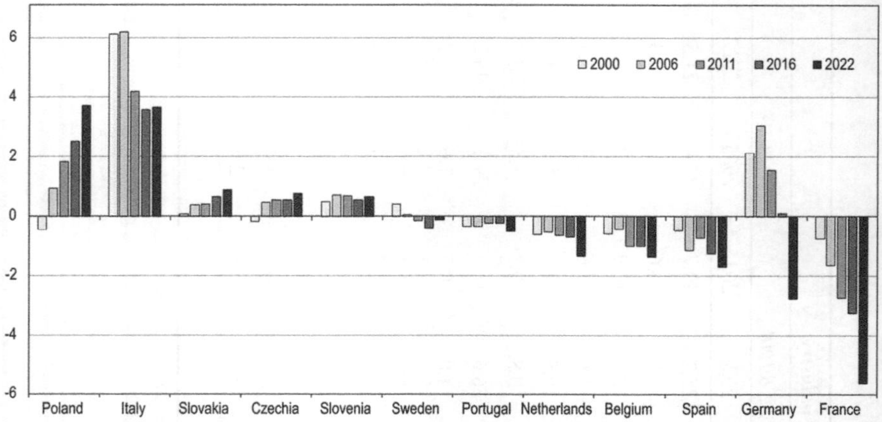

Figure 2.16 Balance of foreign trade in home appliances, 2000–2022 (billion euro)
Source: authors' calculations based on Eurostat data (Comext).

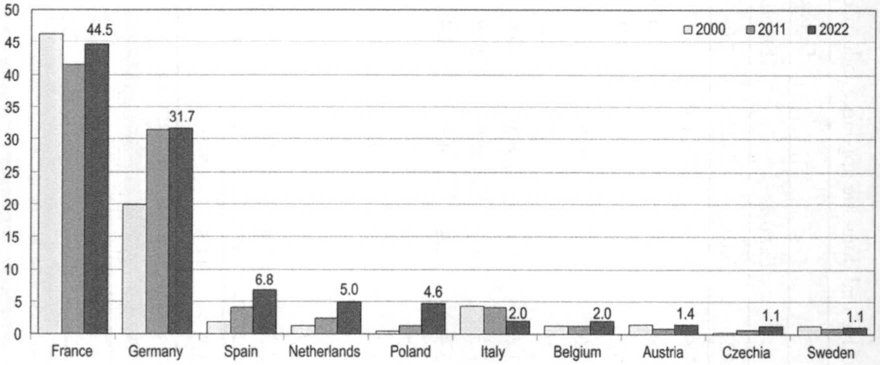

Figure 2.17 Top ten EU exporters of aircraft products in 2000, 2011 and 2022 (billion euro)
Source: authors' calculations based on Eurostat data (Comext).

that the statistics may not include some defence-related production, as countries have different disclosure requirements. This may also explain the significant differences in the reported value of exports between the various sources. In 2022, Central European exports of aircraft products were estimated by Eurostat to be worth €6.6 billion. Most of this value (€3.9 billion) was accounted for by turbojets, propellers and other aircraft engines, followed by aircraft components (€1.8 billion) (Figure 2.18) and aeroplanes and helicopters (€0.8 billion). Between 2000 and 2017, the trade balance of the aircraft industry in CE was slightly negative. Since then, however, the CE countries (excluding Hungary and Slovenia) have recorded an increasing trade surplus, which reached €1 billion in 2022.

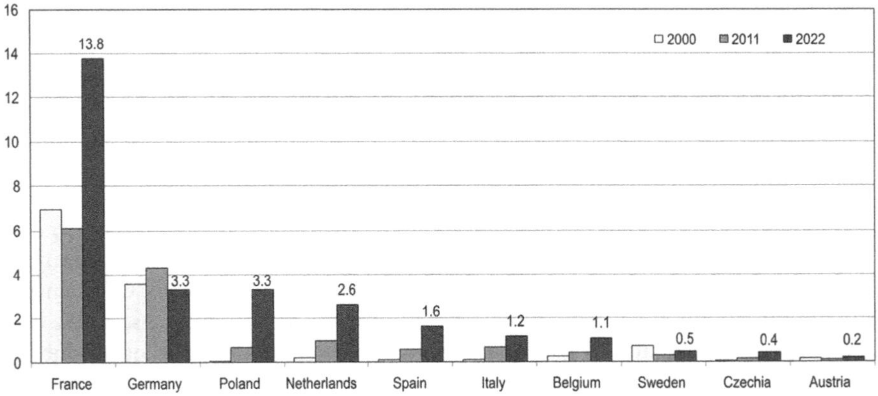

Figure 2.18 Exports of engines, turbojets and propellers for civil aircraft from EU countries in 2000, 2011 and 2022 (billion euro)

Source: authors' calculations based on Eurostat data (Comext).

Conclusions

Historically, Czechia was one of the industrialised areas of Europe, in contrast to other Central European countries. After the Second World War, as part of the Soviet political bloc, all these countries were subject to forced military-oriented industrialisation by large state-owned organisations, with underdeveloped production of consumer goods. This led to a widening technological gap between Western and Central and Eastern European industry. The latter remained relatively isolated until the late 1980s. The rapid transition from state socialism to a market economy, with radical economic restructuring, changes in ownership and a reorientation of trade relations towards the West, led in the initial shock phase to a decline in GDP and high unemployment. Since the early 1990s, however, it has provided the basis for dynamic economic growth, gradually catching up with Western European countries in terms of GDP and quality of life. This has been supported by integration into the EU. Foreign investment has become an important factor in the economic development of the Central European countries. Relative to the size of their economies, they have attracted more capital than Western Europe.

For three decades, there has been a systematic increase in the value of investment in tangible goods, which has contributed to a growing share of CE in EU manufacturing, in terms of both employment (22%) and output (12%). Its share is even higher in terms of the number of enterprises (31%), due to the still-growing number of SMEs, which bears some resemblance to Italian manufacturing. Profitability in CE manufacturing tends to be well above the EU average. Although there has been some progress in reducing the huge gap in labour productivity inherited from the socialist era, it is still 20%–30% lower than in Spain, France and Italy. Despite the increase in the number of researchers and R&D expenditure in CE business enterprises, they account for only 10% of researchers and 6% of expenditure in the EU, which is much lower than their share in overall employment and production. The number of researchers in the six CE countries already exceeds that of Italy's manufacturing sector, but their R&D expenditure is half that of Italy.

The region plays a significant role in the EU automotive industry, accounting for around one-third of employment and one-fifth of production. This is significantly higher than the combined share of France and Italy. Over the last decade, the region has absorbed up to one-third of total EU investment. It is important to note that the investment rate in the automotive sector is higher than in manufacturing in general, although profitability tends to be lower. The share of the six CE countries has become particularly large in the manufacture of automotive parts, where they account for almost half of EU employment and more than one-third of production value – more than Germany. The CE countries also have a strong position in the manufacture of domestic appliances, representing one-third of EU employment and one-quarter of output. However, it is less important in the aircraft sector, where it contributes only 10% of EU employment and around 3% of output.

The automotive industry is important and growing in all six CE countries. Czechia and Slovakia are prominent European producers of motor vehicles, while Poland and Czechia are among the leaders in the manufacture of parts and accessories. Romania, Slovakia and Poland have seen the fastest growth in automotive production and investment, while Czechia has seen the slowest. Slovakia has become extremely dependent on the sector, with 40% of its manufacturing production concentrated there, while in Czechia and Hungary the share is also over one-quarter. However, Slovakia's industry lags behind other CE countries in terms of profitability and productivity. In contrast, Hungary has the highest productivity, followed by Czechia and Poland. In addition, Czechia and Poland lead the region in R&D expenditure in the automotive sector. Poland has become the third-largest producer of domestic appliances in the EU, after Germany and Italy, and their manufacture is also important in Romania, Hungary and Slovenia, but less so in Czechia and Slovakia. The aircraft industry has developed mainly in Poland, Czechia and Romania.

Nothing better reflects CE's integration into European production networks and its increasing role than its rapidly growing exports. The value of broadly defined automotive exports from Czechia and Poland now exceeds that of Italy and is almost equal to that of France. In addition, these exports have become very large in Slovakia, Hungary and Romania. Moreover, the CE countries have the highest trade surplus in Europe, second only to Germany. Czechia, Hungary and Slovakia have some of the highest per capita automotive export values in the world. These three countries are significant exporters of both motor vehicles and their components. By contrast, Poland ranks second in Europe and seventh in the world for exports of automotive parts and accessories, is a leading European exporter of buses and batteries for electric vehicles, second in Europe for trailers and semi-trailers and third for engines, but is not a significant exporter of passenger cars. Czechia ranks second in Europe for exports of buses and fourth for automotive components, while Hungary ranks fifth for engines.

Poland is also one of the world's top ten exporters of domestic appliances, ranking second after China for exports of washing machines and fourth for dishwashers. Other CE countries are also important exporters, and the region accounts for more than one-quarter of EU exports of home appliances, similar to automotive exports. European exports of aircraft and their components are strongly dominated by France and Germany. Nevertheless, Poland ranks fifth in the EU, ahead of Italy, while Czechia and Romania are eighth and ninth, respectively.

All in all, the formerly isolated Central European periphery has become strongly integrated into global, and especially European, production networks and has achieved a significantly improved position. This is reflected in particular in CE countries' systematically increasing share in EU exports, with a growing trade surplus, more exports of complex products and a relative decline in simpler ones. Not surprisingly, countries starting from a lower level, such as Poland, Romania and Slovakia, have made greater progress than the historically more industrialised Czechia. At the same time, the region still lags behind Western Europe in terms of labour productivity and R&D expenditure.

The general success of the CE economies seems to confirm the fundamental role of institutional determinants (Glaeser et al., 2004; Acemoglu & Robinson, 2008) and culture (Landes, 1998; Harrison & Huntington, 2001) in economic development. It is based on the creation of transparent democratic and market institutions, demonopolisation and privatisation of the economy without the emergence of oligarchic structures. Low levels of corruption, high educational aspirations, quality of work and local entrepreneurship would not have been possible without a conducive cultural background. The rapid growth of manufacturing and exports within European production networks was an essential part of this process, taking advantage of the common market, lower costs and geographical proximity to the Western European core.

The following chapters provide an in-depth analysis of the development of three important manufacturing sectors, as well as a closer examination of labour issues and public policies in Poland. Chapter 9 discusses the upgrading processes of the Polish and Central European manufacturing industries and their changing position in the core–periphery perspective.

Note

1 The Laurin & Klement factory, which was founded in 1895, started to produce cars in 1905 and in 1925 it merged with the Škoda military vehicle manufacturer from Pilsen.

References

Acemoglu, D., & Robinson, J.A. (2008). The role of institutions in growth and development. Working Paper 10. Washington, DC: Commission on Growth and Development.

Bachtler, J., Mendez, C., & Oraže, H. (2014). From conditionality to Europeanization in Central and Eastern Europe: Administrative performance and capacity in cohesion policy. *European Planning Studies*, 22(4), 735–757.

Becker, N., & Cieślik, A. (2020). German direct investment in Central and Eastern Europe. In J. Wandel & K. Kamińska (Eds.), *15 Jahre gemeinsam in der Europäischen Union: Errungenschaften und Gegenwärtige Herausforderungen für die Polnische und Deutsche Wirtschaftspolitik* (pp. 79–93). Warsaw: Oficyna Wydawnicza SGH.

Becker, S.O., Egger, P.H., & Von Ehrlich, M. (2010). Going NUTS: The effect of EU structural funds on regional performance. *Journal of Public Economics*, 94(9–10), 578–590.

Castelli, C., d'Hombres, B., de Dominicis, L., Dijkstra, L., Montalto, V., & Pontarollo, N. (2023). What makes cities happy? Factors contributing to life satisfaction in European cities. *European Urban and Regional Studies*, 30(4), 319–342.

Coe, N.M., & Yeung, H.W.-c. (2015). *Global production networks: Theorizing economic development in an interconnected world*. Oxford: Oxford University Press.

Damgaard, J., Elkjaer, T., & Johannesen, N. (2019). What is real and what is not in the global FDI network?IMF Working Paper.Washington, DC: International Monetary Fund.

Dicken, P. (2015). *Global shift: Mapping the changing contours of the world economy*. New York: Guilford Press.

Durand, L., & Espinoza, R. (2021). The fiscal multiplier of European structural investment funds: Aggregate and sectoral effects with an application to Slovenia. IMF Working Paper, WP 21/118. Washington, DC: International Monetary Fund.

EBRD. (2016). *Life in Transition Survey*. London: European Bank for Reconstruction and Development.

European Commission. (2020). *Report on the quality of life in European cities*. Luxembourg: Publications Office of the European Union.

European Innovation Scoreboard. (2023). European Innovation Scoreboard 2023 and Regional Innovation Scoreboard 2023. Brussels: European Commission. https://projects.research-and-innovation.ec.europa.eu/en/statistics/performance-indicators/european-innovation-scoreboard/eis.

Fihel, A. (Ed.). (2011). Recent trends in international migration in Poland. The 2011 SOPEMI report. CMR Working Papers 52 (110). Warsaw: Ośrodek Badań nad Migracjami UW.

Glaeser, E.L., La Porta, R., Lopez-de-Silanes, F., & Shleifer, A. (2004). Do institutions cause growth? *Journal of Economic Growth*, 9(3), 271–303.

Good, D.F. (1984). *The economic rise of the Habsburg Empire, 1750–1914*. Berkeley, CA: University of California Press.

Grodzicki, M. (2018). *Konwergencja w warunkach integracji gospodarczej. Grupa Wyszehradzka w globalnych łańcuchach wartości*. Kraków: Jagiellonian University Press.

Harrison, L., & Huntington, S. (Eds.). (2001). *Culture matters: How values shape human progress*. New York: Basic Books.

Jacobs, A.J. (2017). *Automotive FDI in Emerging Europe: Shifting locales in the motor vehicle industry*. London: Palgrave Macmillan.

Jeffries, I. (2002). *Eastern Europe at the turn of the twenty-first century: A guide to the economies in transition*. London: Routledge.

Klein, A., Schulze, M.S., & Vonyó, T. (2017). How peripheral was the periphery? Industrialization in East Central Europe since 1870. In K.H. O'Rourke & J.G. Williamson (Eds.), *The spread of modern industry to the periphery since 1871* (pp. 63–90). Oxford: Oxford Academic. doi:10.1093/acprof:oso/9780198753643.003.0004.

Kołodko, G.W. (2000). *From shock to therapy: The political economy of post-socialist transformation*. Oxford: Oxford University Press.

Kornai, J. (1992). *The socialist system: The political economy of communism*. Oxford: Clarendon.

Kornai, J. (1997). *Struggle and hope: Essays on stabilization and reform in a post-socialist economy*. Cheltenham: Edward Elgar.

Koźmiński, A.K. (2008). *How it all happened: Essays in political economy of transition*. Warsaw: Difin.

Landes, D.S. (1998). *The wealth and poverty of nations*. New York: Norton.

Lane, P.R., & Milesi-Ferretti, G.M. (2018). The external wealth of nations revisited: International financial integration in the aftermath of the global financial crisis. *IMF Economic Review*, 66(1), 189–222.

Maddison, A. (2010). *Maddison historical statistics database*. Groningen: Groningen Growth and Development Centre. Retrieved from https://www.rug.nl/ggdc/historicaldevelopment/maddison/.

Orłowski, W.M. (2020). Trajectories of the economic transition in Central and Eastern Europe. In G. Gorzelak (Ed.), *Social and economic development in Central and Eastern Europe* (pp. 11–34). London: Routledge.

Pavlinek, P. (2017). *Dependent growth: Foreign investment and the development of the automotive industry in East-Central Europe*. New York: Springer.

Piątkowski, M. (2018). *Europe's growth champion*. Oxford: Oxford University Press.

Piątkowski, M. (2021). How the European Union made Poland European again. In M. Landesmann & I.P. Székely (Eds.), *Does EU membership facilitate convergence? The experience of the EU's eastern enlargement* (Vol. I, pp. 151–172). New York: Palgrave Macmillan.

Pollard, S. (1986). *Peaceful conquest*. Reprint. Oxford: Oxford University Press.

Schulze, M.S., & Fernandes, F.T. (2009). Human capital formation in Austria-Hungary and Germany: Time series estimates of educational attainment, 1860–1910. In K. Halmos, J. Klement, Á. Pogány, & B. Tomka (Eds.), *A felhalmozás Míve. Történeti Tanulmányok Kövér György Tiszteletére* (pp. 275–289). Budapest: Századvég Kiadó.

Turnock, D. (2003). *The human geography of East Central Europe*. London: Routledge.

UNCTAD. (2022). *World Investment Report 2022: International tax reforms and sustainable investment*. Geneva: United Nations Conference on Trade and Development.

United Nations Population Division. (2020). *International migration stock 2020*. New York: United Nations. https://www.un.org/development/desa/pd/content/international-migrant-stock.

Van Zon, H. (2008). *Russia's development problem: The cult of power*. Basingstoke: Palgrave Macmillan.

Williams, A.M., & Baláž, V. (1999). Privatisation in Central Europe: Different legacies, methods, and outcomes. *Environment and Planning C: Government and Policy*, 17(6), 731–751.

3 Automotive Industry

Perhaps no other sector reflects the changing position of the Central European countries in Europe better than the automotive industry (Domański & Lung, 2009; Frigant & Miollan, 2014; Klier & McMillan, 2015; Guzik et al., 2020; Pavlínek, 2018, 2020, 2022). It is also one of the most important industries in the EU, additionally characterised by an extensive supplier network. The authors analyse Poland's dynamic role in this sector on the basis of secondary and primary statistical data, as well as company interviews described in detail in the Introduction. The chapter begins with a brief outline of the history of automotive manufacturing in the country and the post-socialist transformation, followed by a presentation of the size, dynamics and structure of the sector in terms of products and companies, the impact of the shift to electromobility and the development of non-production competences. The upgrading of foreign subsidiaries and the development of domestic firms are discussed in more detail.

Historical background

The contemporary development of the automotive industry cannot be understood without a historical perspective. It is necessary to consider both the demand and supply conditions in the country: to what extent motor vehicles were needed and they could be produced locally.

Czechoslovakia was the only Central European country where domestic manufacturers were able to launch successfully the production of cars and commercial vehicles based on their own designs and capable of long-term development and market expansion. In Poland, the Ford T was assembled in 1918–1920 at the Central Auto Works (CWS) of the Ministry of War in Warsaw. Short-lived, small-scale private assembly initiatives followed. A GM plant began production of Chevrolets in 1928 and a Citroën assembly plant opened in 1930, but both closed during the Great Depression in 1931. In 1932, a licence agreement was signed with Fiat for the assembly and production of cars and light trucks at the state-owned PZInż (formerly CWS). The Fiat 508 became the first mass-produced car in Poland, with some 10,000 vehicles built in Warsaw by 1939; PZInż also manufactured motorcycles. The GM assembly plant was reopened in 1936, followed by others. Nevertheless, production

DOI: 10.4324/9781003430117-4

reached only 1,879 cars in 1938, compared to 14,000 in smaller Czechoslovakia. In 1938 there were only 29,800 cars and 8,600 lorries registered in the country, just over one-third of the number in Czechoslovakia, while Poland's GDP per capita was two-thirds of Czechoslovakia's.

The Second World War caused immense damage with the destruction of manufacturing plants and infrastructure, and the loss of life of millions of people, including engineers. The socialist system of nationalised enterprises created a totally new political and economic situation. The priorities of central decision-makers and the influence of the Soviet Union became vital, while consumer demand lost its importance. Private ownership of motor vehicles was ideologically suspect as a bourgeois need, not to mention that the poor post-war society could not afford to buy cars. What were needed, however, were vehicles for military and industrial transport. As a result, until the late 1960s, the number of trucks produced was greater than the number of cars.

Truck manufacturing began as early as 1948 in the former ironworks in Starachowice. The expanded FSC Star plant supplied both the army and road carriers and remained the largest truck producer in Poland until the 1990s. A new FSC truck plant was built in Lublin in 1951, starting with the assembly of Soviet-licensed GAZ vehicles. From 1959, it specialised in the manufacture of locally built Żuk (Beetle) vans and pick-ups. These used Warszawa car chassis and engines, similar to the Nysa vans and minibuses produced in the town of Nysa since 1958. Two years later, the JZS plant, built on the site of the destroyed German military factory in Jelcz, launched the manufacture of heavy-duty Żubr (Bison) trucks, which were later replaced by new generations of Jelcz trucks (see Figure 6.3). In addition, in 1973, the former FSR repair plant in Poznań began production of Tarpan agricultural pick-ups (Wilk, 2019).

The first coaches were built on the extended chassis of Star trucks from 1952. From 1958, original San buses and coaches were produced in the former railway wagon factory in Sanok, which were replaced by Autosan coaches in 1970. The Jelcz plant also produced coaches under the Czech Škoda licence with Karosa bodies from 1960, followed by city buses from 1963. The latter were replaced in 1973 by buses built under the French Berliet licence.

In the consumer sector, bicycles and motorcycles were the main focus for a long time. In the mid-1960s, Poland was making ten times as many motorcycles as cars, and it was only in the 1970s that car production began to take over.

In 1948, the Polish government signed a licensing agreement with Fiat to build a car factory (Fiat 1100) on the outskirts of Warsaw. It was to be paid for by the export of Polish coal. Under the conditions of the Cold War, the Soviet Union stopped construction in 1949 and granted a licence for the GAZ M20 Pobieda (a 1930s Ford copy), which began assembly in 1951 under the name Warszawa and local engine production in 1953. The main customers were state institutions and companies, as well as political officials. The first car designed in Poland after the war was the low-powered Syrena (Mermaid), also produced by FSO in Warsaw from 1957. Nevertheless, only 24,839 cars were made in the country in 1965, when Poland was allowed to sign a new contract with Fiat. Production of the Fiat 125p at FSO began in 1967. The assembly of the Syrena was then moved from Warsaw to Bielsko-Biała, where the Syrena's engines were manufactured by WSM. Since 1978, Polonez has been a new FSO brand, also prepared in Italy (Szczerbicki, 2017).

Meanwhile, another licence agreement was signed with the Italian partner in 1971. In 1973, FSM (formerly WSM) began producing a tiny Fiat 126p; a new engine factory with a small assembly plant in Bielsko-Biała and a large assembly plant in Tychy were built using Western European loans.

All in all, post-war car manufacturing in Poland began with a Soviet licence for an obsolete model and a small Polish vehicle, but it was Fiat licences that led to mass production of cars in the 1970s (Table 3.1). With 351,000 passenger cars and a total of 424,800 vehicles made in 1980, Poland ranked eighth in Europe and second in the Eastern bloc after the USSR. The number of registered cars rose from 117,000 in 1960 and 479,000 in 1970 to 2,383,000 in 1980. There were also 618,000 registered trucks in 1980. The crisis of the socialist economy in Poland in the 1980s was reflected in a decline in motor vehicle production, about two-thirds of which was supplied by the FSM.

As the volume of car production remained low in the two post-war decades, it was supplemented by imports, but the size of these imports was also moderate, reaching 21,100 vehicles in 1965. Interestingly, Western makes such as Fiat, Chevrolet and Simca were among the most popular in the 1950s, used by state enterprises and institutions. Later, with the growth of production in socialist countries, imports from this direction dominated. Czech Škodas were always popular, as were East German Wartburgs and Trabants, Soviet Moskvichs and Volgas, Yugoslavian Zastavas and Romanian Dacias. In addition, Ikarus city buses were imported in large numbers from Hungary for many years. There were also some imports of Soviet and Czech trucks.

Even when production levels were low, 18%–25% of cars were exported to other socialist countries. In the 1970s and 1980s, exports rose to almost one-third, reaching a record 112,826 units in 1980. The Fiat 125p was the first car made in Poland to be exported in significant numbers (586,376 by 1991, including 140,280 to Western Europe), and later even more Fiats 126p were exported (897,316 by 1992, some to Western Europe). Moderate exports of trucks (15%–20%) went to Hungary, the Soviet Union and some Asian and African countries, while a slightly higher proportion of buses were exported to the socialist countries (Szczerbicki, 2017). Exports and imports of car components were rather limited and took place almost exclusively within the Eastern bloc. The supply of Fiat-designed powertrains manufactured by FSM in Bielsko-Biała for the Fiat 126 produced in Italy, as part of the payment of the licensing contract, was a unique arrangement which required the Polish plant to meet Western quality standards.

The production value of the automotive industry tripled between 1970 and 1979. Employment in the sector reached 134,529 people, i.e. 3.1% of the total number of employees in Polish manufacturing, according to GUS.

Table 3.1 Motor vehicle production and employment in the Polish automotive industry, 1950–2020 (thousands)

	1950	*1955*	*1960*	*1965*	*1970*	*1975*	*1980*	*1985*	*1990*	*1995*	*2000*	*2005*	*2010*	*2015*	*2020*
Total motor vehicle production	0.8	14.8	35.9	59.2	117.0	249.4	424.8	345.0	311.1	401.7	593.0	613.2	865.5	660.6	450.5
Passenger car production	—	4.0	12.9	24.8	64.2	164.3	351.0	283.0	266.0	366.0	532.0	540.1	785.0	472.0	220.9
Employment	NA	NA	70.8	NA	100.1	121.2	133.4	104.7	105.9	102.6	97.2	124.7	146.7	177.0	215.7

Source: authors' compilation based on GUS, ACEA and Eurostat data.

In summary, at the end of the socialist era, Poland had a relatively large motor vehicle production capacity, with three car assembly plants and six commercial vehicle and bus factories. The USSR, Czechoslovakia and Poland were the only Eastern bloc countries to manufacture all types of motor vehicles. The car plants were post-war greenfield investments, whereas most of the commercial vehicle factories were developed within existing production facilities. The production of automotive components increased significantly in the 1970s, mainly through the adaptation and expansion of various metal and mechanical plants. Car engines were manufactured by FSO and FSM, whereas large diesel engines for trucks and buses were supplied by FSC Star, ZM Nowotki in Warsaw, Andoria in Andrychów and WSK PZL-Mielec (British Leyland licence).

The Star truck and Syrena car were the first vehicles designed by Polish engineers of the pre-war PZInż, employed in the central construction bureau of the automotive industry. They were followed in the 1950s by the small Żuk and Nysa vans and San buses. Later, new domestic designs were introduced, mainly for large trucks and some coaches, the development of small commercial vehicles was neglected and the government decided to rely on Western licences for cars and city buses. The research and development (R&D) centres of FSO and FSM focused on introducing minor improvements to cars designed in Italy. As a result, the growth of the Polish automotive industry under socialism did not lead to the development of indigenous design capabilities. In a situation of outdated models of domestically manufactured cars, lack of integration into international production networks and low quality standards, the technological gap between the Polish and Western European automotive industries widened.

The automotive industry in the transformation period

Poland's post-socialist transformation radically changed the macroeconomic and political conditions for the development of the sector. It was a shock for state-owned enterprises, which had no experience of functioning in an opening market economy and had to learn to operate independently in a situation of extreme uncertainty. In addition, hyperinflation made access to capital and the management of supply chains very difficult. Between 1989 and 1991, production of passenger cars dropped from 285,000 to 167,000, i.e. by 42% in two years, while production of trucks and buses fell even more sharply (by more than half and four-fifths, respectively). However, there was an unsatisfied potential domestic demand for passenger cars and small vans with a rapidly growing number of entrepreneurs. With only 127 registered cars per 1,000 inhabitants in 1989 (compared to 233 in Czechoslovakia and 372 in the EU15), Poland appeared to be a promising new market.

Fiat's deal with the Polish government to take over FSM in 1992 proved to be a breakthrough. Production of a new small car, the Cinquecento, was launched in Italy and Poland with engines made in Bielsko-Biała. This can be seen as a path-dependent development of the earlier cooperation between the Turin original equipment manufacturer (OEM) and FSM. By 1998, Fiat had invested a billion dollars in modernising and expanding the Bielsko-Biała and Tychy plants, replacing the Cinquecento with the Seicento and assembling other models.

Finally, in 1996, the Korean company Daewoo set up the Daewoo–FSO joint venture. Nearly $700 million was invested over three years in the assembly and production of several Daewoo models at the Warsaw factory and its dozen component plants. Sales in Poland and Central Europe (CE) were successful, but the Daewoo group ran into financial difficulties in Korea and its assets were sold to GM in 2002. FSO became an independent manufacturer in 2004 and was then taken over by AvtoZAZ (a former Daewoo partner in a joint venture in Ukraine), which assembled Daewoo models and the Chevrolet Aveo under an agreement with GM that lasted until the licence expired in 2011, when car assembly at FSO ceased.

Another key event in the post-socialist development of the sector was GM's decision in 1996 to locate its new European car factory in Poland. The Opel plant in Gliwice, which opened two years later, was the largest greenfield investment in Polish manufacturing in the 1990s ($360 million by 1998) and was later expanded.

The Polish government raised import tariffs to 35% in 1992 as a measure to attract foreign investors. Poland's car production began to grow rapidly with Fiat's investment, doubling in two years to 334,000 vehicles in 1993 and reaching 647,000 units in 1999 with the participation of Daewoo, which captured almost 30% of the Polish market. This also included low-volume semi-knocked-down (SKD) and completely knocked-down (CKD) assembly in the country, e.g. by Fiat, Volkswagen and Ford (vans and cars), which disappeared with the gradual removal of tariff barriers by 2002. Domestic new car sales reached a record high of 640,000 vehicles in 1999 (Krzak, 2004). About 78% of the approximately 4 million new cars registered in Poland between 1990 and 1999 were manufactured by the home industry (Kudłak et al., 2023).

At the same time, the major bus and truck factories Jelcz, Autosan and Star were sold to a Polish investor Zasada Centrum Group in 1994–1995. Jelcz and Autosan gradually lost their market position, leading to a decline in production and employment and eventual bankruptcy in the following decades. Both are now part of the state-controlled military manufacturer Huta Stalowa Wola, with limited production of trucks at Jelcz and buses at Autosan. FSC in Lublin, which made vans and pick-ups, became part of Daewoo's ill-fated investment. After the bankruptcy, Lublin vans and Honker off-road vehicles were manufactured by the British company Intrall and then by new Polish owners, but the firm went bankrupt in 2017.

When it comes to commercial vehicles, foreign investors in Poland initially preferred simple assembly. This was done by Swedish Scania at the Kapena bus repair plant in Słupsk and by Volvo on a greenfield site in Wrocław. Scania developed into a manufacturer of bus frames and bodies as well as complete buses, and for some time the Italian company Cacciamali also produced small buses at the same site. In 1998, Volvo decided to expand the Polish plant into its largest bus factory in Europe. At the same time, a new bus assembly plant was built by the German company MAN in Sady, and a year later MAN bought the Star truck plant from Zasada Centrum. Volkswagen, in a joint venture with FSR, started small-scale SKD assembly of vans in 1993 and gradually took over and expanded the Poznań plant. Entirely new domestic producers of trailers and semi-trailers appeared, such as Wielton.

Foreign involvement in component manufacturing followed Fiat's investment, but it was the new GM plant that gave it a real boost. Magneti Marelli, Teksid and other Fiat Group companies took over former FSM component plants, while Korean Daewoo suppliers bought some FSO factories and a diesel engine plant in Andrychów. The American company TRW developed the production of airbags and seatbelts in two former FSM plants in Częstochowa, while Eaton took over engine valve production from Fiat in Bielsko-Biała (building a new plant) and the truck gearbox factory in Tczew from the Zasada Group. Other major investments in the 1990s included the Delphi plants in Krosno (shock absorbers; now owned by the Chinese company BWI) and Ostrów Wielkopolski (cooling systems), Wabco in Wrocław (air and hydraulic brake systems), Visteon in Praszka (brake systems and oil pumps), Mahle in Krotoszyn (pistons and engine parts) and Bosch in Twardogóra (brake systems), which later moved to a new plant in Mirków in 2003.

The largest greenfield plants built at that time were the diesel engine plants of VW in Polkowice and Isuzu in Tychy, both opened in 1999, GKN in Oleśnica (drive systems), Delphi in Tychy (steering systems), Faurecia in Grójec (metal seat parts) and Kirchoff in Mielec (bodywork and other pressed parts), followed by Toyota in Wałbrzych (gearboxes, later engines), Valeo in Skawina (engine cooling), Faurecia in Legnica (acoustic insulation) and others. In addition, Michelin and Goodyear bought two large tyre factories.

Overall, the automotive sector attracted $3.1 billion of foreign capital in 1989–1998, accounting for 15.5% of total FDI in Polish manufacturing during this period, the second largest after food processing. The protected domestic market was the primary target for early foreign investors, but automotive components and vehicles were increasingly produced in the country for export, e.g. Fiat cars, Volvo buses, VW and Isuzu engines. This led to the construction of large factories that allowed for economies of scale. Daewoo also came to Poland with the strategic goal of using it as an export platform for the EU market. Most of the early investments were in the form of joint ventures or acquisitions of existing companies. New plants have been built since the late 1990s. American component manufacturers were particularly active in the first post-socialist decade, willing to take the risk of investing in Poland. There were also Polish producers of parts and accessories that joined production networks, e.g. Groclin.

The 1990s were therefore a period of increasing car production, in line with the rising incomes of the population. Foreign investment and the emergence of new Polish private companies led to the demonopolisation and diversification of the sector. The number of commercial vehicles produced reached 62,700 units in 1999, mainly vans and pick-ups, with few large trucks. Bus production did not exceed 2,000 units until 2003. The post-socialist development of the industry involved the growth of some enterprises, the development of new, mainly foreign, producers and the decline of others. The effects on employment varied. Privatised enterprises usually reduced the number of employees inherited from the socialist era, despite increasing output, due to improved productivity. Producers with declining output laid off workers. New jobs were created by new enterprises and greenfield investments. The net effect was that employment in the narrowly defined automotive sector (NACE 29) in 1998 was almost the same as in 1989: 112,100 people.

The dynamics and structure of the sector: ownership, manufacturers and products

The positive experience of foreign companies investing in the automotive industry in Poland – good product quality based on the skills and motivation of the workforce, combined with lower costs and accession to the European Union – stimulated further investment and expansion of the sector. Cumulative FDI exceeded $10 billion in 1990–2005 and reached almost $9 billion in 2014–2021, when the country was the fourth-largest recipient of automotive FDI among OECD countries. As a result, Poland has become one of the most important automotive countries in the EU (see Chapter 2), in particular the fourth-largest producer of parts and accessories (7.9% of value added and 13.0% of employment). Output in the narrowly defined automotive sector increased by almost 9 times between 1991 and 2005 (at constant prices) and doubled over the next 15 years, 2005–2021, despite the negative effects of the collapse of Daewoo in 2001–2002, the financial crisis in 2009 and the COVID-19 pandemic in 2020 (Figure 3.1). The number of firms has increased by more than 40% and employment by 75% since 2015, and the sector accounted for 7.3% of the country's total manufacturing workforce in 2021.

The rapid growth of the automotive industry has been achieved through both the expansion of existing plants and the construction of new ones. About 360 greenfield automotive plants were built in Poland between 1991 and 2022.

The authors' analysis, based on their own database (see Introduction), shows that foreign-owned enterprises concentrated 66.3% of employment in the sector in 2007, rising to 78.0% a decade later. Around 60% of the total workforce in the narrowly defined motor vehicle sector NACE 29 (61.7%) is employed in 49 enterprises with at least 1,000 people, including more than one-third (34.4%) in companies with 2,000 or more persons. The share of the other 100 producers with 250–999 employees is 23.8%. Both groups are strongly dominated by enterprises with foreign capital. In addition, there are some 1,550 small and medium-sized, mainly Polish, manufacturers with fewer than 250 employees, representing 14.5% of the workforce. The size and ownership structure of the broadly defined automotive industry do not differ significantly – there are 86 enterprises with at least 1,000 employees (Table 3.2).

The limited role of domestic producers is particularly evident in their small share among IATF 16949 certificate holders.[1] Of the total of 744

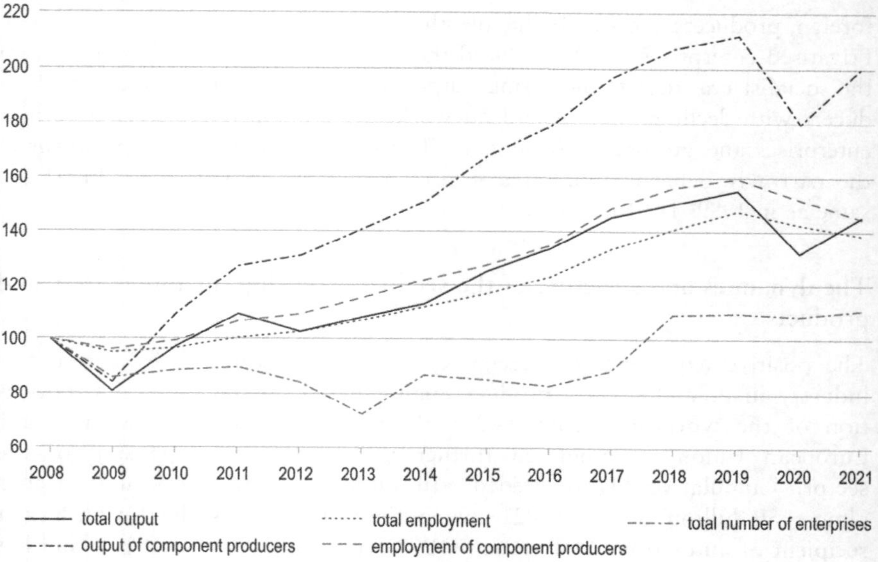

Figure 3.1 Dynamics of the Polish automotive industry, 2008–2021 (2008 = 100)
Source: authors' calculations based on Eurostat data.

plants with these certificates, there are currently 160 factories with Polish capital (21.5%), accounting for 8.3% of employment and 6.0% of revenues.

The origin of the capital of IATF 16949 certificate holders reflects the differentiated ownership structure of the sector in Poland. German enterprises account for one-quarter of total employment, American companies for one-fifth, French firms for 14.3%, Japanese producers for 9.2% and Italian manufacturers for 6.6%.

The Polish car market has changed radically in the 21st century compared to the 1990s (Kołsut & Stryjakiewicz, 2023). The disappearance of tariffs and other barriers with Poland's accession to the EU in 2004, together with the bankruptcy of Daewoo, which had sold cheap cars, and favourable exchange rates, led to a surge in imports of second-hand vehicles. They reached a record level of 1.1 million cars in 2008 and, after lower imports in 2009–2015, have been around 0.9 million units in recent years. Such a dominance of used car imports became unprecedented also in comparison with other CE countries (Kołsut et al., 2023). On the one hand, it led to a more than fivefold increase in the number of cars registered in the country, reaching 687 vehicles per 1,000 inhabitants in 2021. On the other hand, it inevitably had a negative impact on the domestic market for new cars. Only 270,000 new cars were sold in 2009. Since then, however, new car sales have started to rise, doubling to 540,000 vehicles by 2019. Much of the growth has been driven by company cars (now accounting for two-thirds of sales), particularly car leasing by small businesses, which is an important element of the Polish economy (Kisiała et al., 2023).

Table 3.2 Size and ownership structure of automotive enterprises in Poland, 2012 and 2018

A. Narrowly defined automotive							
All firms							
Size of employment	*2012*	*2018*	*Number of plants, 2018*	*2012*	*2018*	*2012*	*2018*
	Number of firms			*Share of employment*		*Share of revenues*	
1,000 and more	57	86	165	62.9%	62.3%	68.3%	65.2%
250–999	113	171	211	27.2%	26.3%	23.5%	26.6%
50–249	135	250	264	9.6%	10.6%	4.4%	7.0%
fewer than 50	24	90	91	0.4%	0.9%	0.2%	0.7%
no data	283	43	47	0.0%	0.0%	3.6%	0.5%
Total	612	640	778	100.0%	100.0%	100.0%	100.0%
Domestic-controlled firms							
Size of employment	*2012*	*2018*	*Number of plants, 2018*	*2012*	*2018*	*2012*	*2018*
	Number of firms			*Share of employment*		*Share of revenues*	
1,000 and more	6	3	5	40.9%	17.2%	35.5%	43.1%
250–999	19	30	43	27.9%	34.2%	31.6%	28.0%
50–249	59	119	126	29.8%	44.5%	24.0%	25.5%
fewer than 50	11	47	48	1.4%	4.0%	0.9%	2.4%
no data	133	23	25	0.0%	0.0%	8.0%	1.1%
Total	228	222	247	100.0%	100.0%	100.0%	100.0%

B. Narrowly defined automotive (NACE 29)

All firms							
Size of employment	*2012*	*2018*	*Number of plants, 2018*	*2012*	*2018*	*2012*	*2018*
	Number of firms			*Share of employment*		*Share of revenues*	
1,000 and more	37	49	99	66.1%	63.5%	73.9%	69.8%
250–999	67	94	117	25.6%	26.8%	21.2%	25.6%
50–249	70	114	119	8.0%	8.8%	3.3%	4.2%
fewer than 50	10	45	45	0.3%	0.8%	0.1%	0.5%
no data	116	16	16	0.0%	0.0%	1.5%	0.0%
Total	300	318	396	100.0%	100.0%	100.0%	100.0%
Domestic-controlled firms							

Size of employment	*2012*	*2018*	*Number of plants, 2018*	*2012*	*2018*	*2012*	*2018*
	Number of firms			*Share of employment*		*Share of revenues*	
1,000 and more	4	2	4	46.5%	22.4%	55.3%	64.6%
250–999	8	12	17	23.3%	26.2%	17.5%	14.5%
50–249	33	64	65	29.0%	47.3%	22.5%	19.2%
fewer than 50	5	21	21	1.3%	4.1%	0.4%	1.7%
no data	65	10	10	0.0%	0.0%	4.3%	0.1%
Total	115	109	117	100.0%	100.0%	100.0%	100.0%

Source: authors' calculations based on annual company reports (full sample).

Nevertheless, the vast majority of new cars sold in Poland are imported rather than domestically made. All this means that car production has become predominantly export-driven.

The total number of motor vehicles produced in the country has been above half a million since 1997 and, after a decline in 2001–2003, grew rapidly to reach a peak of 952,840 units in 2008, including 842,000 passenger cars and 110,840 commercial vehicles. During the crisis of 2009, there was a relatively mild decline in passenger car production, but it fell sharply in 2012 and was below half a million units in the following years. At the same time, production of commercial vehicles has doubled. In 2022, according to ACEA, 246,574 vans were made, more than passenger cars (166,610, the lowest number since 1991). Fiat (Fiat Chrysler, 2014–2021) has been the leading car manufacturer in Poland for several decades, assembling almost 500,000 vehicles in 2008 (Fiat 600, Fiat 500, Panda, Abarth, Ford Ka). The company's decision to locate production of new models in Italy led to lower output in the following years, but production of three new electric models was launched in Tychy in 2023–2024. Corporate policy proved to be even more influential in the case of Opel, which, after its transfer from GM to the PSA Group in 2017, was transformed from a car manufacturer (capacity of 200,000; Opel Astra, Agila, Zafira, Cascada) to a van manufacturer (capacity of 100,000). Stellantis, created by the merger of FCA and PSA in 2021, now includes assembly plants in Tychy (Lancia Ypsilon, Jeep Avenger, Fiat 600, Alfa Romeo) and Gliwice. Volkswagen's growing investment in its Poznań plants has made it the country's second-largest motor vehicle producer, making Caddy and Transporter vans (along with the Ford Tourneo Connect from 2022). A new VW Crafter assembly plant was built in Września in 2016. Production of FSO cars in Warsaw ended in 2011.

Poland has become a major manufacturer of light commercial vehicles (14.9% of the EU total in 2022) and its role has been further strengthened with the Stellantis Gliwice plant reaching full capacity in 2023 and the start of production of the Toyota Proace Max. A greenfield MAN truck plant was built in Niepołomice in 2007 and recently expanded to a capacity of 75,000 vehicles and cabins. Jelcz also produces a small number of medium and heavy military vehicles. In 2022, more than 33,000 trucks were produced in the country.

Poland is the largest EU producer of buses and coaches with 7,362 vehicles in 2019 (25.1% of the EU). Its output has increased fourfold in volume and more than eightfold in value since 2002, reflecting specialisation in the production of modern buses, especially hybrid and electric ones. There are four manufacturers in the country with a capacity of more than 1,500 vehicles: Volvo in Wrocław, Solaris in Bolechowo, Scania in Słupsk and MAN in Starachowice. The latter was a truck plant acquired by MAN, which started production of bus frames and components. Following the construction of a new MAN plant in Niepołomice, trucks were no longer manufactured in Starachowice, where city bus assembly was transferred from Sady in 2016. Solaris was a Polish-owned company founded in 1994, which became the first serial manufacturer of electric buses and their largest European producer. It was taken over by the Spanish company CAF in 2018. Buses are also made by Autosan and others. Bus production has declined in the post-pandemic period to 4,796 units in 2022. Volvo and Scania recently announced the end of unprofitable bus production in Europe, leaving only chassis manufacturing in Słupsk and prompting the sale of the Wrocław factory to Swedish heat pump manufacturer Aira in 2024. In 2023, a new hydrogen-powered NesoBus factory was opened in Świdnik by private Polish investors, with a capacity of 100 vehicles.

There are six major engine plants, accounting for 10.7% of EU production. Two of them belong to Stellantis: in Bielsko-Biała[2] (formerly Fiat) and in Tychy (originally Isuzu, later GM); two others were built by Toyota in Wałbrzych (2002) and near Jelcz-Laskowice (2005). The Volkswagen plant in Polkowice (1999) and the latest Mercedes-Benz plant in Jawor (2019) are also greenfield investments. Engine production peaked in 2011 and stabilised at a lower level in the following decade.

Poland's share of EU production of trailers and semi-trailers is 7.9%, and output has increased more than tenfold since 2002. The Polish company Wielton, based in Wieluń, has become the third-largest manufacturer of semi-trailers in Europe. Other major domestic producers are Zasław TSS in Andrychów and Bodex in Szczerców.

The production of motor vehicles is embedded in an extensive network of suppliers in the country. In 2019, there were 1,127 enterprises producing motor vehicle parts and accessories. According to Eurostat, Poland is one of the EU's main producers of airbags (32.7%), safety belts (23.8%), steering wheels, steering columns and steering boxes (16.2%) and brakes and their parts (15.2%). It also supplies 21.7% of the EU's automotive glass, 18.0% of rubber and rubber-metal products, 9.7% of tyres, 9.3% of wheels and 8.2% of wiring sets. The value of Polish production of automotive parts and accessories more than doubled between 2008 and 2019. The most dynamic growth since 2002 has taken place in brakes, steering systems, plastic parts and glass (at least ten times) and rubber products and wheels (at least five times). There have also been significant increases in the manufacture of airbags, seatbelts and tyres. However, there are components whose output peaked in 2008, e.g. seats, bumpers and suspension systems, and subsequently declined with the decrease in car assembly. It is interesting to note that the cost-sensitive production of wiring harnesses grew only about three times between 2002 and 2017 and has dropped significantly in recent years. The few examples of disinvestment in Poland occurred mainly in plants producing wiring sets and other labour-intensive components during the crisis of 2008–2011. The owners (Sumitomo, Leoni and Takata-Petri) either relocated production to Romania, Egypt and Morocco or consolidated their activities at other locations in Poland.

Exports of passenger cars exceeded 50% of production for the first time in 2000. It continued to grow and has been above 90% since 2003. Nevertheless, car imports exceeded the volume of exports in 1998–2003 and 2018–2021. The total value of exported motor vehicles tripled between 2002 and 2008, but increased by only 20% between 2008 and 2019. The growth in exports was particularly pronounced for light commercial vehicles, buses and coaches (8 times) and trailers and semi-trailers (16 times, including a threefold increase between 2008 and 2021). Exports of engines doubled from 2002 to 2007, then halved. The value of Polish exports of broadly defined automotive parts and accessories (excluding bodies, chassis and engines) has increased more than tenfold between 2002 and 2022: from €2.9 billion to €30.5 billion, and more than threefold since 2008. More than three-quarters of production is exported for steering systems, brakes, airbags, wiring sets, wheels, glass, rubber articles and tyres. The share of exports is now slightly lower for engines (67%) and seatbelts (57%). In 2021, the value of exported lithium-ion batteries made Poland the world's second-largest exporter after China.

Most of the world's leading suppliers from Western Europe, North America, Japan and South Korea have factories in Poland. There are 18 industrial groups with 5 or more plants manufacturing automotive products. The German ZF group has nine production facilities, mainly former American TRW plants for seatbelts, airbags, braking and steering systems, and a Wabco factory for braking and suspension components. There are also nine factories of the French Faurecia (Forvia Group) producing seats, dashboards, interior and door components. Eight plants supplying seating systems (including the former Kongsberg and Guilford facilities) and wiring sets belong to the American company Lear, seven factories of the French company Hutchinson produce fluid transfer systems and plastic parts, while seven plants of the Canadian company Magna supply seats, stampings and lighting. Another American company, Tenneco, has six facilities manufacturing exhaust systems, shock absorbers, pistons and bearings (Federal Mogul). There are also five plants from: French Valeo, which makes lighting, engine cooling, windscreen wipers, electrical and electronic systems; Plastic Omnium, which supplies bumpers and plastic parts; Japanese Toyota (engine parts, gearboxes, castings); American BorgWarner (turbochargers, automatic transmission parts); Cooper Standard, which makes rubber and plastic sealings and hoses; Adient (formerly Johnson Controls), which specialises in seats; and Polish Boryszew, which manufactures rubber connections and plastic parts. A number of large component plants also belong to Volkswagen (seats, castings), American Aptiv (formerly Delphi; wiring harnesses, electrical and electronic systems), Eaton (gearboxes, compressors, valves) and Nexteer (steering systems), Italian Magneti Marelli (lighting, plastic parts, exhaust and suspension systems) and Brembo (braking systems), German Kirchhoff (stamped and welded components) and Coroplast (wire harnesses), French Saint-Gobain (laminated and processed automotive glass), Japanese Sumitomo Riko (rubber components) and Polish Alumetal (aluminium castings).

After the collapse of Daewoo in 2002, employment in the narrowly defined automotive industry fell below 80,000. It continued to grow in the following years, doubling by 2007 and reaching 223,291 in 2019 (210,064 in 2022). Growth has been particularly spectacular in the production of parts and accessories: from just 29,300 in 1996 to 106,136 in 2008 and 169,333 in 2019. The total number of employees reaches around 317,015 if we include manufacturers classified in sectors other than NACE 29 with at least one-quarter of their output in automotive products. There are 2 OEMs and 10 suppliers with more than 5,000 employees. The Volkswagen Group is by far the largest employer, with 17,559 people in 11 plants in 2021 (Table 3.3). Stellantis has a total of 8,104 employees in 5 plants. The German ZF Group is the biggest supplier in terms of employment (10,138). Other major employers include the US companies Lear, Tenneco, Aptiv and Adient, the French firms Valeo, Hutchinson, Forvia (Faurecia) and Michelin, and the Korean LG Energy Solution, which operates a lithium-ion battery gigafactory.

Overall, the Polish automotive industry has experienced significant growth in production and employment in recent decades, mainly driven by foreign investment. The country's position in European production and exports has become particularly prominent in the case of light commercial vehicles, buses and coaches, trailers and semi-trailers, but especially in the manufacturing of automotive parts and accessories. The extensive and diversified component sector, including the production of a wide range of parts in numerous large plants belonging to many companies, is a major strength of the Polish automotive industry. High levels of exports reflect strong integration into European production networks with broad manufacturing capabilities and good quality standards.

Shift to electromobility

The size of the internal combustion engine (ICE) segment in Poland makes it vulnerable at the time of the European shift to electric powertrains and the ban on the sale of ICE-powered cars in the EU from 2035. According to the authors' estimates, in 2018 there were almost 120 suppliers in this segment of the supply chain, employing 52,000 people. These included six engine plants and numerous manufacturers of engine parts, transmissions, thermal management, fuel pumps and fuel tanks (Table 3.4).

The future of this production is now uncertain, with the PSPA-BCG study (Polskie Stowarzyszenie Paliw Alternatywnych & Boston Consulting Group, 2021) predicting a loss of 17,000–23,000 jobs in this segment between 2020 and 2030. Some manufacturers have already started restructuring, such as diversifying into electric motors (e.g. Toyota), the off-highway segment (agricultural and construction machinery, ships, yachts, power generators), other automotive components and/or remanufacturing.

At the same time, the manufacturing of lithium-ion batteries and their components is being developed in the country. In Biskupice Podgórne near Wrocław, the Korean company LG Energy Solution built the largest lithium-ion battery production plant for electric cars in Europe in 2017, with a capacity of 86 GWh, which will be expanded to 115 GWh by 2025. In 2020, Mercedes-Benz built a battery factory for electric cars next to its new petrol and diesel engine plant in Jawor. Battery systems for buses and commercial vehicles are also assembled by the German company BMZ in Gliwice and by the Polish firm

Table 3.3 The largest companies in the broadly defined automotive sector in Poland in 2021

Company (capital group)	*Branches and brands in Poland*	*Number of employees*	*Number of plants / SSCs / R&D*	*Main products*
Volkswagen	Volkswagen, MAN, Scania, Brose Sitech	17,559	11 / 0 / 3	light commercial vehicles, buses, heavy trucks, engines, seats
ZF	ZF, TRW, Wabco	10,138	9 / 6 / 4	safety belts, airbags, drivetrain, steering, braking, electronics and control systems
Stellantis	FCA, Opel, Teksid	8,104	5 / 2 / 0	passenger cars, light commercial vehicles, engines, iron castings
Valeo	Valeo	7,969	5 / 1 / 3	lighting, wiper, thermal, electric and electronic systems
Lear	Lear, Guilford, Kongsberg	7,006	8 / 0 / 3	complete seating systems, frames, mechanisms, foam, connection systems, electronic systems, interiors
TotalEnergies	Hutchinson	6,928	7 / 0 / 0	rubber fluid transfer systems, plastic parts
Tenneco	Federal Mogul, Monroe, Walker	6,774	6 / 0 / 2	exhaust systems, suspension systems, pistons, bearings
Forvia	Faurecia	6,296	9 / 3 / 2	complete seating systems, seat frames, mechanisms, foam, interiors, doors and door panels
Aptiv	Aptiv	5,708	3 / 0 / 1	electrical and electronic parts and systems (connection systems, optical modules, cameras), design of electronic and safety systems
LG	LG Energy Solution	5,501	2 / 0 / 0	lithium-ion batteries for electric cars, separators
Adient	Adient, Johnson Controls	5,256	5 / 0 / 0	complete seating systems, frames, mechanisms, foam
Michelin	Michelin	5,194	1 / 0 / 0	tyres
Mahle	Mahle, Behr	4,776	2 / 1 / 1	cylinders, pistons, valves, cooling modules for engines

Company (capital group)	*Branches and brands in Poland*	*Number of employees*	*Number of plants / SSCs / R&D*	*Main products*
NGK Insulators	NGK	4,408	2 / 0 / 0	ceramic particulate filters for diesel engines
Saint-Gobain	Saint-Gobain	3,739	4 / 0 / 0	laminated and tempered glass for motor vehicles
Toyota	Toyota, Toyota Boshoku	3,543	5 / 0 / 0	engines and their parts, gearboxes, castings
AB Volvo	Volvo	3,193	1 / 1 / 0	buses
BorgWarner	BorgWarner, Delphi Technologies	3,190	5 / 0 / 2	turbochargers, friction and mechanical products for automatic transmissions and torque management products
Goodyear	Firma Oponiarska Dębica	3,031	1 / 0 / 0	tyres
Magna	Magna, Cosma, Olsa	2,995	7 / 0 / 0	seats, folding roofs, lighting, bumpers, pressed parts, mechatronic parts
Bridgestone	Bridgestone	2,978	2 / 0 / 0	tyres
Autoliv	Autoliv	2,960	2 / 0 / 1	airbags
Boryszew	Maflow	2,950	5 / 0 / 1	connections systems, plastic parts
Superior Industries	Uniwheels	2,720	1 / 0 / 0	aluminium wheels
CAF	Solaris	2,454	3 / 0 / 1	buses and trolleybuses
NSK	NSK, AKS	2,448	3 / 0 / 1	steering systems, ball and needle bearings
Marelli	Magneti Marelli	2,405	4 / 0 / 0	lighting, exhausts, fuels, suspension systems, plastic parts
Pass	Pass Polska	2,364	1 / 0 / 0	rubber and plastic parts
Mann+Hummel	Mann+Hummel, Vix Filters	2,363	1 / 0 / 1	filters for passenger cars, trucks, buses and heavy machinery and equipment
Sanok Rubber	Sanok Rubber, Stomet	2,343	2 / 0 / 1	anti-vibration systems and car body sealing

Company (capital group)	*Branches and brands in Poland*	*Number of employees*	*Number of plants / SSCs / R&D*	*Main products*
Nippon Sheet Glass	Pilkington	2,294	2 / 1 / 0	laminated and tempered glass for motor vehicles
Brembo	Brembo	2,162	4 / 0 / 1	braking systems

Source: authors' compilation based on annual company reports.

Note: SSC, shared service centre.

Table 3.4 Combustion engine segment in the Polish automotive industry, 2018

Components	*Number of companies*		*Number of employees*	
	Tier 1	*Tier 2 and lower*	*Tier 1*	*Tier 2 and lower*
Combustion engine	14	40	11,915	17,242
Transmission	8	13	4,076	2,192
Fuel pump	5	13	1,485	5,572
Fuel tank system	7	9	3,604	1,387
Thermal management	3	4	4,169	271
Total	37	79	25,249	26,664

Source: authors' calculations based on annual company reports.

Impact Clean Power Energy in Pruszków. The UK's Johnson Matthey and Belgium's Umicore produce cathode materials, Korea's SK hi-tech and SK Nexilis make battery separators and copper foil for lithium-ion batteries, while China's Shenzhen Capchem and Guoatai-Huarong supply electrolyte and silicon materials. There are already around 70 companies involved in the production of batteries and their components. Poland is also one of Europe's leading countries in the manufacture of high-power charging infrastructure, with Ekoenergetyka providing fast-charging infrastructure to 28 countries, and cities including Berlin, Munich, Paris and Barcelona. Eneli Enelion, EC Engineering and Garo are other significant producers. It is estimated that around 20,000 jobs were created in the electromobility segment in Poland between 2016 and 2022 (PAIiH, 2022).

The country is a European leader in the production of electric buses, VW and MAN manufacture electric commercial vehicles, but the Jeep Avenger became the first electric car made in Poland only in 2023, followed by the Fiat 600 and Alfa Romeo Milano. Mercedes-Benz have announced plans to start production of fully electric vans in Jawor. The government chose China's Geely as a technological partner and supplier of the platform for a Polish electric car, Izera, which the state-controlled company Electromobility Poland is due to start producing by the end of 2025. However, sales of electric vehicles and the development of charging infrastructure have been very slow in Poland. The threat associated with the substitution of ICE cars by electric vehicles, which tend to be more expensive, is a decline in new car sales and an even greater flood of old vehicles from the West (Pardi, 2022).

Non-production competences: R&D and SSCs

The presence and competence of R&D centres are key indicators of industrial upgrading. They facilitate the development of new technologies and products that improve production efficiency and quality, leading to overall industrial upgrading. R&D centres demonstrate industry's capacity to absorb and adapt knowledge. Countries with robust R&D facilities are thus better equipped to absorb, interpret and use the latest technological trends to their advantage, leading to upgrading.

As of the end of 2023, 80 automotive R&D centres have been identified in Poland. Of these, 28 have at least 50 employees and 20 centres employ more than 100 staff. This is a significant increase compared to 2006, when Pavlínek et al. (2009) identified only 16 R&D centres in Poland.[3] In addition to the establishment of new centres, there has also been an expansion of older ones. The best example is the largest R&D centre in Poland, Aptiv in Kraków, which currently employs almost 3,000 people. Other large centres with more than 250 employees include those set up by TRW (now ZF) in Częstochowa and the former Delphi centres in Kraków (now Chinese-owned BWI) and Ostrów Wielkopolski (now Mahle). The largest R&D centre with Polish capital is Bosmal, established as part of FSM in the early 1970s (Table 3.5).

Business R&D expenditure in the Polish automotive sector has increased almost tenfold, from €44 million in 2011 to €407 million in 2021. Over the same period, the number of researchers (full-time equivalent) in the sector rose to 6,835. Although the number of staff is already higher than in Spain and Italy, R&D expenditure is still significantly lower. Thus, despite the dynamic growth in the number and size of R&D centres, the position of Poland and other Central European countries in the global innovation landscape remains relatively limited.

Investors from various countries show significant differences in their willingness to develop R&D competences in Poland. American investors undoubtedly stand out in this respect. At the other end of the spectrum are South Korean and Japanese firms, which typically refrain from building either R&D or SSC capabilities in the country. Considering the number of active companies, there are relatively few R&D centres established by German investors, although some have located significant competences in Poland. ZF is a prominent exception, but it has acquired most of its R&D from the American company TRW. The activities of French investors fall somewhere between these extremes. Furthermore, only one-fifth of Polish producers have certified product design competences, compared to half of foreign companies.

The majority of final assembly manufacturers have made very limited or no investment in Polish R&D departments, Volkswagen being a notable exception with its modestly sized centre. However, this landscape is changing, with Volvo and Stellantis establishing large automotive software R&D centres in the country in 2023. Bus manufacturer Solaris has an R&D centre employing 185 engineers. The development of R&D in Poland has mainly been driven by suppliers of parts and components, in particular Tier-1 companies with a broad production base in the country.

The scope of competence of R&D centres is important. Following Basant and Mani (2012) we classify R&D centres into innovators, which hold patents in the United States Patent and Trademark Office (USPTO) or Patent Office of the Republic of Poland (UPRP), and partial innovators, which do not own

Table 3.5 Major automotive R&D centres in Poland in 2021

No.	*Company*	*Country of origin*	*Location*	*Employment (2021)*	*Year of launch*	*Field of expertise*	*US Pre-Grant Publications (as of 12.07.2023)*	*R&D with the plant*
1	Aptiv Services Poland	USA	Kraków	2,877	2000	advanced electronics and active safety technologies, next-generation infotainment and user experience platforms, electronic control units and smart architecture platforms	126	No
2	ZF Automotive Systems Poland (formerly TRW)	Germany (formerly USA)	Częstochowa	800	2004	belts and airbags, electronics, advanced driver-assistance systems	9	Yes
3	BWI Poland Technologies (formerly Delphi)	China (formerly USA)	Kraków	433	2000	active and passive shock absorbers	1	No
4	MAHLE Behr, (formerly Delphi)	Germany (formerly USA)	Ostrów Wielkopolski	400	2005	powertrain cooling and interior heating systems	7	Yes
5	Bosmal	Poland	Bielsko-Biała	397	1972	various automotive components	3	No
6	Faurecia	France	Grójec, Wałbrzych	344	2004	seat structures, frames and mechanisms	33	Yes
7	Nexteer Automotive	USA	Tychy	272	2016	electric power steering (EPS) systems	1	Yes
8	ZF Steering Systems Poland	Germany	Bielsko-Biała	261	2015	steering assistance systems	11	Yes

No.	*Company*	*Country of origin*	*Location*	*Employment (2021)*	*Year of launch*	*Field of expertise*	*US Pre-Grant Publications (as of 12.07.2023)*	*R&D with the plant*
9	BorgWarner Poland	USA	Jasionka n. Rzeszów	170	2016	turbochargers and their components	5	Yes
10	DIP Draexlmaier Engineering Polska	Germany	Gliwice	220**	2017	software algorithms for electronic modules used for the storage and distribution of electrical energy in vehicles, as well as providing interior lighting for vehicles	0	No
11	ZF CV Systems Poland (formerly Wabco)	Germany (formerly USA)	Wrocław	200*	2014	pneumatic braking systems, expanded in 2020 by launching Global Test Center	48	Yes
12	ZF Automotive Systems Poland	Germany	Łódź	200	2017	designing and testing of ADAS and AD active safety systems	0	No
13	Solaris Bus & Coach	Spain (formerly Poland)	Bolechowo	185	1999	design of buses	0	Yes
14	Tenneco Automotive EE, Monroe European Engineering Center (MEEC)	USA	Gliwice	172	2001	ride control and advanced suspension technologies	7***	No
15	Valeo Autosystemy	France	Skawina	250	2005	engine radiators, oil coolers, turbocharged air coolers, blades, arms, motors and wiper systems	45	Yes

No.	Company	Country of origin	Location	Employment (2021)	Year of launch	Field of expertise	US Pre-Grant Publications (as of 12.07.2023)	R&D with the plant
16	Tenneco Automotive Polska	USA	Rybnik	134	2000	exhaust systems	7***	Yes
17	Autoliv Poland	Sweden	Jelcz-Laskowice	100–200*	2006	airbag modules	7	Yes
18	Sanok Rubber	Poland	Sanok	100–150*	n.d.	rubber compounds and products made from elastomers, plastics and their functional combinations with metal and other materials	0	Yes
19	NSK Bearing Poland	Japan	Kielce	100–150*	n.d.	bearings and steering columns, engine and gearbox components	0	Yes
20	Volkswagen Poznań	Germany	Poznań	130	2014	mechatronic and electronic systems, luggage and cargo space	0	Yes
21	DIP Draexlmaier Engineering Polska	Germany	Jelenia Góra	110**	2016	electrical harnesses for combustion and electric vehicles	0	Yes
22	Lear Corporation	USA	Tychy	83	2010	upholstery for car seats	0	Yes
23	Valeo Electric and Electronic Systems	France	Czechowice-Dziedzice	74	n.d.	electric car starters, air throttles, electric compressors	6	Yes

No.	Company	Country of origin	Location	Employment (2021)	Year of launch	Field of expertise	US Pre-Grant Publications (as of 12.07.2023)	R&D with the plant
24	Bury Technologies	Poland	Rzeszów	70	n.d.	electronics, software development and testing, printed circuit board design	5	No
25	Lear Corporation	USA	Legnickie Pole	70	2014	validation of the production concept during single and small batch production of metal structure prototypes for car seats	0	Yes
26	Robert Bosch	Germany	Mirków	70	2012	brake fluid reservoirs, and components for power units (iboosters)	3	Yes
27	Wielton	Poland	Wieluń	50–100*	2014	trailers and semi-trailers	0	Yes
28	Brose Sitech	Germany	Polkowice, Wrocław	50	2013	metal seat frames and elements of suspension	4	Yes

Source: authors' compilation based on annual company reports.

Notes: *estimation; **division by locations according to office space; ***combined for locations in Rybnik and Gliwice, there is no way to credibly divide patents between these two locations.

patents. They further distinguish the types of R&D activities carried out in these centres, including product design, new product development, new process development, product improvement, process improvement and technology support. Pavlínek et al. (2009) categorise R&D centres into routine R&D centres – those that design a unique class of automotive components for an entire TNC or its European division (referred to as "product specialists") – and centres dedicated to basic research and higher R&D functions. The authors further distinguish between stand-alone R&D centres and those co-located with manufacturing facilities.

The vast majority of R&D centres in Poland (21 out of 28 with at least 50 employees) are located next to manufacturing plants. Many of them have primarily development competences, i.e. focus on optimisation of technological processes, testing of prototypes, validation and modification of products in cooperation with large R&D centres in Western Europe or the USA, e.g. Lear and Brembo. Broader R&D functions of product design – from preparation of the concept through design, simulations and prototypes to the final product – can be found in about 20 subsidiaries of large TNCs operating in Poland as Tier-1 suppliers. Some of them are responsible for designing new products for manufacturing plants in Poland that have a so-called product mandate, e.g. Mahle Behr in Ostrów Wielkopolski, Faurecia in Grójec, Brose Sitech in Wrocław, Nexteer in Tychy, ZF in Bielsko-Biała, Tenneco in Rybnik, Autoliv in Jelcz-Laskowice, NSK in Kielce and Draexlmaier in Jelenia Góra.

At least 11 R&D centres have even more advanced competences, designing products for an entire division in Europe or globally. The Aptiv Technical Centre in Kraków is the company's largest R&D centre worldwide, specialising in advanced electronics and active safety technologies, including infotainment and 3D gesture recognition, and has built a Smartrack for testing its prototypes. ZF Automotive's engineering centres in Częstochowa and Łódź are responsible for designing safety systems (airbags and seatbelts) for the group, while the centre in Bielsko-Biała works on steering systems and transmissions for electric vehicles. Valeo in Skawina and Czechowice-Dziedzice develops thermal systems, including heat exchangers for electric vehicles, electric starters and compressors. The Monroe European Engineering Centre in Gliwice, one of Tenneco's five global R&D centres, creates concepts and patents for ride control and advanced suspension technologies. Shock absorbers are designed by BWI in Kraków, which is also home to a BorgWarner Mobility technical centre, which recently moved into new facilities to provide solutions for the electromobility segment (on-board chargers, DC/DC converters and battery management systems), as well as a new Volvo Cars Tech Hub, which develops software for electric vehicles. Draexlmaier has a software engineering centre in Gliwice that provides algorithms for electronic modules used to store and distribute electrical energy in vehicles, and Bosch in Mirków is involved in the design of brake fluid expansion tanks and iboosters. Interestingly, several of these R&D centres are now working on new solutions for electric and/or autonomous vehicles.

Using the number of patent applications to the USPTO as a measure of innovation, as suggested by Basant and Mani (2012), the most advanced centres appear to be Aptiv in Kraków, ZF CV in Wrocław (formerly Wabco), Faurecia in Grójec, ZF in Częstochowa and Valeo in Skawina. Aptiv's R&D operation in Kraków stands out, contributing 11% of all patent applications by Aptiv to the USPTO. The Polish centres of ZF and Faurecia account for a significant 3% of the group's global patent applications. In total, 22 R&D centres have generated at least one patent application filed in the USA. Automotive companies with Polish capital do not file patents in the USA (with the exception of Bury Technologies), but do generate domestic patents, with Wielton leading the way.

Over the past two decades, the offshoring of knowledge-intensive business services (KIBS) has been a major shift in corporate strategy. Firms often transfer business services from developed to less developed countries in order to reduce labour costs and enhance their unique capabilities, either to serve the home market or to support the firm's global operations (Massini & Miozzo, 2010; Richter & Brühl, 2017; Müller & Franz, 2019). No country illustrates these trends better than Poland. The number of jobs in business process outsourcing (BPO), R&D, information technology outsourcing (ITO) and SSCs increased tenfold between 2008 and 2022, exceeding 400,000 employees by 2022, according to ABSL. The automotive industry has also contributed to this growth.

As of the end of 2021, 25 automotive companies with SSCs were identified in Poland, employing a total of 8,000 people. The first SSCs tended to emerge alongside large manufacturing plants. One of the factors was the ability to recruit SSC staff from the pool of office workers already employed by the company. SSCs began to appear in the early 2000s and were primarily associated with OEMs, e.g. Fiat services in Bielsko-Biała in 2001, Volvo accounting and IT services in Wrocław in 2004 and MAN SSC in Poznań in 2006. Major suppliers followed suit, locating their SSCs near factories (e.g. TRW in Częstochowa, Timken in Sosnowiec, Valeo in Skawina) or near Polish headquarters (e.g. Delphi in Kraków, Robert Bosch in Warsaw). The pace of creation of new centres accelerated after 2010 (e.g. Cooper Standard in Bielsko-Biała, Exide and Bridgestone in Poznań, Pilkington in Sandomierz, General Motors in Tychy, Faurecia in Łódź) and especially after 2015, when 40% of the currently operating centres appeared (Mahle, Federal Mogul, 3M, Toyota, Wabco, Faurecia, Huf, Volkswagen, Schaeffler, Gates, BCS Automotive Interface Solutions). The majority of recently established centres are located in major cities, with the highest concentration in Wrocław. What appears to be more important than proximity to an existing operation is the companies' access to a broad labour market, which is particularly important for recruiting managerial staff and coping with the high turnover specific to the BPO/SSC/ITO sector.

Undoubtedly, the main motivation for establishing SSCs in Poland was to reduce operating costs and improve the quality of processes performed within the organisation. SSCs typically started their operations with fairly simple competences, such as standard functions (e.g. transactional accounting), requiring average skills and a team of several dozen people. While few SSCs remained at this level, the majority acquired new, more advanced functions, such as IT and purchasing, which required significantly higher skills. This was accompanied by an increase in staff numbers. This evolution was well summed up by one of the managers:

> What is necessary to win more advanced processes? The basis is to establish credibility as a partner. First you have to prove that you can handle simple processes, and then you can move up step by step. That takes a couple of years. In our case, it took three years of hard work to build up our information technology and human resources capabilities.

Production and functional upgrading of foreign subsidiaries: company-level analysis

The in-depth study of major producers, including analysis of annual reports, IATF certificates and interviews, provides a deeper insight into production and non-production competences and how they change over time. The analysis, carried out for the 184 largest enterprises with revenues of more than PLN 50 million (about €10 million) between 2007, 2012 and 2019, shows an increasing value creation and value capture by automotive companies in Poland (Table 3.6).

There is a noticeable upward trend in value added per employee for all companies, regardless of the type of capital. Between 2007 and 2019, it increased from PLN 127,400 to PLN 162,200. Foreign-controlled enterprises show significantly higher productivity: PLN 135,500 in 2007 and PLN 165,800 in 2019. Polish-owned producers are lagging behind, but their growth is faster: from PLN 64,300 in 2007 to PLN 121,900 in 2019, i.e. it almost doubled in this period.

Table 3.6 Value created and value capture in the Polish automotive industry

Value	*Ownership*	*Year*		
		2007	*2012*	*2019*
Share of value added in revenues (%)	Total	15.1	17.5	19.3
	Foreign-owned	14.8	17.2	18.9
	Polish-owned	22.9	25.1	28.6
Share of wages in revenues (%)	Total	5.3	6.1	8.2
	Foreign-owned	5.0	5.9	8.0
	Polish-owned	11.4	12.6	13.5
Share of depreciation in revenues (%)	Total	3.9	3.6	4.0
	Foreign-owned	3.9	3.6	4.0
	Polish-owned	3.4	3.6	4.5

Source: authors' calculations based on the financial reports for the 184 largest enterprises with revenues exceeding 50 million PLN (about €10 million) including 40 domestic firms.

The data show a steady increase in the share of value added in the revenues of automotive firms from 15.1% in 2007 to 19.3% in 2019. This reflects the increasing efficiency of the sector as a whole. Interestingly, domestic companies have a higher share of value added in revenues: 22.9% in 2007 and 28.6% in 2019, as well as its continuous improvement. For foreign producers, the figures are 14.8% and 18.9%, respectively, which corresponds to the generally lower profits of foreign affiliates in Poland.

There is also a continuous upward trend in the share of wages and salaries in revenues, from 5.3% in 2007 to 8.2% in 2019. This is the result of both rising wage levels and an increase in employment. The share of wages and salaries is much higher in Polish companies than in foreign-owned enterprises (13.5% and 8.0%, respectively, in 2019), although the difference is somewhat reduced by the stronger growth in TNCs (in 2007 it was 11.4% in domestic and 5.0% in foreign firms).

Smaller changes are observed in the share of depreciation in revenues, which was 3.9% in 2007 and very similar (4.0%) in 2019, but temporarily fell to 3.6% in 2012, probably as a result of the financial crisis of 2008–2009. This reflects the trend among foreign producers. In the case of companies with Polish capital, we see a steady increase from 3.4% in 2007 to 4.5% in 2019. This confirms continued investment activity in the automotive sector, with Polish firms showing a slightly more aggressive investment pattern.

Overall, there have been positive structural changes in the automotive sector over the period 2007–2019. Labour productivity has improved, value creation has increased as measured by the share of value added in revenues, and value capture has risen as reflected in the growing share of wages in value added and the high investment rate. Although the scale of operations and productivity of domestic producers are much lower, they are able to create and capture more value. It is important to emphasise that this only reflects the situation of the largest enterprises, as conditions in local SMEs may be different.

As we have seen, the volume of production has grown systematically, and as a result many of the Polish plants are among each company's largest in Europe, and in some cases they are the biggest or even the only facilities manufacturing certain products. For example, within the Volkswagen Group, the expanded MAN truck plant in Niepołomice has the highest production capacity and Polkowice is the only place where diesel engines are still manufactured; LG operates the largest battery production plant in Europe and Umicore the first European battery cathode material factory.

There is also little doubt that product upgrading has taken place, both at the level of the sector as a whole and at individual company level. The former is reflected in an increasing share of more complex, high value-added products, such as steering systems, brakes and their parts, of which Poland is now a leading European exporter, while the country's role in the production of simpler, standard components, such as wiring harnesses and stampings, has declined. Most Polish factories now make more advanced and sophisticated products than they did 10 or 20 years ago, and some have become the lead plants for their companies in Europe, introducing new generations of products. This reflects both the general move in this direction by entire corporations and the expanded responsibilities of their Polish subsidiaries. This has been shown by Olejniczak (2019) in an in-depth longitudinal study of Japanese affiliates between 2003 and 2018.

At the same time, the progress of technological processes varies considerably. On the one hand, in the first phase of post-socialist transformation, technological lines and equipment could be transferred from Western Europe to Poland. On the other hand, most production now comes from newly built or expanded and modernised factories, some of which, such as the new Mercedes-Benz plant in Jawor, are state of the art. Nevertheless, Krzywdzinski's (2017) study of automotive suppliers in Germany and CE shows that technology is generally less advanced in the latter. And the overall level of automation and robotics in the Polish industry is lower than in the Czech one. In 2022, there were 75 robots per 10,000 manufacturing workers in Poland, and about four times more in the automotive sector, which was still almost three times less than in Italy (IFR, 2023). This may be related to lower labour costs and, until recently, higher labour availability. The latter has changed dramatically, as discussed in Chapter 7, which, together with the pressure for higher efficiency, stability of the production process and quality, is pushing towards the adoption of more automated solutions; the latter facilitates the wider employment of women on the shop floor. In 2022, the number of new robot installations in Poland was the fifth highest in Europe, after Germany, Italy, France and Spain, and ahead of the UK (IFR, 2023).

The automotive industry is a leading sector in Polish manufacturing when it comes to implementing Industry 4.0 solutions, although there are significant differences within the sector. Large plants of major suppliers are emerging as leaders, some of which have implemented world-class solutions, e.g. in the area of digital twin technology, machine learning and artificial intelligence. On the other hand, there is a significant group, mainly SMEs, that do not see Industry 4.0 as a long-term strategy to move to a higher level in the value chain. According to interviews conducted by the authors in 2019, automotive companies in Poland are mainly interested in Industry 4.0 solutions in the area of predictive maintenance (Gwosdz et al., 2020). A more recent pilot survey, conducted in 2022, shows that the Industry 4.0 technologies most frequently adopted by automotive suppliers are those that are considered mature. The main benefits associated with the adoption of Industry 4.0 by the companies surveyed are improved efficiency, production stability and increased profitability. The main barriers to the use of Industry 4.0 technologies are a lack of investment capital and cybersecurity concerns, a concern expressed by more than 42% of respondents in the survey (Gwosdz et al., 2022).

The enhanced position of automotive producers from Poland in European production networks, especially Tier-1 and many Tier-2 suppliers, is reflected both in the diversification of their customers – large plants typically supply parts for several vehicle models and various companies – and in the increasing number of plants producing components for the premium segment.

The production of some automotive TNCs in Poland is supported by technical (engineering) centres. Their number, size and competences have increased significantly over the last two decades, as discussed in detail above. A few dozen of them are mainly development centres focusing on the modernisation of technological processes, routine validation tasks and product modifications for local plants. There are about 20 foreign-owned Tier-1 suppliers that operate R&D centres involved in pre-competitive new product design projects, half of which prepare product concepts and designs for global or European markets, generating a significant number of patents. In addition, advanced shared service functions such as IT and purchasing for an entire division in Europe are performed by some TNCs in Poland.

Development of Polish domestic firms

There are different types of domestically controlled enterprises in the sector. Many state-owned carmakers have been taken over by foreign investors, while others have been privatised by local capital, often through management buy-outs. New private Polish manufacturers have also emerged. Some companies and/or plants have been acquired by local investors from foreign owners, and a few ailing producers have been integrated into the state-controlled military group PGZ. Domestic firms that were unable to integrate into European supply chains had to switch to manufacturing spare parts or other products, and some went out of business.

Firms with predominantly domestic capital employed about 45,000 people in the narrowly defined automotive sector in 2018 (22% of total employment), and at least 63,000 together with automotive producers classified in other industries. Their employment has increased by about 50% since 2012. There were 33 Polish-owned companies with more than 250 employees and a large number of SMEs. One hundred and sixty Polish-owned factories held the IATF 16949 certificate in April 2022, confirming their suitability to supply vehicle manufacturers.

Domestic suppliers represent all segments of automotive production, with the largest number of manufacturers of plastic, metal and stamped parts, castings, forgings and electrical parts. Three-quarters of domestic manufacturers are mainly Tier-2 and Tier-3 suppliers. About 30% of Polish enterprises supply part of their production directly to OEMs, although only 11% are mainly Tier-1 suppliers, the rest supplying more components as Tier-2, Tier-3 or for the aftermarket. The automotive sector is the main customer for two-thirds of domestic suppliers, while the remaining one-third sell most of their products to other manufacturing sectors, mainly household appliances, electronics and construction. Polish component producers usually started supplying a single customer and, if successful, could expand their market reach, including supplies to the premium segment.

A common view among many of the managers interviewed is that Polish-owned producers integrated into the supply networks are able to achieve good manufacturing capabilities, becoming reliable suppliers and meeting high quality standards. What they often lack are indigenous design competences. This, together with limited economies of scale and a lack of brand names, is a fundamental barrier to improving their position in the supply networks. There are exceptions that deserve a brief mention.

The Zasada Group, owned by former rally driver Sobiesław Zasada, was a Polish company that became an early investor in the mid-1990s, taking over ailing state-owned bus and truck manufacturers Jelcz, Autosan and Star, as well as some component plants. However, the strategy of specialising in the production of low-cost vehicles for the domestic market proved unsuccessful. Insufficient capital and know-how in the face of growing competition from Western imports and new manufacturers such as Solaris, which offered high-quality products increasingly sought after by Polish road carriers and municipalities modernising their fleets, forced the Zasada companies out of the market. They were eventually taken over by foreign TNCs (Star) or the state-controlled military conglomerate (Jelcz and Autosan).

Groclin became the largest Polish automotive supplier in the first decade of the 21st century. It began as a small workshop in Grodzisk Wielkopolski in 1977 and grew into a Tier-2 supplier of leather and fabric seat covers to state-owned assembly plants in the 1990s. The company was controlled by its founder, Zbigniew Drzymała, and was listed on the Warsaw Stock Exchange, allowing it to raise capital and build three factories in Poland and one in Ukraine in 2004, with another under construction there in 2008, when total employment reached 3,100. The financial crisis and the loss of premium segment contracts from Volvo, Porsche and BMW led to difficulties and eventually the takeover of Groclin in 2013 by Germany's Kabel-Technik, which had developed a wiring business. The latter was sold to the Finnish PKC Group in 2017 and the home plant in Grodzisk was bought by a Polish furniture manufacturer in 2019, while it was announced that vehicle trim production would be concentrated in Ukraine and Bosnia to reduce costs. A radical change in the business model came in 2021, when the production of electric bicycles began and a merger with CountMe took place, creating a group of Less brands specialising in buying used items (clothes, toys, books) and putting them back on the market.

The Polish OEM to achieve international success is Wielton. The company was established in the 1990s in Wieluń, repairing used semi-trailers imported from the West. In 1996 it started its own production of semi-trailers for the domestic market and continued to grow, taking advantage of the increasing demand from Polish and Central European carriers, who were becoming the leaders in EU road transport. Wielton tried to expand in Eastern Europe by opening its assembly plant near Moscow in 2012, but changed its strategy after the Russian annexation of Crimea and decided to target Western European markets. Between 2015 and 2021, it acquired brand manufacturers Fruehauf in France, Rimorchi (Viberti) in Italy, Langendorf in Germany, Lawrence David in the UK and Guillén in Spain, making Wielton the third largest semi-trailer manufacturer in Europe and one of the top ten worldwide. The company now has 9 factories and 4 R&D centres in 7 countries, with half of its revenues (€732 million in 2022) generated abroad and 3,100 employees in 2021.

A few other Polish producers also expanded internationally through foreign acquisitions (Micek et al., 2021; Sass & Tabajdi, 2023). Sanok Rubber, founded in 1931, was one of the first automotive suppliers to be privatised by an American equity fund in 1993. It was listed on the Warsaw Stock Exchange in 1997 and 6 years later a local management buyout took place. A joint venture to produce rubber for the construction sector was established in Russia in 1995, but major investments in automotive sealing and anti-vibration systems followed. The acquisition of German firm Draftex (sealing systems) and French company Colmant Cuvelier (belts and couplings) in 2014–2015 were the first steps towards internationalisation; the acquisition of Qingdao Masters of Rubber and Plastic in China (sold in 2022) and the construction of a greenfield plant in Mexico in 2016–2018 marked a new, global stage of expansion. Sanok Rubber now has 5 factories and 2 R&D centres in 5 countries, with around 3,000 employees, including 2,200 in Poland. It is a Tier-1 supplier to a large number of OEMs (60% of automotive sales) and a Tier-2 supplier to other customers.

The largest automotive supplier with predominantly Polish capital is the Boryszew Group. It takes its name from a town near Warsaw where a synthetic silk factory was opened in 1911. It was privatised in 1992 as a producer of antifreeze and brake fluids, and in 2000 became part of a large industrial group controlled by Roman Karkosik. Specialising in industrial chemicals and non-ferrous metals, the Boryszew Group established an automotive division as part of its diversification strategy. Between 2010 and 2014, it acquired the Italian company Maflow, which produces aluminium and rubber tubes, four medium-sized German producers of plastic components and tools for the automotive industry, and Japanese Tensho subsidiaries in Poland and Germany. It also built greenfield plants in India (2011), Russia (2014), Mexico (2016), Poland and Germany (2017). Boryszew's automotive division now comprises 20 factories in 11 countries, including France, Spain, Czechia, Brazil and China, as well as R&D centres in Italy, Germany and Poland, generating sales of around €400 million in 2022 (€1,450 million for the group as a whole).

Other major Polish producers include Alumetal, Izoblok and Bury. Alumetal, whose beginnings date back to 1953, is one of the leading European producers of secondary aluminium casting alloys, with 90% of its sales to the automotive sector ($732 million in 2022). It has 3 factories in Poland, including 2 newly built ones, and a greenfield plant in Hungary (2016). Izoblok specialises in the production of expanded polypropylene (EPP) mouldings. It was founded in 1998, acquired by a foreign investor a few years later, but soon taken back by the Polish founder. In addition, Izoblok bought German company SSW Pearl-Foam in 2016, making it a leader in the European EPP market. Founded in 1987 as a small family business, Bury manufactures automotive information, communication and connectivity systems in Mielec and Mexico, has an R&D centre in Rzeszów and software development units in Poland and Germany, and employs a total of 2,200 people.

The success of these companies shows that there are domestic manufacturers with the brand, decision-making, marketing and design capabilities to build strong market positions in the core economies of Western Europe, Asia and Latin America. However, their number is very limited.

In general, the integration of domestic suppliers into European production networks and the upgrading of the position of some of them has been an evolutionary process. They often started by producing for the aftermarket and/or winning contracts from foreign Tier-2 or Tier-1 suppliers or OEMs. Good performance in terms of product quality and delivery reliability built trust, which could lead to winning larger contracts and new customers, including in more demanding market segments, manufacturing more complex components and/or moving to a Tier-2 or Tier-1 position. Company growth, increased financial capacity and customer pressure encouraged process improvement, including greater automation and robotisation.

The relatively large size of the automotive sector in Poland and in CE as a whole, together with its continuous growth, provided room for international expansion for some companies. Success on the domestic and/or Central European market was followed by decisions to seek new markets (Wielton, Sanok Rubber) or lower costs by investing in Russia or Ukraine (Groclin), and since 2010 also in Western Europe. Acquisitions of original brand manufacturers in the core economies represented a window of opportunity after the global financial crisis of 2008–2009, while greenfield investments in the emerging markets of Asia and Latin America were the result of a follow-the-customer strategy. This would not have been possible without a gradual build-up of confidence and ambition to achieve a prominent position in Europe, advanced manufacturing, organisational and financial capabilities linked to past success, capital raised on the stock market and involvement in other industries. There has been a combination of traditional cost advantages with greater flexibility linked to experience of operating in difficult and rapidly changing environments, which has enabled Wielton, for example, to offer a wide range of products tailored to the needs of a large number of medium-sized customers. All in all, this reflects the interdependence between developing country-specific and firm-specific advantages (Micek et al., 2021).

Successful manufacturers such as Wielton, Sanok Rubber, Bury and Boryszew have developed their indigenous design capabilities, including simulation and/or prototyping and testing, enabling them to meet the requirements of a wide range of customers. This is also the case for some Tier-2 suppliers, such as FA Krosno, which manufactures gas springs for European and American manufacturers and acquired the French company Airax in 2023. There is no doubt that the position in GPNs of domestic suppliers which achieve technological capabilities and diversification of customers is far more advantageous. Nevertheless, there are many Tier-2 and Tier-3 suppliers that rely on blueprints provided by their customers, which makes them highly dependent. Only one in five

Polish companies certified to the IATF 16949 standard has design capabilities. There are only a handful of Polish manufacturers that can be classified as original design manufacturers. The story of the decline of Zasada and Groclin illustrates the formidable barriers faced by expanding domestic producers and their vulnerability, especially firms specialising in cost-sensitive, labour-intensive products, and the failure of low-cost strategies.

There are also independent Polish R&D companies. Bosmal, a former R&D unit of FSM in Bielsko-Biała, is the largest and operates as a subcontractor for various Tier-1 suppliers, providing them with solutions for specific components, preparation of prototypes and validation. A relatively new trend is the emergence of independent start-ups, backed by Polish capital, providing design and R&D services to the automotive industry. Kraków-based Endego (formerly Cadm Automotive) is a leading Polish provider of engineering and software services to the sector. EC Engineering, which specialises in design for the transport sector, including e-mobility and automotive, has grown from a small business with just 3 employees in 2000 to a company employing 150 engineers by 2022.

Interestingly, expanding production generates multiplier effects that primarily benefit domestic firms, even in foreign-dominated industries such as automotive. Domestic companies provide auxiliary services to manufacturers, such as tooling, maintenance, repair and logistics. In particular, we are witnessing the growth of Polish IT firms and integrators that provide Industry 4.0 solutions to manufacturers. Many of them work mainly for foreign-owned clients, both in Poland and abroad, as cooperation between SMEs and R&D centres and technical universities is generally weak.

Conclusions

Poland inherited a medium-sized automotive sector from the socialist era that, apart from a few licensing agreements, was poorly connected to the Western European core. It became a target for foreign investment in the 1990s; Fiat was the first major OEM to take over the largest Polish carmaker, FSM, while GM (Opel) decided to build a new assembly plant. These were followed by an increasing number of acquisitions and greenfield investments. Whereas early investors were often attracted by the Polish market, later ones were predominantly export-oriented. The availability of skilled, albeit relatively cheap, labour and geographical proximity were key factors. Accession to the European Union and government incentives provided a favourable institutional framework.

Massive investment fuelled the dynamic growth of the automotive industry, making Poland a significant exporter strongly integrated into European automotive production networks. The country's role in different segments of the sector has evolved, with initially increasing and then decreasing passenger car assembly, and now a particularly prominent position in the manufacture of light commercial vehicles and buses. However, the main strength is a vast and diversified components sector, where Poland has become the second-largest European exporter after Germany. It is made up of many lead firms from different countries and numerous medium-sized and small domestic enterprises, which makes automotive production well embedded in the country. Importantly, the construction of new plants, the expansion of existing ones and the launch of new products (e.g. new Stellantis, Toyota and Mercedes-Benz vehicles recently) have been accompanied by very few disinvestments, apart from the spectacular global collapse of Daewoo.

Many of the plants located in Poland are among the largest in Europe and are sometimes the main or even the only manufacturer of certain products for their companies. The improvement in their position is also reflected in the diversification of their customers, i.e. supplying several companies for different car models and the premium segment. There is a general trend towards the manufacture of more complex products and towards technological modernisation, i.e. product and process upgrading. All this is reflected in an increasing share of value added and labour costs in company revenues, although labour productivity still lags behind Western European levels. The current shift away from ICEs in the European Union is a clear challenge for many suppliers operating in the country, although it is too early to assess its long-term impact. At the same time, significant investments are already being made in the manufacture of batteries for electric vehicles and their components.

The technological gap between Poland and Western Europe, created under state socialism, has not disappeared in the post-socialist period with the arrival of foreign investors, as they have tended to focus on manufacturing activities in Poland. However, there has been a gradual development of R&D functions, especially in the last decade. Advanced functional upgrading is a selective process that takes place mainly among some Tier-1 suppliers. It is most common in American companies, less so in European and Asian ones. Overall, the scope of non-production competences of foreign affiliates is still smaller than their production capacities in Poland, which shows that product and process upgrading is much stronger than functional upgrading.

Domestic producers generally play a secondary role in the automotive industry. Many of them have developed good manufacturing capabilities that allow them to be integrated into European production networks as lower-tier suppliers. There is a narrow group of Polish-owned firms with distinct product design competences, some of which have started to expand internationally. Finally, there are spillover effects outside the automotive sector, e.g. in tooling companies and firms specialising in the implementation of Industry 3.0 and 4.0 solutions.

Notes

1 IATF 16949 is an international quality management standard specifically tailored for the automotive industry. It is recognised by automotive manufacturers worldwide and often determines the ability to work with OEMs.

2 In January 2024, Stellantis announced its planned closure.
3 At least 30 new centres were created after 2009. No information was found on the date of establishment of 23 smaller centres (with fewer than 30 employees), some of which may have existed before 2009.

References

Basant, R., & Mani, S. (2012). Foreign R&D centres in India: An analysis of their size, structure and implications. Indian Institute of Management Ahmedabad (IIMA) Working paper no. 2012-01-06.Ahmedabad: IIMA.

Domański, B., & Lung, Y. (2009). The changing face of the European periphery in the automotive industry. *European Urban and Regional Studies*, 16(1), 5–10.

Frigant, V., & Miollan, S. (2014). The geographical restructuring of the European automobile industry in the 2000s. MPRA Paper No. 53509. Munich: MPRA. Retrieved from https://mpra.ub.uni-muenchen.de/53509/.

Guzik, R., Domański, B., & Gwosdz, K. (2020). Automotive industry dynamics in Central Europe. In A. Covarrubias & S.M.R. Pérez (Eds.), *New frontiers of the automobile industry: Exploring geographies, technology, and institutional challenges* (pp. 377–397). Cham: Palgrave Macmillan.

Gwosdz, K., Baron, M., Budka, M., Hetmańczyk, K., Hetmańczyk, M., Sobala-Gwosdz, A., & Szczepanek, R. (2022). *Does geographical proximity matter? The role of strategic coupling of automotive industry and digital entrepreneurs as the mechanism of new path creation in Polish regions*. Gerpisa Colloquium, Detroit. Retrieved from https://www.gerpisa.org/en/node/7061.

Gwosdz, K., Micek, G., Kocaj, A., Sobala-Gwosdz, A., & Świgost-Kapocsi, A. (2020). Industry 4.0 and the prospects for domestic automotive suppliers in Poland. In J. Drahokoupil (Ed.), *The challenge of digital transformation in the automotive industry: Jobs, upgrading, and the prospects for development* (pp. 89–105). Brussels: European Trade Union Institute.

IFR. (2023). *World Robotics 2023 report*. Frankfurt: International Federation of Robotics.

Kisiała, W., Kudłak, R., & Kołsut, B. (2023). The market for new cars: Another dimension of the core-periphery pattern. In B. Kołsut & T. Stryjakiewicz (Eds.), *The economic geography of the car market: The automobile revolution in an emerging economy* (pp. 45–70). London: Routledge.

Klier, T., & McMillan, D. (2015). Plant location patterns in the European automobile supplier industry. *Growth and Change*, 46(4), 558–573.

Kołsut, B., Kisiała, W., & Kudłak, R. (2023). Import of second-hand cars: Evidence of individual entrepreneurship and social networks? In B. Kołsut & T. Stryjakiewicz (Eds.), *The economic geography of the car market: The automobile revolution in an emerging economy* (pp. 72–95). London: Routledge.

Kołsut, B., & Stryjakiewicz, T. (Eds.). (2023). *The economic geography of the car market: The automobile revolution in an emerging economy*. London: Routledge.

Krzak, J. (2004). *Skutki akcesji Polski do UE dla branży samochodowej*. Raport nr 224. Warsaw: Kancelaria Sejmu, Biuro Studiów i Ekspertyz.

Krzywdzinski, M. (2017). Automation, skill requirements, and labor use strategies: High-wage and low-wage approaches to high-tech manufacturing in the automotive industry. *New Technology, Work and Employment*, 32(3), 247–267.

Kudłak, R., Kołsut, B., & Kisiała, W. (2023). Driving gears of car ownership transformation. In B. Kołsut & T. Stryjakiewicz (Eds.), *The economic geography of the car market: The automobile revolution in an emerging economy* (pp. 24–43). London: Routledge.

Massini, S., & Miozzo, M. (2010). Outsourcing and offshoring of knowledge-intensive business services: Implications for innovation. In F. Gallouj, & F. Djellal (Eds.), *Handbook of innovation and services: A multi-disciplinary perspective* (pp. 469–500). Cheltenham: Edward Elgar.

Micek, G., Guzik, R., Gwosdz, K., & Domański, B. (2021). Newcomers from the periphery: The international expansion of Polish automotive companies. *Energies*, 14(9), 2617.

Müller, P., & Franz, M. (2019). Transnational labour migration and the offshoring of knowledge-intensive business services within global production networks: The case of a German automotive company in Turkey. *Environment and Planning A: Economy and Space*, 51(6), 1350–1369.

Olejniczak, T. (2019). *Japońskie fabryki hybrydowe w Polsce i Europie Środkowo-Wschodniej*. Warsaw: Poltext.

PAIiH. (2022). *Elektromobilność w Polsce: Inwestycje, trendy, zatrudnienie*. Warsaw: Polska Agencja Inwestycji i Handlu.

Pardi, T. (2022). *Heavier, faster and less affordable cars: The consequence of EU regulations for car emissions*. Brussels: European Trade Union Institute.

Pavlínek, P. (2018). Global production networks, foreign direct investment, and supplier linkages in the integrated peripheries of the automotive industry. *Economic Geography*, 94(2), 141–165.

Pavlínek, P. (2020). Restructuring and internationalization of the European automotive industry. *Journal of Economic Geography*, 20(2), 509–541.

Pavlínek, P. (2022). Relative positions of countries in the core-periphery structure of the European automotive industry. *European Urban and Regional Studies*, 29(1), 59–84. doi:10.1177/09697764211021882.

Pavlínek, P., Domański, B., & Guzik, R. (2009). Industrial upgrading through foreign direct investment in Central European automotive manufacturing. *European Urban and Regional Studies*, 16(1), 43–63.

Polskie Stowarzyszenie Paliw Alternatywnych & Boston Consulting Group. (2021). *Jak elektromobilność zmieni rynek pracy w Polsce? Zielone sektory przyszłości*. Warsaw: Polskie Stowarzyszenie Paliw Alternatywnych (PSPA) & Boston Consulting Group.

Richter, P.C., & Brühl, R. (2017). Shared service center research: A review of the past, present, and future. *European Management Journal*, 35(1), 26–38. doi:10.1016/j.emj.2016.08.004.

Sass, M., & Tabajdi, G. (2023). Automotive outward FDI from the Visegrad countries and Austria: Do indigenous companies invest abroad? In *23rd International Joint Conference Central and Eastern Europe in the Changing Business Environment, Proceedings*, 18–19 May 2023, Prague, Czech Republic – Bratislava, Slovakia (pp. 225–235). Bratislava: Vydavateľstvo EKONÓM. doi:10.18267/pr.2023.kre.2490.18.

Szczerbicki, T. (2017). *Polskie samochody osobowe z lat PRL. Produkcja seryjna*. Czerwonak: Vesper.

Wilk, H. (2019). Motoryzacja w Polsce (1945–1989). *Polska 1944/45–1989*, (17), 331–348.

4 Aircraft Industry

The aircraft (aviation) industry is one of the most advanced sectors of modern manufacturing. Based on two major pillars, civil and military, it is generally resilient to external shocks. It has also undergone significant technological (e.g. additive manufacturing, see Wagner & Walton, 2016) and operational changes to meet the growing need for climate mitigation (e.g. Bows-Larkin, 2015), leading to the adoption of sustainable low-emission aviation (Ranasinghe et al., 2019). However, the contemporary development and spatial patterns of the aircraft industry cannot be studied without discussing the past economic and technological conditions. Therefore, the next section provides a brief historical overview of the development of the sector.

Historical background

The history of the Polish aircraft industry dates back to the First World War. In his review paper, Suwala (2018) distinguished four stages in the development of the sector in Poland (the interwar period 1914–1939, the Second World War 1939–1945, the communist period 1945–1989 and the restructuring phase since 1990). This subsection examines the first three phases, while the next is devoted to a discussion of the disruptive changes that took place in the restructuring period.

The origins of the Polish aircraft industry can be traced back to enthusiastic aviation pioneers (Cynk, 1971) and the resulting establishment of aircraft associations and flying clubs (Jane, 1913). Referring to Glass (1992), Suwala (2018) argues that Warsaw (with its PZL P.7, P.11, P.24 and PZL.23 Karaś fighters and a PZL.37 Łoś bomber) became the centre of the interwar aircraft industry, with some smaller sites in Wielkopolska and eastern Poland.

Until the mid-1930s, the domestic market was relatively small and the Polish government was the dominant customer during the Great Depression. Furthermore, in the early 1930s there was a massive nationalisation of the nascent Polish aviation industry (Cynk, 1971). The sector became one of the state's priorities in the face of the emerging military threat. This was reflected in the introduction of a major industrialisation plan and the creation of the Central Industrial District (COP) from the mid-1930s. It resulted in the construction of

DOI: 10.4324/9781003430117-5

an aircraft factory in Mielec and an engine plant in Rzeszów (now in south-eastern Poland), which did not reach full capacity before the Second World War (see Figure 6.3). These investments laid the foundations for a modern aircraft industry in Poland. Some military aircraft (bombers and fighters) were exported, e.g. to Greece, Turkey, Romania and Bulgaria. Both imports and exports of aircraft to/from Poland played a rather complementary role to domestic aircraft production before the Second World War.

During the war, aircraft factories were not completely destroyed, except in Warsaw-Okęcie. Most of them survived, but in poor conditions and with a considerable lack of machinery (Glass & Kubalańca, 2013), and some were used by the German army. Suwala (2018, p. 26) argues that they "unintentionally contributed to the establishment of an aviation industry network in Poland after the Second World War, which has survived to this day (e.g. Wrocław, Kalisz, Krosno)".

Under socialism, the industry functioned within the USSR-dominated Comecon and technological development was based on cooperation with the Soviet Union. Between 1945 and 1984, the majority of Polish aircraft production was exported, including 72% of aircraft, 90% of helicopters and 85% of engines (Glass, 1984). As a strategic industry in Comecon, the sector had to export its products (aircraft, helicopters, wing and tail components etc.) to the Soviet Union, which accounted for 92% of all exports (excluding gliders) (Glass, 1984; Glass & Kubalańca, 2022). Production focused mainly on the manufacture of Polish variants of Soviet aircraft, as well as small agricultural and utility planes and helicopters.

Both civil and military helicopters were made at WSK PZL-Świdnik. The Mi-2 was the only helicopter designed in the USSR that was not mass-produced there, but at WSK PZL-Świdnik. From the mid-1980s, the Świdnik plant began manufacturing its own design, the PZL W-3 Sokół, which was produced in various versions for transport, naval, landing, assault and battlefield support.

Three trends worked against the total dominance of USSR-oriented manufacturing. The first was Poland's specialisation in the production of utility and agricultural aircraft and their components within the Eastern bloc. This led to their export to a number of countries around the world, not just communist ones (Glass, 1984). Secondly, the production of gliders (as civil aircraft) was dominated by Polish firms independent of the Soviet Union, with a growing position in international non-Comecon markets from the mid-1960s. Thirdly, with the liberalisation of the mid-1970s, engine production opened up to American companies. WSK PZL-Rzeszów bought a licence from Franklin to manufacture piston engines. In 1976, a long-term contract was signed between Pratt & Whitney (P&W) and the Polish government for the production of numerous parts and assemblies for one of their aircraft engines. On the basis of American licences and imported equipment, the Polish aviation industry delivered its certified products to its US partners (Fiszer & Bluj, 2007). This resulted in a relatively small share of engines being exported to the USSR.

Glass (1984) estimates that in the first 40 years of socialist Poland some 15,500 airplanes, 5,750 helicopters and 4,670 gliders were produced, as well as 50,600 aircraft engines. Output peaked in 1973, when 927 aircraft and helicopters were built. This figure fell to 710 in 1980, when the sector employed a maximum of 60,000 people. At the end of the 1970s, the sector consisted of two aircraft factories (Mielec, Warsaw-Okęcie), one helicopter plant (Świdnik), two aircraft engine plants (Rzeszów, Kalisz), eight auxiliary plants and four glider factories. The first R&D units were created in 1971, when the R&D Centre for Aircraft Propulsion was established at WSK PZL-Rzeszów.

The aircraft industry in the transformation period

In the early 1990s, the sector entered a painful restructuring phase. The negative impact of the collapse of Comecon was a severe loss of orders, which resulted in an 80% production cut in Polish aviation factories (Kinder & Suwala, 2012; Suwala & Micek, 2018). This can be illustrated by the decline in the number of aircraft and helicopters manufactured from 433 in 1990 to only 55 two years later. Employment in the sector decreased by three-quarters between 1990 and 2000 (Glass & Kubalańca, 2022), with significant layoffs in the largest companies and the collapse of their branch plants. Suwala and Micek (2018) show that in just five years between 1989 and 1994, employment at the Rzeszów factory fell from 10,960 to 6,050 and at the Mielec plant from 20,112 to 8,750. In 2003, the Mielec factory employed only 1,800 people (10% of the 1980 workforce).

At the same time, the government tried to help the major aircraft factories through the Industrial Development Agency (ARP; established in 1992), which provided loans and guarantees for restructuring. On the basis of past cooperation from the socialist era, Poland's second-largest aircraft engine manufacturer, WSK PZL-Kalisz, entered into a joint venture with P&W Canada in 1992. In 1996, the factory was fully acquired by P&W. In the same year, P&W Canada signed a ten-year cooperation agreement with WSK PZL-Rzeszów (Fiszer & Bluj, 2007). In 1999, after more than three years of cooperation with Coltec Industries, the landing gear manufacturer WSK PZL-Krosno was taken over by American Goodrich, and subsequently by UTC in 2012. Long before the foreign takeover, PZL-Świdnik had been producing airframes for several types of aircraft manufactured by the Anglo-Italian company AgustaWestland since 1996. The plant also supplied components for Eurocopter and Bell (Smura et al., 2021).

In summary, during the post-socialist transformation of the 1990s, many Polish aircraft plants entered into cooperation or joint venture partnerships with Western corporations. However, there were no significant changes in the ownership of the companies. Cooperation with foreign aircraft manufacturers was a must, as employment fell fourfold and the number of aircraft and helicopters produced fell more than 20-fold between 1980 and 2000. The collapse of the market led to a sudden deterioration in the economic performance of the aircraft firms.

In the first decade of the 2000s, the largest aircraft factories were sold to foreign capital. In 2002, WSK PZL-Rzeszów was bought by the American company United Technologies Holdings (UTH), which owned the P&W brand. Five years later, UTH bought shares in PZL Mielec and began assembly and manufacturing of the Sikorsky S-70i Black Hawk helicopter. The last major plant acquired by foreign investors was WSK PZL-Świdnik, which had been producing helicopters since the late 1950s. It was bought by AgustaWestland (now Leonardo Helicopters) in 2010. At the same time, all major aircraft and helicopter plants (in Mielec and Świdnik) continued to repair and maintain older aircraft models out of a manufacturer's commitment to maintaining service capability.

The dynamics and structure of the sector: ownership, manufacturers and products

The beginning of the second decade of the 21st century saw the emergence of greenfield investments in the aircraft industry. Most of them were led by UTH and its subsidiaries: the first factory for auxiliary power units (APUs) and an engineering centre were opened by Hamilton Sundstrand in Rzeszów. This investment, together with the acquisition of large state-owned plants, can be seen as a revival of the Polish aircraft industry.

The position of Poland in the EU aircraft industry has been growing since the mid-2000s. It is one of three CE countries, along with Czechia and Romania, where this sector is significant. In the broader Eurostat category "manufacture of air and spacecraft and related machinery" (C303), Poland's production value almost quadrupled between 2008 and 2021. The country's share of EU value added has increased from 1.4% in 2005 to 2.1% in 2019 and 2.0% in 2021. However, it is less than one-sixth that in Italy and one-quarter that in Spain. According to the PRODCOM database, the highest growth in output was observed for turned metal parts for aircraft, spacecraft and satellites (8.4% of the EU total in 2021) and parts of turbojets or turbo-propellers for use in civil aircraft (7.0%). The country accounted for 4.9% of employment in the sector in the EU in 2021. The most dynamic increase is in the number of enterprises registered in the Polish aircraft industry (Figure 4.1). In 2011, 5.8% of EU27 companies were active in Poland, while their share almost doubled to 9.7% in 2021. Only Germany, France and Italy host more aircraft firms.

In terms of employment, Poland's share in the EU is fairly stable. However, the number of persons employed in the broadly defined aircraft industry in the country increased by 67% between 2000 and 2019, reaching over 42,000 people. This figure also includes employment in enterprises that are not classified under NACE 303 but supplying aircraft components and military customers. These two reasons make a difference to the Eurostat data, which show 19,613 employees in NACE 303 in 2019 and 16,667 employees in 2021.

The Russian invasion of Ukraine, which began in 2022, has led to an expansion of military aircraft production in Poland. Poland increased defence

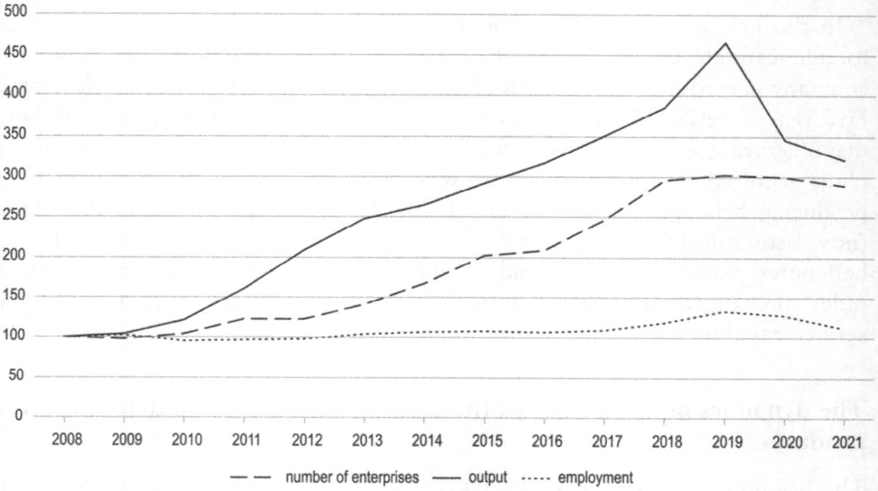

Figure 4.1 Dynamics of the Polish aircraft industry, 2008–2021 (2008 = 100)
Source: authors' calculations based on Eurostat data.

spending towards 4% of GDP by 2023. Some companies will benefit significantly. This includes the €1.4 billon order for AW149 helicopters, which accounts for 8.1% of the Leonardo group's total new orders in 2023. Many firms specialising in aircraft repair have also profited from the current war-related demand.

The ownership structure of the sector has changed with the acquisition of large state-owned enterprises. Domestic companies dominated in 2006, but by 2019 about 65% of the workforce was employed by foreign firms.

At present, the US company Raytheon Technologies (UTH until the merger in 2020), through its Collins Aerospace and P&W brands, is the major foreign investor in the Polish aircraft industry (Table 4.1); it is the second-largest global producer in the defence sector (after Lockheed Martin) and the second biggest in the aircraft industry in terms of revenues (after Boeing). Following the sale of the UTH-owned plant in Mielec to US-based Lockheed Martin in 2015, Raytheon (UTH) accounted for 27% of total employment in Poland in 2019. Raytheon Technologies controls seven plants in Poland, located in Rzeszów, Wrocław, Kalisz, Niepołomice and Krosno. In Rzeszów, it operates the largest aircraft factory in Poland, P&W Rzeszów (approximately 4,500 employees with an R&D and engineering centre). Located on the premises of former WSK PZL-Rzeszów, it carries out assemblies and sub-assemblies for aircraft engines (including intermediate fuselage and geared turbofan transmission systems) and supplies components for advanced aircraft models such as the Airbus A320NEO, Boeing 747-400 and Airbus A380 (Smura et al., 2021). In addition, the plant has recently become a maintenance and repair centre for P&W engines, not

Table 4.1 The largest companies in the broadly defined aircraft industry in Poland in 2019

Company (capital group)	*Branches and brands in Poland*	*Number of employees*	*Number of plants / R&D*	*Main products*
Raytheon Technologies	Collins Aerospace, Pratt & Whitney	8,165	7/3	aircraft engines, assemblies and sub-assemblies for aircraft engines (sheet elements and complex static structures as well as aircraft engine gearboxes, pipe assemblies)
Leonardo Helicopters	Wytwórnia Sprzętu Komunikacyjnego PZL-Świdnik	2,811	1/1	helicopters; helicopter structures, composite hulls, tail beams, rotor blades and tail rotor blades
Polska Grupa Zbrojeniowa	WSK PZL-Kalisz, WZL no. 1, WZL no. 2, WZL no. 4	2,171	4/1	repairs of aircraft, helicopters, their engines and hydraulic, pneumatic, electrical and electronic equipment of aircraft; production of spare parts for aviation equipment; galvanic and painting services; radial piston aircraft engines; repair of engines; assemblies, subassemblies and parts of aircraft engines; products for flow engines; industrial services within thermal treatment and thermal-chemical treatment
Lockheed Martin	Polskie Zakłady Lotnicze (PZL Mielec)	1,616	1/0	S-70 Black Hawk helicopter and M28 fixed-wing short takeoff and landing aircraft in civil and military versions; fuselage of F-16
Thoni Alutec	Thoni Alutec	1,520	1/0	aluminium castings
EDC	EDC	1,400*	1/1	design and development of parts of units of aircraft engines
MTU	MTU Aero Engines	964	2/1	low-pressure turbine parts such as blades and vanes, seals and disks; assembly of turbine centre frames; repair of engine components

Company (capital group)	*Branches and brands in Poland*	*Number of employees*	*Number of plants / R&D*	*Main products*
Airbus	Airbus	800	1/1	aviation structures and components for CASA C295 and C235, Airbus A-320 aircraft; modernizations and repairs
Safran	Safran, Aero Gearbox (joint venture with Rolls-Royce)	879	4/0	mechanical components for accessory drive trains for aircraft engines; accessory drive trains for Rolls-Royce civil aviation engines
General Electric	Avio Aero	592	1/1	design and development of aircraft engine components and modules; stator and rotor blades for civil and military engine turbines; low-pressure turbine nozzles
MB Aerospace	MB Aerospace, Vac Aero	525	2/0	engine housings and structural frames; key rotating hardware such as rotating seals, shrouds and flanges; high-performance treatments and coatings for aero-engine components
Gardner	Gardner Aerospace	934	4/0	precision machining of components for the aviation and automotive industries
ATI	ATI ZKM Forging	500	1/0	die forging, heat treatment forgings, non-destructive testing and mechanical processing for various industries

Source: authors' elaboration based on company annual reports and websites.

Note: * Total employment of GE Aerospace and Łukasiewicz Research Network - Institute of Aviation.

only for the Polish Army. P&W Kalisz manufactures large and complex parts (gears, steering devices, main engine shafts) for the wide range of P&W engine models and employs about 1,600 people.

The final assembly sites for aircraft and helicopters (Mielec and Świdnik) remain in operation, but their products are significantly different. Within the global and corporate production network, PZL Mielec has become the largest Lockheed Martin manufacturing site outside the USA. It has received $1.8 billion in investment over the past decade and produces cabins for UH-60M Black Hawk helicopters for international customers, including the US Army. An assembly line for the S-70i helicopter – a weaker export version of the Black Hawk family of attack helicopters – has also been launched in Mielec. The plant has also recently started producing parts for the F-16 fuselage. By 2024, the plant is expected to produce 80% of the fuselage structure. The company retains production capacity for its earlier designs, namely the M28 and M28B Bryza transport and passenger aircraft (the only non-light aircraft designed in Poland) and the M18 Dromader agricultural and fire-fighting aircraft (Smura et al., 2021). PZL Mielec also supplies elements of aircraft structure to P&W, which increases domestic trade between foreign companies in Poland.

PZL-Świdnik, part of Italy's Leonardo with 2,900 employees, is the only OEM with full helicopter design, manufacturing and support capabilities, making Poland one of five such EU member states. With 7,500 helicopters delivered to over 40 countries in its long history, PZL-Świdnik ranks third in the world in terms of the number of helicopters produced. Under the Leonardo brand, PZL-Świdnik not only supplies its flagship W-3A Sokół, but also assembles Leonardo-designed models such as the AW101 and AW149 for the Polish Ministry of Defence. The latter are Polish versions: the airframe structures are built in Świdnik and the integration of sensors, avionics and advanced weapons and self-defence systems takes place on the assembly line. PZL-Świdnik also manufactures components for many of Leonardo's helicopters, such as the AW101, AW139, AW169 and AW189 (Smura et al., 2021).

The Polish aircraft industry is characterised by a relatively high degree of organisational concentration. The three corporations operating in the country (Raytheon, Lockheed Martin and Leonardo) concentrate about half of the total workforce and turnover of the 42 largest aircraft companies. There are several foreign and domestic firms that weaken this dominance (see Table 4.1).

The growth of the sector has been strongly influenced by exports and corporate demand. Polish exports ranked fifth in the EU in 2022, overtaking Italy (see Chapter 2). Over the past 15 years, Poland has become a major European producer and exporter of turbojets, turbo-propellers and their parts. Although the origins of turbojets and their components are historical, exports have grown from €275 million in 2008 to €2,397 million in 2021 (Figure 4.2), through not only foreign acquisitions (P&W Rzeszów and Kalisz) but also greenfield investments. The latter include new engine component plants by Germany's MTU Aero Engines and US-based MB Aerospace in the Podkarpackie Science and Technology Park at Jasionka airport near Rzeszów.

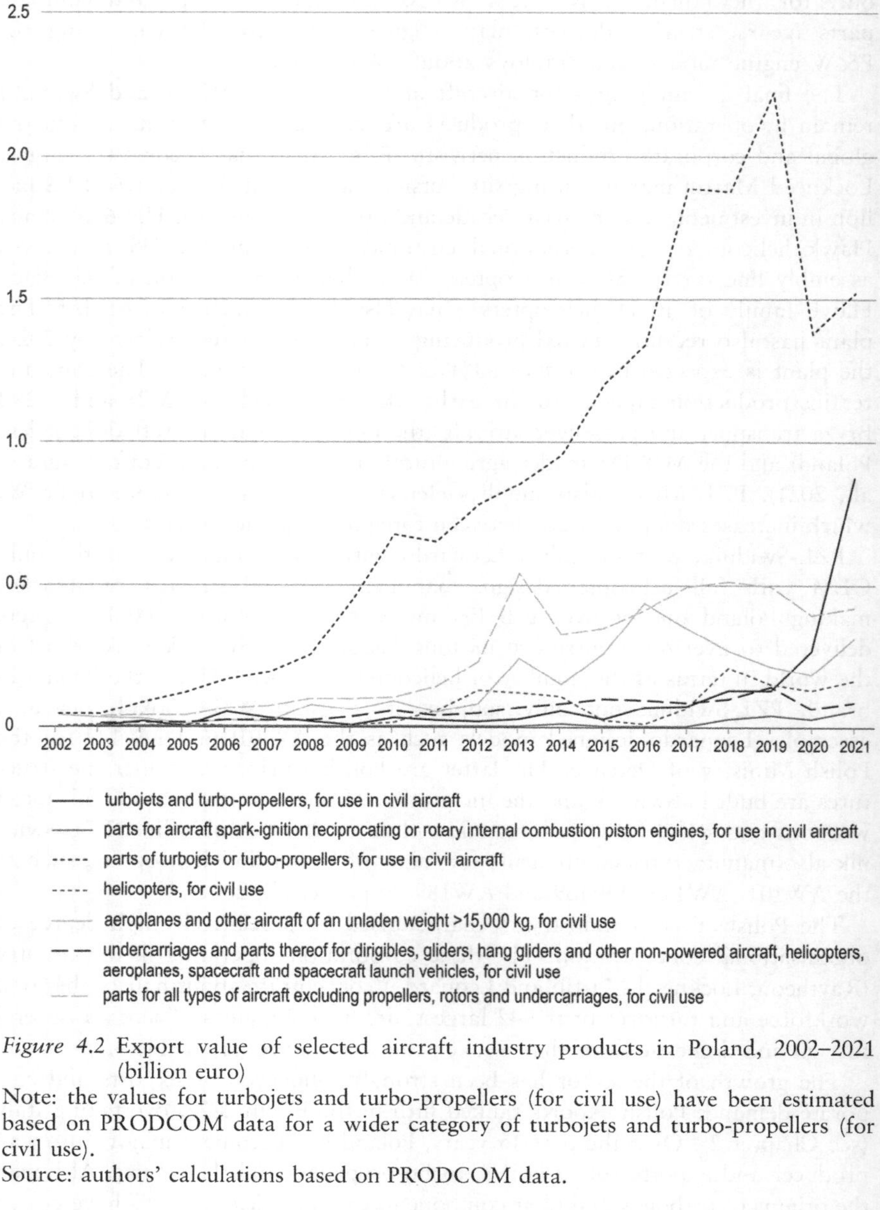

Figure 4.2 Export value of selected aircraft industry products in Poland, 2002–2021 (billion euro)

Note: the values for turbojets and turbo-propellers (for civil use) have been estimated based on PRODCOM data for a wider category of turbojets and turbo-propellers (for civil use).

Source: authors' calculations based on PRODCOM data.

The aircraft industry, especially the manufacture of advanced aircraft parts, is highly competitive compared to other CE locations. One of the representatives of the sector claimed: "Foreign managers of large corporations constantly look at Poland as an attractive destination." Another manager of a medium-sized foreign Tier-2 company argued: "In terms of efficiency, we are still outperforming emerging markets in the aircraft industry, such as Bulgaria and Romania (they are not yet good in terms of quality and efficiency). The key for us is still to improve efficiency."

Non-production competences

R&D spending in the Polish aircraft and spacecraft sector has seen a nearly twofold increase, from €32 million in 2011 to €63 million in 2019. Over the same period, the number of researchers (full-time equivalent) in the Polish aircraft sector doubled.

In 2021, there were at least 11 R&D centres in the aircraft industry in Poland (Table 4.2), mostly operated by Tier-1 suppliers. Large engineering teams are located at PZL-Świdnik (650 employees), P&W AeroPower Rzeszów (400 people) and P&W Rzeszów (300 staff). The latter not only assembles new APU engines, but also operates the R&D centre with a modern design office, prototype workshop, materials laboratory and test bed for testing turboprop, turboshaft and APU engines. The design department at PZL-Świdnik has evolved from the R&D centre established in the 1960s and is currently an approved design organisation. It also performs ground and flight tests. The laboratories of the Raytheon-owned Global Engineering Centre UTC Aerospace Systems in Wrocław are involved in various regional, national and international R&D projects, such as the application of 3D printing in the production of aircraft parts and the development and design of aircraft hydraulic systems. The Engineering Design Center (EDC), established in 2000, is an engineering alliance between General Electric and the Łukasiewicz Research Network – Institute of Aviation. It conducts research and design not only in the field of aviation, but also in gas power and renewable energy. EDC is one of GE's global facilities outside the USA. It cooperates closely with similar GE R&D centres in the USA, India, Mexico and Turkey. EDC engineers are involved in the design and improvement of aircraft engine components; they are responsible for the development of the Genx turbofan jet engines that power the Boeing 787 and 747-8, among others. After 20 years of activity in Poland, Safran Transmission Systems opened an R&D centre in Rzeszów in 2023, which will employ 250 engineers by 2027. Its research focuses on aero-engine component design and geometric and multidimensional analysis. Domestic companies have some limited R&D capacity. The state-owned WZL No. 2 tests engines after renovation or improvement and conducts engine development tests.

Engine maintenance has recently become one of the core activities of the aviation industry in Poland. One of the newest facilities, EME Aero, is a joint venture of Lufthansa Technik and MTU Aero Engines and is one of the largest MRO (Maintenance, Repair, Overhaul) centres for P&W engines with a planned capacity of 450 engines serviced per year.

If we take the number of patents granted by the United States Patent and Trademark Office (USPTO) as a measure of innovation, the Polish subsidiaries of the American Boeing, P&W and General Electric, the German MTU Aero

Table 4.2 Major aircraft R&D centres in Poland in 2021

No.	*Corporation*	*Country of origin*	*Location*	*Employment (2021), estimation*	*Year of launch*	*Field of expertise*	*US Pre-Grant Publications (as of 12.07.2023)*	*R&D with the plant*
1	General Electric	USA/Poland	Warsaw	1,400*	2000	design and improvement of parts of aircraft engine units	n.d.	No
2	Raytheon Technologies	USA	Rzeszów (×2), Wrocław	800	2016/2014	design and construction of modules for the latest engines; new engine development projects; APU R&D; hydraulic systems	215	Yes/Yes
3	Leonardo Helicopters	Italy	Świdnik	650	1967	Design and Computation Centre, Engineering Laboratory and Flight Test Department	9	Yes
4	Boeing	USA	Gdańsk	600	1991	Development of Global Data Management software and systems	27	No
5	Lockheed Martin	USA	Mielec	NA	1969	advanced composite structures R&D and design	1	Yes

No.	*Corporation*	*Country of origin*	*Location*	*Employment (2021), estimation*	*Year of launch*	*Field of expertise*	*US Pre-Grant Publications (as of 12.07.2023)*	*R&D with the plant*
6	MTU	Germany	Tajęcina	175	2018	engine component design, thermal and durability analysis	15	Yes
7	General Electric (Avio Aero)	USA/Italy	Bielsko-Biała	100	2001	engine component and module design and development	5	Yes
8	Airbus (ETC PZL Aerospace Industries)	France/the Netherlands	Warsaw	70	1984	simulation and virtual reality development	9	Yes
9	Safran	France	Rzeszów	50	2021	R&D in aero-engine components, in particular aircraft gearboxes	0	No

Source: authors' elaboration based on company annual reports and websites.

Notes: R&D centres include design/engineering centres and in-house design/engineering departments. *total employment of GE Aerospace and Łukasiewicz Research Network – Institute of Aviation.

Engines and the French Airbus appear as the most advanced centres (27, 22, 5, 15 and 9 patents, respectively). Within the Raytheon group, the Polish centres in Wrocław and Rzeszów (UTC Aerospace Systems and P&W AeroPower Rzeszów) play the most important role, accounting for 5.4% of the global patent contribution. In summary, 11 out of 32 large and medium-sized foreign aircraft companies operating in Poland have generated at least one US patent. Aircraft firms with Polish capital do not file patents in the USA. Despite the growth in the number and size of R&D centres, the role of Poland and other Central European countries in the global innovation landscape remains limited.

Public research institutes also play a role in aircraft R&D. The largest, the Łukasiewicz Institute of Aviation, which dates back to 1926, employs around 1,500 engineers and researchers. The Institute cooperates with the major aircraft manufacturers such as Boeing, GE, Airbus and P&W, as well as the European Space Agency and some unmanned aerial systems (mainly drones) suppliers. The second institution, the Military Air Force Institute of Technology, has conducted tests of the PZL M-28, PZL-130 Orlik, PZL I-22 Iryda and PZL W-3RM Anaconda helicopters and continues its own research, e.g. in the field of air targets. It also devotes considerable attention to drones (Smura et al., 2021). The Cold Flow Turbine Test Facility Polonia Aero, established by Avio Aero and WZL No. 2 in cooperation with technical universities and co-financed by EU funds, is a rare private–public initiative. It carries out experimental testing of low-pressure turbines used in the aviation and power generation industries under cold flow conditions.

It should be noted that the common model in the aircraft industry is long-term R&D cooperation between research teams from technical universities and companies. Such large-scale cooperation exists between Rzeszów University of Technology, P&W Rzeszów and other Aviation Valley firms. Avio Polska is also extensively involved in joint projects with universities, such as Warsaw University of Technology (Czakon & Klimas, 2011).

There are also smaller R&D firms supporting the aircraft industry. The British company Domin Fluid Power provides actuation and control technology with a potential weight saving of 550 kg per aircraft. It should not be forgotten that Polish (mainly domestic) companies have expertise in the design and assembly of drones. These include relatively large producers such as Farada Group, Flytronic and uAvionics Technologies. In addition, public enterprises also focus on drones (e.g. the Unmanned Aerial Vehicles Competence Centre of WZL No. 2).

Poland does not design complete aircraft and helicopters, and the pool of engineers with experience in this specific field is very limited. However, R&D and engineering centres have sufficient competence and talent for the design of various aircraft components. A good basis for R&D is provided by the close cooperation between technical universities and Aviation Valley companies. In addition, there is a network of 12 training centres for numerical control machine operators (in technical schools or in practical training centres) established by Aviation Valley firms. The industrial companies influence the curricula, provide teaching materials and train teachers. Practical training takes place in conditions that are as close as possible to those encountered by real aircraft manufacturers.

Shared service centres of aircraft companies are not common in Poland. One of the exceptions is Boeing (formerly Jeppesen) in Gdańsk. With its 600 employees and the Boeing Aviation Engineering Centre, it focuses on Global Data Management software and systems development, supporting Boeing's entire portfolio of digital analytics and geospatial services for pilots and airlines. After ten years of operation in Poland, the Polish MTU has started to provide IT services to all MTU sites worldwide. The separate, well-developed sector of auxiliary services is related to engine repair. It includes both state-owned enterprises such as WZL and private operators. Collins Aerospace runs a service centre in Poland for evacuation slides for large wide-body aircraft.

Foreign-owned companies in Poland that supply major aircraft manufacturers lack the autonomy to find customers. Large contracts with the army or the Ministry of Defence are usually signed at the TNC headquarters. One of the exceptions is Meyer Tool, which is free to acquire new contracts and customers. Many firms sell their products and services to other subsidiaries within their capital group and to parent companies (e.g. P&W, Gardner AeroSpace Mielec, Recaro Aircraft Seating and Magellan AeroSpace show over 90% of total sales within the group). It can be estimated that only about one-third of Polish aircraft manufacturers have significant direct customers outside their own capital structure, e.g. MB Aerospace, MTU Aero Engines, Admill, which cooperate with Raytheon Technologies, Airbus and/or GE-owned companies.

Production and functional upgrading of foreign subsidiaries and domestic firms: company-level analysis

The aircraft industry is one of the sectors with a large number of suppliers. Boeing aircraft consist of between 400,000 (737 model) and 6,000,000 (747-8 model) parts (Boeing, 2023), making the final product one of the most complex in manufacturing. Subsidiaries of large corporations operating in Poland are also woven into complex domestic production networks. One of Poland's largest factories, PZL Mielec, reports that it cooperates with 1,233 foreign and domestic suppliers in Poland. The fact that American companies have extensive production and, to some extent, design capabilities in Poland means that Polish subsidiaries are included in production networks with their owners and other leading American producers.

The analysis, conducted for the 42 largest enterprises with revenues of more than PLN 20 million (about €4.5 million) between 2007, 2012 and 2019, shows the increasing value added and value capture by aircraft companies in Poland (Table 4.3). The impact of ownership and position in the supply chain (for all firms excluding the OEM plants in Mielec and Świdnik) can be considered here.

Due to vertical (intra-corporate) integration and integration within GPNs, aircraft companies operating in Poland show a high degree of openness to

Table 4.3 Value created and value capture in the Polish aircraft industry

Share of value added in revenues (%)			
	2007	*2012*	*2019*
Total	44.37	44.73	45.81
Polish-owned companies	36.26	50.71	56.78
Foreign-owned companies	44.99	42.89	43.41
All companies without OEMs	43.19	45.23	46.39
Share of wages in revenues (%)			
	2007	*2012*	*2019*
Total	24.74	21.03	20.38
Polish-owned companies	27.39	28.89	25.11
Foreign-owned companies	24.07	18.42	19.31
All companies without OEMs	24.27	21.30	20.54
Share of depreciation in revenues (%)			
	2007	*2012*	*2019*
Total	6.59	5.73	6.17
Polish-owned companies	4.24	5.38	4.45
Foreign-owned companies	7.18	5.84	6.54
All companies without OEMs	6.77	5.88	6.40

Source: authors' calculations based on the financial reports for the 42 largest enterprises with revenues exceeding PLN 20 million (about €4.5 million), including 8 domestic firms.

foreign markets. Based on the annual reports of the 36 largest aircraft producers, the share of exports in total revenues has been calculated: the mean was 69% and the median 87% in 2019. Around 72% of the firms studied export more than half of their output. The skewness of the distribution confirms the export orientation of the majority of aircraft manufacturers. The exceptions are two plants of WZL No. 1 and WZL No. 4, which focus on domestic repairs of military aircraft and helicopters.

There is a moderate upward trend in value added per employee (labour productivity) for all enterprises. Its faster growth is observed in Polish-owned firms, where the value added per employee increased from PLN 214,550 in 2007 to PLN 246,590 in 2019. The productivity of foreign-owned enterprises is slightly higher (PLN 254,810).

The data show a slight increase in the share of value added in revenues for the Polish aircraft industry, from 44.4% in 2007 to 45.8% in 2019 (Table 4.3). This is a lower growth rate than for the automotive sector, but it should be borne in mind that this share is generally much higher in the aircraft industry. The rising share of value added in revenues reflects the increasing efficiency of the sector as a whole. Interestingly, from 2012 onwards, domestic producers show a higher share of value added in revenues (56.8% in 2019), illustrating their continuous improvement. The corresponding figure for foreign manufacturers is 43.4%. If we exclude OEMs, the growth in the share of value added in revenues is higher (from 43.2% in 2007 to 46.4% in 2019).

Surprisingly, there is also a steady decline in the share of wages and salaries in revenues, from 24.7% in 2007 to 20.4% in 2019. However, it should be noted that these figures are still almost three times higher than in the automotive industry. Aircraft manufacturers' revenues have increased dramatically, while wage growth has been slower (although the fastest of the industries surveyed – see Chapter 7).

Small changes can be observed in the share of depreciation in revenues, which is a proxy for investment and reinvestment activity. It was 6.6% in 2007 and similar (6.2%) in 2019, but fell temporarily to 5.7% in 2012, probably as a result of the 2008–2009 financial crisis. This reflects the trend among foreign producers. There are also fluctuations for companies with Polish capital, with a significant decrease between 2012 (5.4%) and 2019 (4.5%). This indicates lower investment activity by domestic firms, for which the lack of capital may be an obstacle.

In summary, some positive structural changes can be observed in the aircraft industry, especially between 2012 and 2019. Labour productivity has increased, as has value creation, as measured by the share of value added in revenues. However, less value has been captured, as reflected in the declining share of wages in value added.

Further investigation of the main producers, including analysis of annual company reports, interviews and internet resources, sheds light on the processes of upgrading and their change over time. Polish subsidiaries of foreign companies maintain relatively strong technical competences in component manufacturing and are constantly acquiring new products. However, there is a limited number of manufacturing plants in Poland that supply unique components in corporate structures. Examples include some of Raytheon Technologies' factories. Firstly, within the first five years after the acquisition of WSK PZL-Rzeszów, the company closed or sold low-value, auxiliary (e.g. metallurgical) and non-core (e.g. transport, accommodation and recreation) activities. In addition, the firm abandoned most non-UTC contracts (with French, Italian and British companies, see Fiszer & Bluj, 2007) and focused on core competences within the UTC aircraft engine value chain with novel equipment and improved processes. Thirdly, UTC Aerospace Systems in Krosno started as a relatively small producer of chassis elements and then became a significant manufacturer of complete aircraft landing gear (e.g. Boeing 737, 747, 767, 777, Airbus A380 and A350, F-35) and an important supplier for the F-16.

Many foreign firms focus primarily or exclusively on manufacturing activities in Poland. Some of their facilities here are among the largest in Europe. Collins Aerospace (Raytheon's brand), for example, has over 6,500 employees at four Polish sites (Wrocław, Kalisz, Krosno and Jasionka), accounting for 43% of Collins' total employment in Europe. Mielec is Lockheed Martin's biggest factory outside the USA. There are a few American companies whose only European plants are in Poland, such as Meyer Tool.

Much of the process upgrading is taking place at company level. There are many foreign plants that have introduced state-of-the-art machinery and assembly lines. This has provided a basis for know-how development and process innovation. The progress of the aircraft industry is illustrated by the 32 European Union Aviation Safety Agency (EASA)-Approved Production Organisations (POAs) in Poland, compared to 26 POAs in Spain and 44 POAs in Czechia.

Product upgrading in the sector can be seen in the manufacture and export of more advanced, higher value-added products than in the past, such as complex engine parts, complete engines, landing gears etc. PZL Mielec is a good example of product upgrading as it has recently started assembling Black Hawk helicopters in VIP versions and started production of F-16 fuselage in the newly established production department. By 2024, 80% of the entire F-16 fuselage structure will be assembled in Mielec.

There is a spectrum of attitudes among foreign investors towards Polish aircraft plants, but two opposing types of strategy are the most common. The majority of companies recognise the potential of Polish subsidiaries and allow them to develop their own know-how and process innovations. One of the managers of a medium-sized foreign Tier-2 supplier argued that, "Polish engineers learn rapidly and we are already a medium-cost country. We are top in performance and quality, but no longer low-cost." The opposite strategy is represented by firms that still treat Poland as a low-cost country, with limited product and process upgrading. There are some affiliates that have little local autonomy and their operations are largely controlled by the parent companies. More strikingly, different subsidiaries belonging to the same group but operating in separate production segments may have different models of local autonomy.

In addition to corporate strategy, one of the key determinants of industrial upgrading is the pool of active local managers. Half of the 36 foreign aircraft companies surveyed employ foreign CEOs. This is common for some UK (e.g. Gardner Aerospace), French (Airbus) and US (MB Aerospace, Meyer Tool) investors. However, the largest aircraft and helicopter manufacturers have Polish CEOs. This illustrates the maturity of the sector in Poland. As one of the representatives of a small R&D centre argued:

> The direct involvement of Polish managers is crucial for upgrading; they must have the will to develop know-how in the subsidiary. If the local

management of the subsidiary does not have higher aspirations than to maintain the low-cost country status, the results will get worse from year to year and the company will no longer invest in Poland.

Among domestic manufacturers, there has been notable process upgrading in Tier-2 and Tier-3 suppliers and service providers. For example, Ultratech in Sędziszów Małopolski, which employs about 100 people, has obtained NADCAP (National Aerospace and Defence Contractors Accreditation Program) approval for non-destructive flaw detection on the special fluorescent penetrant inspection line. This enables the firm to supply its products to the majority of global manufacturers operating in Poland.

Industrial upgrading (both process and product) is supported by cluster organisations. Given the relatively small size of the aircraft industry, it has created several business clusters. The largest (180 members) and oldest (founded in 2003) is the Aviation Valley Association. Its main objectives are to integrate the aircraft industry community, attract investors to existing facilities, develop the network of small and medium-sized enterprises that supply the large factories, and train existing and future employees. Today, the vast majority of the world's modern aircraft models have parts manufactured by Aviation Valley companies. Secondly, Aviation Valley firms are responsible for 90% of the production of the aircraft industry in Poland (Rzeczpospolita, 2018). In addition to Aviation Valley, there are clusters of aircraft and related industries in Kalisz, near Bielsko-Biała, and Legnica.

Conclusions

History has played an important role in the development of the Polish aircraft industry. It should be noted that the Soviet bloc had a relatively good technological level in this military-oriented sector, so there were many engineers at the very beginning of the transformation period. After the collapse of the Soviet market, there was a significant drop in output. Production in Poland was weakly linked to the Western European core, except for a few licensing agreements. In addition, foreign investment in the sector came later than in the automotive industry, mainly in the first decade of the 21st century. In the early years, the domestic market for aircraft products was very limited and FDI was largely export-oriented. Investment took place in existing plants, using skilled and relatively cheap labour. However, a recent shift towards medium-cost manufacturing has led to new investment, including in R&D, over the past decade. The country is now a major producer of helicopters and has become a hub for the manufacture of specialised turbojets, turbo-propellers and metal parts for aircraft. There are several foreign manufacturers of aircraft engines and components, as well as many medium-sized and small domestic suppliers. Despite dynamic growth, the output of the aircraft industry as a whole is still well below that of Spain and Italy. Recent domestic military demand (e.g. orders for the

AW149 from PZL-Świdnik) is slightly changing the dominance of export-driven growth. Poland has also become a centre for engine maintenance and repair.

Polish plants are involved in the production of parts for global aircraft manufacturers, helicopters and, to a lesser extent, military and civil aircraft and drones. Domestic producers definitely play a secondary role in the sector, often acting as Tier-2 and Tier-3 suppliers. Diversification of customers is very slow, as the majority of customers are TNCs with dominant intra-company trade. Moreover, there are no firms in Poland capable of designing an aircraft for the world market.

Factories located in Poland are rarely among the largest in Europe or the main manufacturers of certain products for their companies. However, product upgrading is clearly taking place in the sector. Aircraft components are made in Poland for increasingly complex products. Functional upgrading is limited in scope, but can be observed to a large extent in individual cases of some Tier-1 suppliers that have made advances in the design and manufacturing of aircraft parts.

References

Boeing. (2023). World class supplier quality. Retrieved September 27, 2023, from https://787updates.newairplane.com/787-Suppliers/World-Class-Supplier-Quality.

Bows-Larkin, A. (2015). All adrift: Aviation, shipping, and climate change policy. *Climate Policy*, 15(6), 681–702. doi:10.1080/14693062.2014.965125.

Cynk, J.B. (1971). *Polish aircraft 1893–1939*. London: Putnam.

Czakon, W., & Klimas, P. (2011). Anchoring and the orchestration processes: The case of Aviation Valley. In S. Lachiewicz & A. Zakrzewska-Bielawska (Eds.), *Fundamentals of management in modern small and medium-sized enterprises* (pp. 304–321). Lodz: Technical University of Lodz Press.

Fiszer, M., & Bluj, M. (2007). *Od Pegasusa do F-100-PW229. Wypisy z siedmiu dekad historii WSK "PZL-Rzeszów" S.A (1937–2007)*. Warsaw: Magnum-X.

Glass, A. (1984). *Polskie skrzydła*. Warsaw: Interpress.

Glass, A. (1992). Realizacja koncepcji rozwoju przemysłu lotniczego. In A. Glass (Ed.), *Polska technika lotnicza do roku 1939* (pp. 44–79). Warsaw: IHNOit.

Glass, A., & Kubalańca, J. (2013). *Polskie konstrukcje lotnicze* (Vol. V). Sandomierz: Stratus.

Glass, A., & Kubalańca, J. (2022). *Polskie konstrukcje lotnicze* (Vol. VII). Sandomierz: Stratus.

Jane, F. (Ed.). (1913). *Jane's all the world's aircraft 1913*. London: Sampson Low Marston.

Kinder, S., & Suwala, L. (2012). Rzeszów und das "Aircraft Valley" – Perspektiven für eine dynamische Wirtschaftsentwicklung in Südostpolen. *Polen-Analysen*, 7(118), 1–13.

Ranasinghe, K., Guan, K., Gardi, A., & Sabatini, R. (2019). Review of advanced low-emission technologies for sustainable aviation. *Energy*, 188, 115945.

Rzeczpospolita. (2018, November 26). Jaka będzie przyszłość polskiej branży lotniczej? Retrieved September 27, 2023, from https://regiony.rp.pl/archiwum/art17634431-jaka-bedzie-przyszlosc-polskiej-branzy-lotniczej.

Smura, T., Truppo, A., Czulda, R., & Zięć, K. (2021). Przemysł lotniczy w Polsce – możliwości, wyzwania i perspektywy. Pulaski Foundation. Retrieved from https://pulaski.pl/wp-content/uploads/2023/06/6316da0a5da68578af0523cbfbd5c6f6-1.pdf.

Suwala, L. (2018). Between location, persistence and relocation – early historical and spatial trajectories of the Polish aviation industry. In P. Capik & M. Dej (Eds.), *Relocation of economic activity: Contemporary theory and practice in local, regional and global perspectives* (pp. 15–31). Cham: Springer. doi:10.1007/978-3-319-92282-9_2.

Suwala, L., & Micek, G. (2018). Beyond clusters? Field configuration and regional platforming: The Aviation Valley initiative in the Polish Podkarpackie region. *Cambridge Journal of Regions, Economy and Society*, 11(2), 353–372. doi:10.1093/cjres/rsy010.

Wagner, S.M., & Walton, R.O. (2016). Additive manufacturing's impact and future in the aviation industry. *Production Planning & Control*, 27(13), 1124–1130. doi:10.1080/09537287.2016.1199824.

5 Home Appliance Industry

The production of domestic appliances is now one of Poland's most important export-oriented industries, and the country has become the largest manufacturer of household appliances in Europe in some of its segments. This development cannot be understood without the historical background presented at the beginning of this chapter. The current structure and dynamics of the sector are then described. This is followed by an analysis of the non-production competences and upgrading of foreign and domestic companies.

Historical background

Home appliances were manufactured in Poland before the Second World War. However, their popularity was low, mainly due to their high prices, limited access to electricity in many rural areas and the low production capacity of the domestic industry. Many of the first solutions appeared through imports and dealerships of Bitter-Polar, Electrolux, General Motors and Siemens, which operated in large cities (Miliszkiewicz, 2012). Polish production of refrigeration equipment developed from the late 1920s, mainly in Warsaw, Kraków and Lviv. Manufacturing of other large appliances such as gas cookers, washing machines and smaller electrical appliances took place in Warsaw, Poznań, Łódź, Kielce, Grudziądz and Bydgoszcz. Household appliances were produced in enamel factories: Enamel Plant in Grudziądz (later a manufacturer of Westphalian kitchens and Śnieżka refrigerators), Światowid in Myszków (later a producer of washing machines, centrifuges and gas cookers) and Emalia in Olkusz (later known for the production of washing machines). However, the production of household appliances was a new activity, as evidenced by the fact that it was not distinguished in the statistics.

In the first decade after 1945, low-volume production carried on in factories continuing pre-war traditions. At the same time, there was a gradual expansion of mechanical, metalworking and electrical engineering factories, some of which later began to produce household appliances. This was the case with the SHL company in Kielce, which manufactured motorcycles and in 1953 started the first post-war production of Frania washing machines. This was a washing machine with a fixed drum and rotor, which was particularly popular until the

DOI: 10.4324/9781003430117-6

1970s. Washing machines of this type were also made by Światowid (Białas et al., 1974), Emalia, Pometal in Poznań and Agromet in Czarna Białostocka. The production volume of this simple model reached more than 400,000 units and was geographically dispersed during this period. Some of the plants later began to specialise in other products, for example after 1964 Pometal concentrated on the manufacture of induction motors and their starters. By 1986, more than 6 million Frania units had been produced. A breakthrough in the production of washing machines in Poland, in terms of both quality and quantity, was the decision to manufacture washing machines with a moving drum by Polar. Founded in Wrocław in 1952, the company began producing refrigerators in 1957 and in 1971 became the first Polish manufacturer of automatic washing machines under licence from the Yugoslavian firm Gorenje. Initially, the machines were simply assembled, but later models were made using domestically produced components. Tourist washing machines and a range of parts for home appliances were made by Eda in Poniatowa, while Termet (Świebodzice) produced programmers for washing machines as well as gas cookers. At the end of the socialist period, the main centres of washing machine manufacturing were Polar, Światowid and Emalia, which employed 9,600 workers and sold a total of 0.7–0.8 million units. This was more than in Czechoslovakia (0.4 million), Hungary (0.3 million) and Romania (0.2 million), but much less than in Italy (4.3 million).

The first refrigeration products were made in the mid-1950s. From 1954, WSK PZL-Mielec built two series of refrigerators of its own design in cooperation with Czechoslovakia. Manufacturing continued in Mielec until 1966. Meanwhile, Polar started production of the Mewa refrigerator. In the years that followed, new models were created and Polar became the largest refrigerator manufacturer in Poland during the socialist era, celebrating its millionth unit in 1967 and specialising in this production for several years. The second major producer was Silesia in Rybnik, which had been making refrigerators since 1962. Smaller refrigerator manufacturers were Agromet, Pometal and POiE Grudziądz (production was later moved to Wrocław). Like washing machines, refrigerators were produced by only a few specialised companies. The picture of the industry that emerged in the 1970s persisted until the 1990s. This was also the period when production peaked at 0.7 million units in socialist Poland, which was the leader in this part of Europe. At the end of socialism, Polar provided three-quarters of Poland's refrigerators and freezers, with Silesia producing the rest. Together, Polar and Silesia employed more than 9,000 people. In 1989, Poland manufactured fewer refrigerators (0.5 million units) than East Germany and about the same as Czechoslovakia, i.e. the smaller CE countries. The production volume in West Germany or Italy was several times higher (4.0–4.5 million units).

Poland was also a major producer of cooking equipment of various types. In the first post-war decades, these were mainly coal and coal-gas cookers. From the early 1960s, freestanding cookers and gas cookers with ovens were gradually developed. Wromet in Wronki was a pioneer in this field, and Polmetal in

Radom was another important manufacturer (see Figure 6.3). Gas cookers, electric cookers and tourist kitchens were also periodically made in smaller quantities by Mesko in Skarżysko-Kamienna, Wrozamet in Wrocław, Termet, Światowid and Selfa in Szczecin. In the early 1980s, a record 0.85 million units were manufactured; at the beginning of the market economy in 1989, 0.6 million units were produced.

Small household appliances were made in large quantities. They were produced in many factories, including those that did not belong to the Predom association. Selfa and Dezamet in Nowa Dęba manufactured toasters, kettles, electric cookers and irons. Eda made juicers but was also an important supplier of components, as were Termet and Metrix in Tczew. Farel in Kętrzyn provided hairdryers and fan heaters. Small home appliances were also periodically produced by Agromet (vacuum cleaners), Silesia (kettles, ice-cream makers, laundry centrifuges), Prespol in Niewiadów and Mesko. Zelmer of Rzeszów was the leader in equipping Polish households with small domestic appliances (SDAs). It introduced vacuum cleaner production in 1953 and by the 1980s was making more than 1.0 million units a year. By comparison, Germany manufactured more than 6.0 million units in the same period and the USSR more than 5.0 million. Zelmer also produced food processors (0.9 million units in the late 1980s), malaksers, grinders, mincers and mixers.

Employment in the sector is difficult to estimate. For some industrial plants, the manufacture of domestic appliances was the only product range, for others it was an auxiliary but permanent part of their activities, whereas for some it was only an episode of a few years. The secondary production of home appliances often took place together with the manufacturing of armaments (the so-called "S" department) and was a kind of civilian "screen" to hide the dominant specialisation of the enterprise. Some civilian production was carried out in the arms factories of Dezamet, Łucznik and WSK, among others. The 1960s and 1970s saw a significant increase in the output of household appliances, with intensive development in the production of gas cookers, washing machines, refrigerators and small electrical appliances. In 1960, 49,000 people were employed in the manufacture of domestic appliances and touring equipment (Table 5.1). Five years later there were 62,800 workers, but by the end of socialism only about 30,000 remained.

Factories nationalised after 1945 were part of single or multi-plant enterprises supervised by central boards or associations (which managed individual sectors), which in turn were supervised by ministries controlling a group of industries. Between 1945 and 1989, the production of household appliances underwent frequent organisational changes as it was fragmented among several industrial associations. Predom was a specialised association managing more than a dozen enterprises producing mechanised domestic appliances, but also heating equipment and bicycles. Research and design skills were also centralised in Predom-OBR, established in 1973 (formerly the Predom centre for the development of industrial consumer goods, in existence since 1968).

Table 5.1 Production of major domestic appliances and employment in the sector in Poland, 1955–2020 (thousands)

	1955	*1960*	*1965*	*1970*	*1975*	*1980*	*1985*	*1990*	*1995*	*2000*	*2005*	*2010*	*2015*	*2020*
Washing machines (including washer-dryers)	28	531	429	423	620	809	739	482	419	564	1,481	4,048	6,509	6,772
Refrigerators and freezers	3.4	37.7	289	444	715	694	578	604	585	693	1,674	1,867	3,349	3,518
Gas stoves with oven	0.0	35.1	246	461	722	858	758	507	204	161	774	645	455	263
Employment	NA	49.0*	62.8*	NA	NA	NA	NA	NA	NA	NA	25.3	25.9	26.9	29.4

Source: authors' calculations based on GUS and Eurostat data.

Note: *data for home appliances and touring equipment.

In addition to domestic production, household appliances were also imported from abroad. Refrigerators and freezers were a dominant imported item, rising from 375,000 units per year in the mid-1970s to more than 600,000 units a decade later. Imports of washing machines appeared relatively late in the 1980s, reaching more than 400,000 units in 1989. Poland has exported mainly gas cookers since the 1960s, at around 300,000 units per year.

The growth in production and imports improved the equipment of Polish households. At the beginning of the 1960s, there were only 19 washing machines per 100 households. By 1988, there were 136 washing machines per 100 households, of which 55 were automatic. This was the second-best result in the Eastern bloc after Czechoslovakia, but the level was two times higher in Western Europe. Refrigerators were even rarer in 1960, with only 1.8 per 100 households. By 1988, the figure had risen to 123. The number of vacuum cleaners per 100 households doubled between 1970 and 1990, reaching 97 units.

The home appliance industry in the transformation period

At the start of the economic transition, Polish households were less equipped with domestic appliances than their Western counterparts. The general orientation of socialist industry towards non-consumer goods led to shortages in the supply of home appliances. Polish companies produced a narrow range of equipment compared to Western companies, in a limited number of models and in quantities too small to meet domestic demand. The opening up of the Polish economy meant an opportunity to meet consumer needs, but also a threat to domestic producers, who had to learn how to operate in new conditions. Refrigerators and freezers were made in similar quantities of around 500,000–600,000 units per year during the transition period. Vacuum cleaner production was stable at around 1 million units. The situation was more difficult for washing machines and gas cookers, where output fell by 50%. In 1989, 811,000 washing machines were manufactured and in 1991 only 336,000 units. Wrozamet, Polmetal and Wromet produced 757,000 gas cookers in 1988 and 345,000 in 1992.

The 1990s were a period of difficult adaptation to new operating conditions. The major companies in the sector (Polar, Wrozamet, Emalia, Światowit and Wromet) remained state-owned and were looking for potential investors. There were also reorganisations of multi-plant and multi-product companies, for example the closure of Polar's Miłków plant and the spin-off of its Żagań factory under the name Zamex. Dezamet, which produced for the defence industry but also engines and small home appliances (irons), was split into separate companies, and the production of domestic appliances was continued by Dezal. However, no leading manufacturer went out of business during the transition shock. In 1994, 1.5 million units of major domestic appliances (MDAs) were produced in Poland. There were 35 plants employing 27,000 people. Washing machines were made by Wrozamet, Polar and Świątowid. The tradition of manufacturing refrigerators and freezers was continued by Polar with a 72%

share of output, Zamex (18%), Argos in Bytów (7%) and Silesia (3%). Gas cooker production was dominated by Wromet (since 1993 under the name of Amica) with a 44% share of domestic output, Wrozamet (30%) and Polmetal (later Acanta Kitchen Factory) with a 20% share. Smaller home appliances were supplied by companies specialising in more than just household appliances, such as Metrix (cooker hoods, ironing machines), Prespol (coffee grinders and food processors), Mesko (juicers), Farel (hairdryers, electric cookers) and Dezal (irons). However, the dominant position in this segment was held by Zelmer, which produced more than 1 million vacuum cleaners and more than 500,000 food processors in 1993.

Another key event was the arrival of global domestic appliance manufacturers in Poland. In 1992–1993, Electrolux, Indesit, Bosch and Whirlpool set up sales offices in the country and a few years later they decided to start production. Geographical location, the large domestic market, human resources, labour costs and rich manufacturing traditions were among the main reasons for their growing interest in Poland. The introduction of special economic zones in 1995 also encouraged investment decisions in the white goods industry. In 1996, Electrolux began cooperation with Światowid in the production of washing machines (the factory was later moved to Siewierz). BSH started assembling its appliances in Poland in 1994 and opened its first washing machine plant in 1998. Indesit launched the production of cookers in 1999, having previously been an importer. Total foreign investment in the 1990s exceeded $190 million and was concentrated mainly in Wrocław and Łódź (Domański, 2001). For a few years, Daewoo was also involved in the manufacturing of washing machines. By 2010, these companies had built up their production potential in Poland, either by investing in the construction of new plants or through acquisitions. Such a strategy was followed by Samsung, which bought refrigerator and washing machine plants from Amica in 2009. Similarly, Whirlpool expanded its presence by acquiring Polar from Moulinex-Brandt in 2002 and Indesit in 2014. LG started producing televisions in Biskupice Podgórne in 2005, and washing machines and refrigerators have been manufactured there since 2017.

Domestic producers adopted different development strategies after 1989. Amica expanded its capabilities by producing refrigerators (1996) and washing machines (2000), but eventually sold these two plants to Samsung and sourced these products from China and Türkiye in the following years. Polar was taken over by French capital, then by Whirlpool, and the Polar brand eventually disappeared. Wrozamet, which began cooperating with Fagor in 1997, was taken over by Fagor in 2002. In 2015 it was sold to BSH. One of the initiatives involving Polish capital was the production of freezers and washing machines by Argos. In 1997 it employed more than 700 people in 3 plants in Bytów, Miastko and Lębork and made more than 50,000 units of refrigerators. The company closed down in 2003, but its traditions are partly carried on by Byfal. Other Polish brands did not survive the difficult transition period. By the mid-1990s, household appliances bearing the Metrix logo were no longer produced. In the following years, Farel in Kętrzyn and Metal Products Factory in Jawor (a stove manufacturer) went bankrupt. In 2002, the history of the well-known sewing machine manufacturer Łucznik and the freezer producer Zamex came to an end.

All in all, the 1990s were a period of rebuilding and increasing production capabilities, despite the transformation shock. In the area of major household appliances, output reached historic highs between 1997 and 2006, surpassing the maximum of the socialist period. Only the production of gas cookers showed a clear downward trend due to their substitution by a new heating solution (electric hobs and ovens). These changes were accompanied by a reconfiguration of exports and their geography. At the beginning of the 1990s, exports and imports declined significantly; major household appliances were exported to the former Comecon countries as well as to Western Europe, but Russia remained the dominant partner for historical reasons. By the early 2000s, the direction had changed and exports to Germany, Italy and the UK now dominated. These trends have intensified in subsequent years.

The dynamics and structure of the sector: ownership, manufacturers and products

The increased involvement of international domestic appliance manufacturers in Poland in the late 1990s and early 2000s has led to the country's growing role on the European stage. The value of production exceeded €6.7 billion in 2021 and accounted for 12.9% of EU output. Poland has become one of the largest producers in the sector in Europe, especially in the field of major home appliances. More than 55% of European dishwashers, washing machines and dryers and 43% of refrigerators and freezers are made in Poland. The high share in the volume of equipment produced has been achieved with significant employment potential (13.8% of EU employment). Production capacity, as measured by the number of factories, has expanded with a relatively stable number of enterprises (9% increase over the last decade), despite the clear impacts of the 2008–2009 crisis, the COVID-19 pandemic and the ongoing war in Ukraine.

Employment in the manufacture of domestic appliances (NACE division 27.5) amounted to more than 30,640 people in 2021 (an increase of 11% since 2008 – Figure 5.1), the vast majority of whom worked in foreign-owned enterprises (80.9%). The share of foreign firms in employment rose by almost five percentage points over the decade to 2021. The sector is dominated by large companies with more than 1,000 employees (6 enterprises), which account for 72% of employment. Big foreign firms account for 64% of all employees in the sector, and only one Polish company, Amica, has a similar workforce. Three manufacturers, Electrolux, BSH and Whirlpool, have around 5,000 employees or more (Table 5.2). In contrast, enterprises with 250–999 personnel account for 24.7%. There are also a few suppliers with more than 1,000 employees and consumer electronics manufacturers involved in the production of white goods.

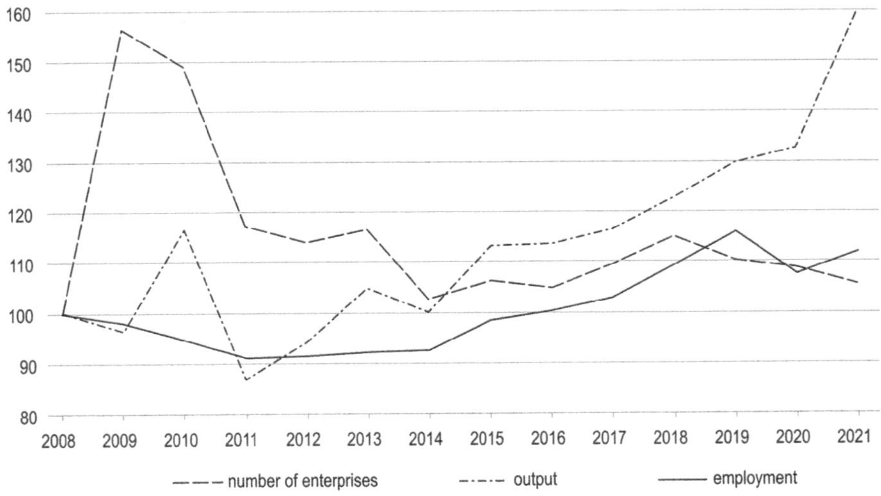

Figure 5.1 Dynamics of the Polish home appliance industry, 2008–2021 (2008 = 100)
Source: authors' calculations based on Eurostat data.

Until 2002, the production range of Polish household appliances was relatively stable, continuing trends that were well established in the socialist era, such as the production of gas and coal stoves and non-automatic washing machines. In the period 2000–2002, massive foreign investment brought about profound changes.

In laundry production, new plants by Electrolux, Amica and BSH, among others, helped to double output from a level of 400,000 units in the late 1990s to around 800,000 units in 2001. Since then, production has risen steadily to 6.5–6.7 million units, with further investments by Electrolux, Indesit, Samsung and Whirlpool and a new greenfield plant by Miele opening in 2017. Clothes tumble dryers are a new product whose assembly and subsequent manufacturing was started by Electrolux in Siewierz. BSH joined in 2005 and Whirlpool in 2018. Poland, with a 7% share of EU production of washing machines and dryers in 2004, became the European leader in 2010, overtaking Italy. In 2018, about 3 million units were made, representing 55% of EU output.

Dishwasher manufacturing was launched in the country in 2002 by BSH and has grown dynamically in the years since. New plants were built by Electrolux (2006), Indesit (2008) and FagorMastercook (2010). This has been the fastest-growing segment of MDA production, along with washing machines and dryers. In 19 years, the number of dishwashers produced has exceeded 5.9 million units (Figure 5.2). Poland became the European leader in 2019, now accounting for 48% of EU output.

The first new refrigerator factory was built by Amica in 1996. A major expansion of production capacity took place between 2002 and 2004, when Whirlpool took over Polar and Indesit started production on a greenfield site.

Table 5.2 The largest companies in the home appliance industry in Poland

Company (capital group)	*Branches and brands in Poland*	*Number of employees (2018)*	*Number of plants/SSCs/ R&D*	*Main products*
Electrolux	Electrolux	5,589	5/1/1	dishwashers, washing machines, dryers, cookers, ovens, hoods
Whirlpool	Whirlpool, Hotpoint-Ariston, Indesit	5,012	6/1/1	washing machines, dishwashers, dryers, cookers, ovens, refrigerators
BSH	Bosch, Siemens, Gaggenau	4,959	6/2/2	washing machines, refrigerators, dishwashers, dryers, ovens, SDAs
Samsung	Samsung	2,537	2/0/1	washing machines, refrigerators
Amica	Amica, Gram, Hansa, CDA, Fagor	2,290	1/0/1	cookers, hoods, refrigerators, dishwashers
Diehl	Diehl	1,161	1/0/1	electronic user interfaces and advanced electronic control systems
Biazet	—	933	1/0/0	SDAs, vacuum cleaners
Bitron	Bitron	863	2/0/1	electromechanical and electronic components

Source: authors' compilation based on annual company reports.

After the financial crisis of 2008, there was a significant drop in production. Another important moment was the acquisition of the FagorMastercook factories by BSH in 2015. After their modernisation was completed in 2017, the upward trend in Polish refrigeration production was reinforced. In 2021, almost 4 million units of refrigeration equipment were made in Poland (43% of the refrigerator-freezers produced in the EU and 25% of the refrigerators), compared to 0.7 million units in 1998.

There have been significant changes in the manufacturing of cooking equipment. Two historical centres in Wronki (Amica) and Wrocław (formerly Wrozamet and FagorMastercook, now BSH) have survived, whereas the tradition of production in Radom (Polmetal) has come to an end. Amica produces around 1.4 million units of cooking appliances, with a high growth rate for built-in ovens. Together with electric cookers, built-in ovens have become a new mainstay of cooker manufacturing in Poland in recent years. This is due to investments by Electrolux (2006), Indesit (1999) and the continuation of Wrozamet

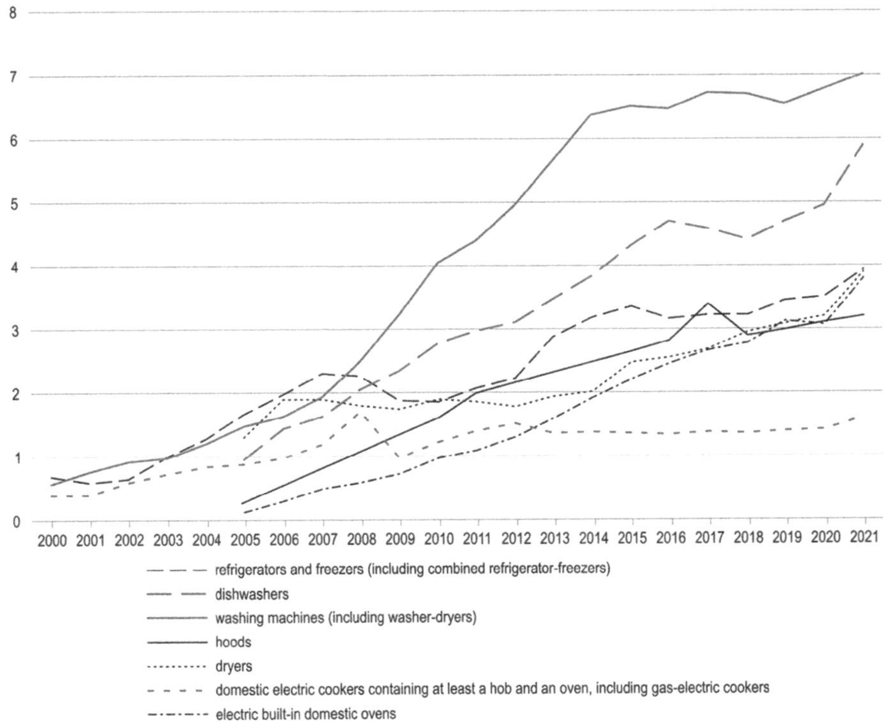

Figure 5.2 Production of home appliances in Poland, 2000–2021 (million units)
Source: authors' calculations based in GUS data.

production by BSH. The production of built-in hobs is less dynamic: 0.3 million units are made. With 40% of cookers and ovens and 37% of built-in ovens manufactured in the EU, Poland is the European leader.

Poland has also become an important manufacturer of cooker hoods. The tradition of their production by Predom Metrix has been strengthened mainly by companies with Polish capital. Ciarko in Sanok remains the leader in this group. Other important Polish producers are MAAN (Podole), Akpo (Laski) and Solgaz (Świdnica), most of which were established in the late 1980s. Foreign capital in this segment is represented by Elica (Jelcz-Laskowice) and Best (Zabrze). Both started production in 2005, although Best was a local company that was taken over by Electrolux in 2018. In 2013, Indesit (now part of the Whirlpool group) opened its cooker hood factory. These foreign investments, together with a gradual increase in the production capacity of domestic firms, meant that output rose from 0.3 million units in 2004 to over 3.2 million units in 2021.

There is also a group of domestic producers of small home appliances in Poland. Historically, Zelmer was the largest manufacturer. For many decades it was the only producer of vacuum cleaners, providing more than 1.9 million units in 1999. The company's activities were gradually expanded to 36 product groups in 2010, including food processors, meat mincers, grinders and mixers. Zelmer also manufactured major built-in household appliances such as ovens, dishwashers and cooker hoods. It was the leader in the small appliances segment in Poland and the third largest in CE. In 2013, the firm was sold to BSH, which began producing its own brands. In 2019, the production of appliances with the Zelmer logo was finally discontinued. Today the company makes BSH equipment, including vacuum cleaners and coffee machines.

Several domestic manufacturers of small household appliances also have a longer history. Mesko-AGD, which was spun off from the Mesko Group in 2000, focuses on kitchen equipment for the catering industry. Niewiadów AGD is the heir of a company known for making car trailers, coffee grinders and mixers, and now specialises in the production of food dryers. Dezal-Pro continues the traditions of Dezamet, manufacturing toasters and waffle irons, while Radix makes Prumel electric baking trays. Biazet in Białystok is a large Polish contract manufacturer (933 employees in 2018). The company produces and assembles small household appliances for global leaders such as coffee makers, fryers and vacuum cleaners for Philips, espresso machines for Lavazza and vacuum cleaners for Electrolux. Białystok is also home to the coffee maker factory of the Dutch company Bravilor Bonamat. Overall, Polish production of small household appliances has been declining in recent years, especially small electric kitchen appliances (mixers, food processors) since 2015. Today, around 4 million units are made annually.

Non-production competences: R&D and SSCs

Research and development are advanced non-production functions in industry. They build relationships with other activities such as IT, automation and robotics, the academic and professional communities, and are channels for knowledge transfer so that factories can implement the latest solutions in appliance manufacturing, such as Internet of Things (IoT), energy efficiency, home energy management and storage. R&D centres in the home appliance sector in Poland are working on some of these issues. By mid-2023, there were at least 12 centres operating in the country, 7 of which had 100 or more employees, belonging to OEMs and some Tier-1 suppliers.

Samsung's largest R&D centre employs more than 600 people in Warsaw and Kraków. Its wide-ranging activities include the creation of artificial intelligence solutions, software platforms and voice assistant technologies that can be implemented in home appliances. Other centres have competences focused exclusively on domestic appliances. Whirlpool employs more than 300 engineers in Wrocław and its refrigerator and dishwasher projects are implemented globally, especially in American factories. The Polish centre is one of the company's 9 patent centres, with 1.4% of Whirlpool's patent applications to the United States Patent and Trademark Office (USPTO) coming from Poland. BSH has two R&D centres in Poland. The larger one, with 200 employees working in the laundry and tumble dryer segments, has been operating in Łódź since

2019. Another 100 people work on new projects in the SDA segment at the Rzeszow branch, following the Zelmer tradition. According to the company, new vacuum cleaners made in Poland are almost entirely designed here. Amica has also expanded its R&D capabilities. Its department of more than 100 people in Wronki and Poznań creates new solutions for the company's products, especially cooking appliances. More limited non-production activities in Poland are carried out by Electrolux, which has had a small dishwasher development centre in Żarów since 2015. The company's SSC is much larger.

In addition to OEMs, there is significant R&D potential in some companies that supply electronics for household appliances. They design and manufacture electronic circuits and controls for a wide range of products. The largest is Diehl Controls in Wrocław, employing about 100 engineers. Bitron, JM Elektronik and Geco have smaller centres with 25–35 employees. Jabil has recently expanded its design capabilities by opening a 30-engineer centre in Wrocław. There are also process support departments in the manufacturing plants. They operate under different names (competence centres, product care) and employ some research personnel. Some of them, such as the BSH Dryer Competence Centre launched in 2007, later became the basis for the creation of an R&D centre.

What is important is the implementation of solutions developed by R&D centres. According to the USPTO databases, the most important are the research centres of Samsung (98 applications) and Whirlpool (41). A smaller number of patents were filed by BSH (11 applications), Diehl Controls (9 applications – 18% of the company total) and Bitron (7).

Similarly to TNCs in other industries, white goods companies in Poland have expanded their advanced services in the form of SSCs/Information Technology Outsourcing (ITO) centres. The oldest and largest is Electrolux's centre in Kraków, which has been operating since 2005 and currently employs 760 people. It provides finance and accounting services for the Electrolux Group, serving 25 countries in Europe and North America. There are also several other business support functions such as an IT team, service manuals, property management and payroll. BSH develops services for the company in Łódź, which is also its production centre. It started with IT services in 2007, and later moved other processes, including finance and accounting, purchasing and foreign trade, increasing the workforce to 350. Also in Łódź, Whirlpool took over the SSC created by Indesit. It focuses mainly on financial processes in the Europe, the Middle East and Africa (EMEA) region and employs 270 people. The latest investment is the opening of the SSC for the Miele Group in Poznań, which employs 330 people and provides accounting, controlling, reporting and sales support.

Production and functional upgrading of foreign subsidiaries: company-level analysis

The analysis, carried out on 61 companies with revenues of more than PLN 50 million (around €10 million) between 2007, 2012 and 2019, shows that value creation and value capture by household appliance manufacturers in Poland are increasing.

Upgrading processes in the sector are reflected in the steadily growing value added per employee. It stood at PLN 76,175 in 2007, rising to PLN 100,647 in the next 5 years and PLN 127,035 in 2019. Productivity growth is observed both in companies with foreign and domestic capital. For the former, it was PLN 85,672 in 2007 and PLN 131,003 in 2019, exceeding that of Polish-owned firms. However, the latter, starting from a much lower level, showed a higher growth rate and has somewhat narrowed the gap, reaching PLN 116,870 in 2019. An interesting but still open question is whether Polish producers, given their current position in the value chains, will be able to reach the level of foreign companies.

The share of value added in revenues for the manufacture of domestic appliances was 19.6% in 2007. There was a slight increase to 20.3% in 2012 and a faster rise to 22.5% in 2019 (Table 5.3). A higher share of value added in revenues is characteristic of Polish enterprises, where it went up from 20.7% in 2007 to 25.7% in 2012 and then decreased somewhat to 24.3% in 2019. Foreign affiliates experienced slower growth, from 19.1% in 2007 to 21.7% in 2019. Detailed case studies seem to confirm the growing share of advanced processes in foreign companies, especially in large enterprises.

Wages and salaries accounted for 12.7% of revenues in 2019, compared with 10.0% in 2007. Most enterprises recorded a significant increase in employment during this period, but it was also a period of steady wage growth. When broken down by source of capital, Polish companies recorded a higher level and greater increase in the share of wages and salaries. It was 10.7% in 2007 and reached 15.4% in 2019 for this group. The share of wages in revenues of foreign entities decreased slightly between 2007 and 2012, but rose to 11.5% in 2019.

Table 5.3 Value created and value capture in the Polish home appliance industry

Value	*Ownership*	*Year*		
		2007	*2012*	*2019*
Share of value-added in revenues (%)	Total	19.6	20.3	22.5
	Foreign-owned	19.1	19.8	21.7
	Polish-owned	20.7	25.7	24.3
Share of wages in revenues (%)	Total	10.0	10.6	12.7
	Foreign-owned	9.7	9.3	11.5
	Polish-owned	10.7	13.5	15.4
Share of depreciation in revenues (%)	Total	3.8	4.0	3.6
	Foreign-owned	2.4	3.3	3.1
	Polish-owned	4.3	4.3	3.8

Source: authors' calculations based on the financial reports for the 61 largest enterprises with revenues exceeding PLN 50 million (about €10 million), including 17 domestic firms.

The situation is different for depreciation as a percentage of revenues. It rose from 3.8% to 4.0% between 2007 and 2012, but fell to 3.6% in 2019. For foreign-owned enterprises, it remained stable at 4.3% between 2007 and 2012 and then dropped to 3.8% in 2019. This may reflect the slowdown of their investments in Poland after their peak in the earlier period. Interestingly, the situation was different for Polish-owned firms, where the share of depreciation increased significantly from 2.4% to 3.3% in 2012 and then decreased slightly to 3.1% in 2019.

All in all, positive changes are taking place in the home appliance industry. There has been a clear increase in value created in large companies, regardless of the origin of the capital. Moreover, there is no doubt that value capture, expressed in terms of the growing share of wages in revenues, is increasing. Polish producers are dynamically improving their ability to create and capture value, often at a higher rate of change, which may allow them to close the gap with foreign-owned producers.

A more detailed picture of these changes can be obtained from company reports and interviews. They shed light on qualitative changes in manufacturing capabilities and the development of non-manufacturing competences over time.

There are currently 35 manufacturing plants producing finished white goods in Poland. Most of them (27) produce MDAs, whereas others supply SDAs. The dominant role is played by 19 TNCs, each with several large plants and other non-production units (Table 5.2). Polish capital is more strongly represented among SDA producers and component manufacturers.

The largest foreign companies are concentrating their efforts mainly on developing their production capacities in Poland. This is clearly visible in the MDA segment. Amica and Solgaz are the only Polish-owned manufacturers in this segment, with the exception of cooker hoods. The production of refrigeration equipment, tumble dryers and dishwashers is entirely carried out by TNCs. Production volumes for these groups of appliances have reached record levels in recent years (see Figure 5.2).

For example, it took BSH 14 years to produce its first 10 million dishwashers in Poland, but only 6 years to double that number. The expansion of production capacity goes hand in hand with the growth of factories. One measurable effect is the increase in employment in TNC subsidiaries. BSH employed 1,700 people in Poland in 2012 and 6,688 in 2022. Polish subsidiaries are becoming increasingly important within individual corporations, as they can be one of the largest and sometimes the only factories manufacturing a particular appliance. BSH's new factory is its biggest and most modern dishwasher facility, which is also reflected in exports to demanding and new markets in North America, Asia and Australia. Poland is also home to BSH's only tumble dryer plant. Tumble dryers, the smallest but fastest-growing MDA production in Poland, are also important for Electrolux. Its Polish factory is the only one on the continent. For Whirlpool, its Polish dryer plant is its most important production centre in this part of the world and its refrigerator factory is its only one in Europe. The Pass (rubber parts) plant in Poland is the company's largest subsidiary in the world.

In addition to the increase in production capacity, changes can be observed that indicate product upgrading and the expansion of TNCs' non-production activities in Poland, as well as an increase in employment. The reasons for this process can be found in the company reports of both OEMs and their suppliers. Aweco supplies valves to demanding customers such as Miele, which manufactures premium domestic appliances. The design, testing and introduction of more sophisticated products are evident at Bitron and Diehl Controls, leading suppliers of electronic control systems and user interfaces for many categories of equipment. The Diehl Controls facility began as a joint venture making parts for a plant in Germany. It then moved into manufacturing complete components, was given the opportunity to develop cooperation with technical universities and opened its R&D centre in Wrocław in 2014. Today, the subsidiary manufactures advanced products, half of which are developed locally. More complex and sophisticated production is also evident among final manufacturers of domestic appliances. In BSH, product upgrading is visible, among other things, in the introduction of a heat pump in dryers, new washing machine models with automatic detergent dispensers, water and electricity savings and easier ironing. The number of appliances with web-based communication capabilities is also increasing. Samsung's refrigerators are more sophisticated and advanced side-by-side models. For cooker hoods, the option of controlling the extractor fan from the level of the induction hob has been introduced, e.g. by Electrolux in Zabrze from 2018.

Progress in production processes appears to be more pronounced, but also more varied in the sector. On the one hand, a number of new factories built in Poland are among the most modern in the company and in the industry as a whole. These include the new plants for Whirlpool dryers, BSH dishwashers and Miele washing machines. Home appliance manufacturing is still labour-intensive, but the automation and robotisation of production and the implementation of Industry 4.0 solutions have accelerated in recent years. Jabil, an electronics supplier, has been implementing several automation projects every year since 2018. Autonomous vehicles are in use at BSH's plants, and problems in recruiting workers are prompting Samsung's factory to invest in automation. Samsung promotes its factories in Poland as the most modern manufacturing centres in Europe. Electrolux emphasises the implementation of Industry 4.0 solutions in its cooker hood plant in Zabrze and dishwasher factory in Żarów. However, the automation of internal logistics, which streamlines plant operations, dominates, while the robotisation of other processes is less common. The progress of Polish plants in terms of production processes is particularly evident when compared to the first years of TNC investment in Poland, when some investors transferred assembly lines from their factories abroad, e.g. Electrolux and BSH.

Development of Polish domestic companies

Producers with Polish capital employed around 5,300 people in the narrowly defined white goods industry in 2018. Due to the pandemic crisis, the number of employees fell to 4,900 in 2020, but was still 20% higher than in 2012. SMEs predominate, with only one company employing more than 1,000 people and another five with more than 200. Most domestic manufacturers differ from TNCs in terms of production capacity, distribution network and non-manufacturing competences. Their analysis reveals an interesting evolution.

One of the peculiarities of the home appliance sector, unlike the automotive and aircraft industries, is the operation of OEMs with domestic capital. Amica is the largest Polish MDA manufacturer. The company originated from a privatised stove producer (cooking equipment accounts for 64% of sales), then entered other market segments at the turn of the millennium, only to withdraw from their production after a few years (replaced by refrigerators and other MDAs made under its brand in China). It has its own R&D and maintains a stable domestic market share of around 18% for MDAs. Amica has had a successful international expansion based on six brands recognised in Europe. The company offers appliances mainly in the mid-price range, with some in the upper mid-price segment (CDA brand). It has developed its manufacturing expertise, for example in the production of hobs with its own technological solutions, and strives to keep up with the latest trends in other product innovations.

There is a group of prominent hood makers that began their history in the 1980s and 1990s. The largest Polish manufacturers produce both under their own brand and for foreign contractors. The exception is Akpo, which has developed its own brand from the very beginning. Major producers such as Ciarko, MAAN and Akpo have gained recognition both at home and abroad. Ciarko exports more than 60% of its production, while other Polish manufacturers exceed 30%. They have their own laboratories with design competence, especially Ciarko. The latter is trying to strengthen its position in the upper price segment by developing Ciarko Design – a line of the most advanced products.

Biazet is a large manufacturer whose business strategy has evolved. In the early post-socialist period, it won contracts with Western customers as a manufacturer of parts and then complete television sets. At the end of the 1990s, this activity was replaced by the production of lighting and automotive components. In 2002, the company began manufacturing household appliances, specialising in coffee machines. At a time when production of small home appliances was moving en masse to Asia, the company decided to stay in this field as a European contract manufacturer for several well-known SDA brands. Production capacity has increased significantly (from 1 to 14 production lines), as have process improvements in the form of a tool room and modern machinery. For several years, Biazet has been working on its own branded end product, trying to acquire complementary R&D and sales firms, but this is proving more difficult than expected.

MPM took a different strategy. It started by importing household appliances and gradually moved to its own production of kettles and then other products. In 2008, it also introduced MDAs. The company is developing its expertise by introducing Wi-Fi-enabled products and working closely with large distributors present in big-box stores. MPM offers appliances under its own brand, but is also a distributor of foreign brands. It has subcontracted part of its production to Smile. Smile makes more than 160,000 white goods, mostly small appliances, for MPM.

ZMM Maxpol and Zelmotor are medium-sized SDA manufacturers that have their origins in Zelmer. The former started its business with the production of plastic parts. In 2007 it began working with Zelmer, which continued with BSH after the takeover. Four years later, in addition to supplying plastic components to BSH and then Electrolux, it became a manufacturer of its own brand of juicers, fruit and vegetable dryers and home comfort equipment. Zelmotor, founded in 2009 as a spin-off from Zelmer, specialises in the production of electric motors for small household appliances. In 2019, it decided to launch its own production of slicers and mincers under the SMAPP brand. It already has six product groups for the kitchen, as well as vacuum cleaners and air purifiers.

Polish-owned component suppliers include both older plants and newly established firms. They represent all segments of white goods manufacturing, with the largest number of producers of plastic, metal and stamped parts, castings, forgings and small electrical parts. The household appliance industry is a dominant customer for around 80% of suppliers. Some companies also supply the automotive sector, which appears to be a growing trend. Most Polish component manufacturers are not Tier-1 suppliers, but some have achieved a significant position, for example by providing control electronics.

The home appliance industry also comprises a group of firms involved in advanced electronics assembly. The largest are foreign-owned (Bitron, Jabil, Diehl Controls), but several smaller domestic companies are also successful. Inventronics in Jawor specialises in, among other things, microprocessor controllers for household appliances and heating, ventilation and air conditioning (HVAC) equipment, with a production capacity of 40 million units per month. Geco supplies automation solutions, in particular controllers used in cooker hoods, ovens, induction hobs and refrigerators by leading manufacturers in various EU countries. The company carries out R&D activities in electronic and electrical production and currently employs 120 people.

The example of Polish manufacturers shows that, despite the dominance of foreign OEMs, there is also a group of local companies that are improving their position in the domestic and international markets. They are developing not only as component suppliers but also as final producers, sometimes successfully building their brand in Western and Central-Eastern Europe. However, no Polish company has yet expanded abroad through greenfield investments and acquisitions. Many domestic manufacturers of plastic, rubber or metal components are upgrading their technological processes and adapting their production to customer demand. Some white goods suppliers are successfully entering more demanding markets such as the automotive industry. Together with significant exports, this demonstrates their ability to meet high quality standards. However, the evolution of domestic suppliers from advanced products and processes to the role of OEM is rare in this sector.

Biazet's postponement of the introduction of its own brand and difficulties in acquiring R&D may reflect limited opportunities for rapid progress in this area. Many companies have laboratories with testing capabilities, but have chosen not to seek greater added value through in-house R&D. There may be both financial and organisational barriers.

Conclusions

The manufacturing of household appliances in Poland developed gradually from the 1950s onwards, but it was not until 20 years later that companies specialising in their production began to appear. Large factories replaced scattered activity in many locations, often accompanying armaments production. However, the level of investment was too low in relation to domestic demand, licensing agreements were rare and failed to replace often obsolete technology. Socialist-era factories survived the transition period and were privatised. Major global home appliance manufacturers came to Poland, taking over existing producers (Fagor) or deciding to build new plants (BSH, Indesit). There was a parallel development of companies with Polish capital; Amica remains the largest domestic manufacturer today.

Foreign investors have integrated Poland into European production networks, changing the dominant direction of distribution from domestic to export markets. Production capacity has been greatly expanded in recent years, both in modernised existing plants and in new factories. Many of them are now the only or the main European production centres for a given range within the group. While new domestic final producers are rare, there is a growing number of suppliers, particularly manufacturers of metal and plastic components. As a result, Poland has become the most important producer of household appliances in the EU in terms of volume. At the same time, there has been a successful expansion of some Polish brands into European markets, e.g. Amica and manufacturers of cooker hoods. This success has been accompanied by a relatively small number of bankruptcies, e.g. Daewoo and Fagor (although the latter found a buyer).

Today, home appliances made in Poland are advanced, modern products. The country's non-production competences play a certain role in this. They are mainly developed by TNCs, but have also become important in domestic firms. The strategies of foreign companies in developing R&D and SSCs are diverse, even in such a small sector. These competences are still smaller than the production potential would suggest.

References

Białas, T., Sygit, W., & Walocha, T. (1974). *Myszkowska Fabryka Naczyń Emaliowanych Światowid 1899–1974*. Myszków: MFNE.

Domański, B. (2001). *Kapitał zagraniczny w przemyśle Polski: Prawidłowości rozmieszczenia, uwarunkowania i skutki*. Kraków: Institute of Geography and Spatial Management, Jagiellonian University.

Miliszkiewicz, G. (2012). Problematyka wyposażenia dworów ziemiańskich na tle obrazu produkcji artykułów gospodarstwa domowego w II Rzeczypospolitej. In H. Łaszkiewicz (Ed.), *Praca i życie codzienne w majątku ziemiańskim: Materials of the 5th Scientific Session held at the Zamoyski Museum in Kozłówka on 12–14 October 2011* (pp. 99–119). Lublin: Wydawnictwo Werset.

6 Regional Differentiation

Spatial dynamics of manufacturing in Poland

The post-socialist transformation brought about a major shift in the industrial structure of the country, which led to significant changes in the geographical distribution of production (Domański, 2015; Churski & Kaczmarek, 2022). The decline of coal mining and the steel industry severely affected Poland's largest industrial region, Upper Silesia (Śląskie voivodeship), while the decline of another traditional sector, textiles, led to high unemployment in the Łódź region in the 1990s.

At the same time, new manufacturing sectors began to develop rapidly, contributing to the restructuring and diversification of both old industrial districts. Upper Silesia became the main concentration of the fast-growing automotive industry in the country, as well as the development area of several other sectors. Łódź and its surroundings attracted considerable investment, especially in the household appliance industry.

The strongest growth in manufacturing over the past two decades has been in the two historically developed regions of western Poland, Wielkopolskie and Dolnośląskie (Lower Silesia), especially in the metropolitan areas of Poznań and Wrocław. The share of metropolitan areas in Polish manufacturing has generally increased, with the interesting exception of the capital region of Warsaw. The south-eastern region of Podkarpackie proved to be the relatively fastest growing in the historically less industrialised eastern Poland. It has the largest concentration of the aircraft industry, which dates back to the 1930s. The quality of the labour force appears to be a prominent factor in attracting the location of plants to regions and towns where skilled workers with technical skills can be found. This explains the large investments and rapid development of manufacturing in the historically industrialised regions and towns, including the old industrial districts of Upper Silesia and Łódź, as well as Podkarpackie. In addition, Upper Silesia and Łódź benefit from favourable road accessibility thanks to the junction of the main north–south A1 motorway with the west–east A2 and A4 motorways, while Podkarpackie became the first region in eastern Poland to be connected to western Europe by the A4 motorway.

DOI: 10.4324/9781003430117-7

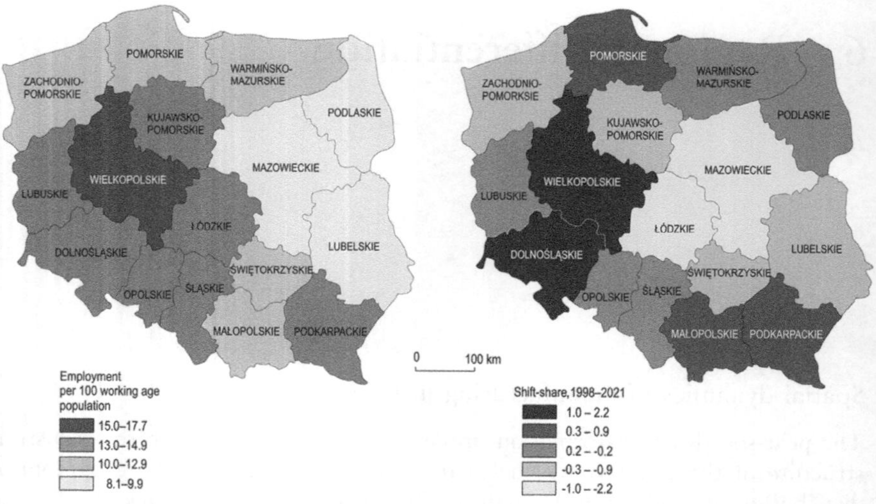

Figure 6.1 Spatial dynamics of Polish manufacturing by NUTS2 regions
Source: authors' calculations based on Statistic Poland data.

The general orientation of Polish manufacturing towards Western European markets also supports the trend for manufacturing to be located in the western and south-western regions of the country (Figure 6.1). The internal market favours location in the southern regions, which are characterised by a higher concentration of population and economic activity, as well as in metropolitan areas. The relative decline in the role of the Warsaw region in manufacturing reflects the strong service orientation of its economy and possibly the impact of the high costs of the capital city. Large cities, including Warsaw, are the main beneficiaries of the development of research centres and advanced producer services, due to the availability of skilled personnel and cooperation with universities. At the same time, a greater propensity to use temporary labour is also observed in metropolitan areas, probably due to greater competition and labour shortages in the local labour market.

Aims and scope of the chapter

The main objective of this chapter is to identify how the major changes that have taken place in the industries studied over the last three decades have translated into changes in their spatial structure. The main theme is the question of change and continuity in spatial organisation of manufacturing. Within this main problem, answers were sought to the following specific questions:

1 How does the location behaviour of firms in the automotive, aircraft and household appliance industries influence the dynamics of regional development in Poland?

2 Do these industries strengthen or weaken territorial disparities, especially core–periphery dynamics?
3 In which types of areas are more advanced activities concentrated? What factors affect this distribution?
4 To what extent have the dynamics of these sectors contributed to the restructuring of traditional industrial regions and towns?
5 What are the dominant forms (ideal types) of spatial concentration?

In particular, it is interesting to see whether upgrading processes in the broadly defined automotive, aircraft and domestic appliance industries are reflected in changes in the territorial organisation of production. That is, the extent to which simple spatial structures, such as TNC-led export platforms, evolve into more complex entities. Such a transformation may be accompanied by a greater embeddedness of industrial firms, reflected, *inter alia*, in an increasing diversity of suppliers, the establishment of non-production functions and the development of regional cluster initiatives.

Two territorial dimensions – regional (NUTS2) and metropolitan/non-metropolitan – are considered in the analysis.

Geographical patterns and territorial upgrading in the automotive, aircraft and domestic appliance industries

a The automotive industry

At the end of state socialism, the country's automotive industry was concentrated in two main regions: the capital region of Warsaw in central Poland, and the Upper Silesian industrial district, which also extends to the Bielsko-Biała area in the south. Warsaw was the historical nucleus of the sector, with its origins dating back to pre-war assembly activities. This region experienced significant growth following the establishment of FSO in 1950, supported by a plethora of branch plants and component suppliers in the area. In contrast, the Upper Silesian industrial district largely emerged as a result of the establishment of FSM in 1971, with an engine factory in Bielsko-Biała and a car assembly plant in Tychy, which opened in 1975. There were also about a dozen component plants in the region. Other automotive facilities, including two truck plants in Starachowice and Lublin and a bus factory in Sanok, were scattered across the south-east of the country. A few plants were also located in western Poland, namely in Jelcz, Nysa and Poznań. However, these smaller factories lacked a wider network of suppliers to support their operations.

Despite significant changes in ownership during the 1990s, the geographical distribution of the motor vehicle industry was broadly similar to that of the previous decade. More than two-thirds of employment in the sector remained concentrated in four regions in 1998: Śląskie, Podkarpackie, Mazowieckie and Wielkopolskie. The decline of the truck plant in Starachowice led to a decrease in the importance of Świętokrzyskie within the industry.

After a period of relative stabilisation in the spatial configuration of the sector in Poland during the 1990s, the first two decades of the 21st century witnessed a significant geographical realignment (Figures 6.2 and 6.3). Two

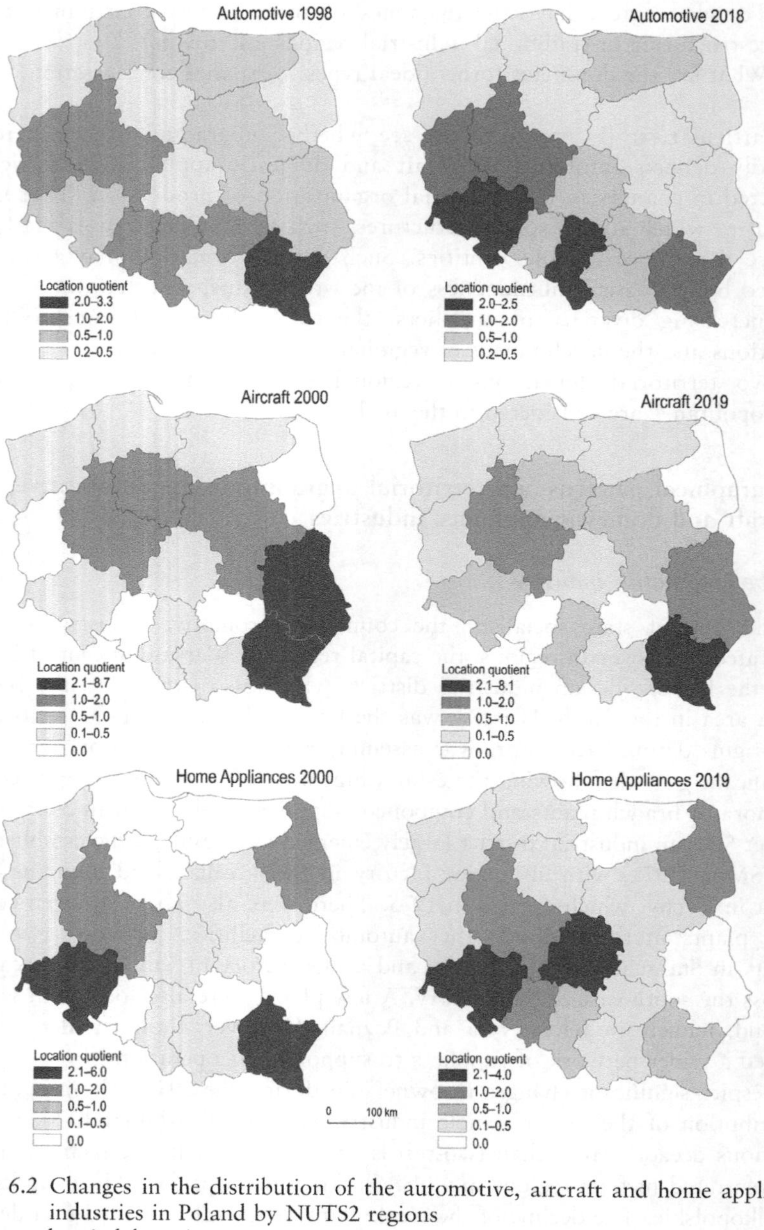

Figure 6.2 Changes in the distribution of the automotive, aircraft and home appliance industries in Poland by NUTS2 regions

Source: authors' elaboration.

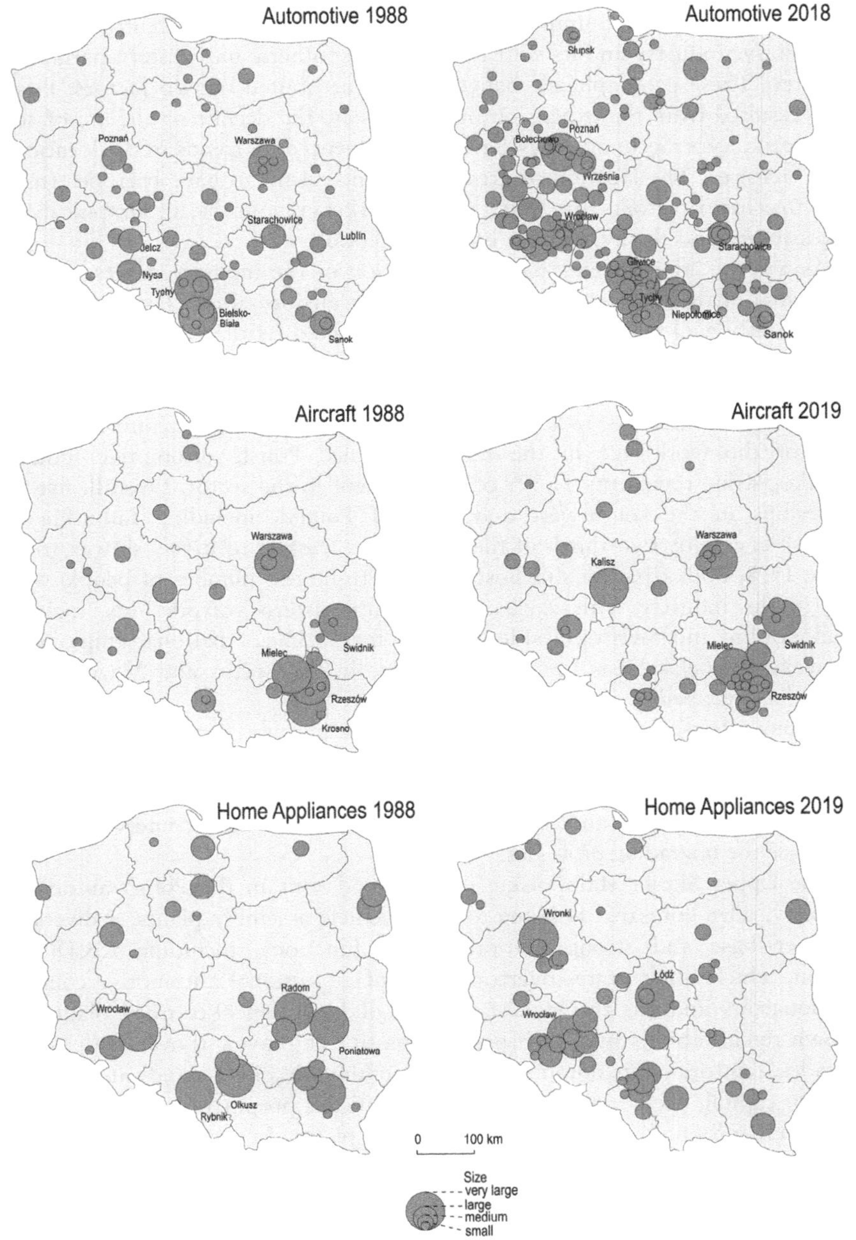

Figure 6.3 Changes in the distribution of automotive, aircraft and home appliance production centres in Poland

Source: authors' elaboration.

processes occurred simultaneously: the increasing spatial concentration of the automotive industry and its shift towards the southern and western parts of the country. These geographical changes can be attributed to two factors. Firstly, they resulted from the expansion or, conversely, the decline or closure of some large producers. Secondly, they have been influenced by trends in the location of new factories. The location of greenfield plants seems to have been determined by three main factors: proximity to the market, favourable geographical road accessibility and the availability of skilled labour.

As a result, the current spatial distribution of the industry differs markedly from that of the first decade of post-socialist transformation. The sector is now significantly agglomerated in south-western Poland, with a new central hub in Śląskie voivodeship, extending to the Kraków metropolitan area in Małopolskie. The share of Śląskie in national employment has risen to 29%, while that of Dolnośląskie is 18%. Thus, these two voivodeships account for almost half of the workforce in the broadly defined Polish automotive industry. Wielkopolskie represents 11.3% of employment in the sector. Overall, five voivodeships in the south-west and west of Poland, including Lubuskie and Opolskie, employ two-thirds of the workforce. Despite relatively slower growth since 1998, Podkarpackie still hosts the fourth-largest number of people working in the industry with 9.3%. Three south-eastern voivodeships, including Małopolskie and Świętokrzyskie, account for 17.8% of national employment. However, Lubelskie has lost its importance in this sector and Mazowieckie's share has dropped to just 2.7%.

A comprehensive analysis of each of the major automotive regions is carried out using a range of performance indicators. This provides a deeper insight into their specific development trajectories and allows an understanding of the different regional characteristics and capabilities, as well as the strategic interventions that influence the upgrading processes.

The Upper Silesia-Małopolskie region stands out in the Polish automotive industry. This core area is home to three vehicle assembly plants, a diversified supplier base and strong non-production functions, including R&D. The region, which concentrates over one-third of all national automotive company headquarters and has the highest number of IATF 16949-certified plants, has shown remarkable growth in broad automotive employment over the past two decades, reinforcing its dominant status. Notably, despite a significant inflow of foreign capital, the region is home to a significant proportion of Polish-owned suppliers, accounting for 26% of all domestic plants. In terms of the number of R&D centres and cluster initiatives, Upper Silesia and Małopolskie also appear to be the most innovative automotive region in the country (see Figure 6.4). It is currently the only area in Poland that can be classified as a "developing cluster" according to Enright's (2003) classification or as an "advanced production system" according to Baron (2016). Moreover, it demonstrates the ability to forge a new Industry 4.0 path through a critical connection with its IT capabilities (Micek et al., 2022). This strategic development has been facilitated by the active role of the Silesian Automotive and Advanced Manufacturing

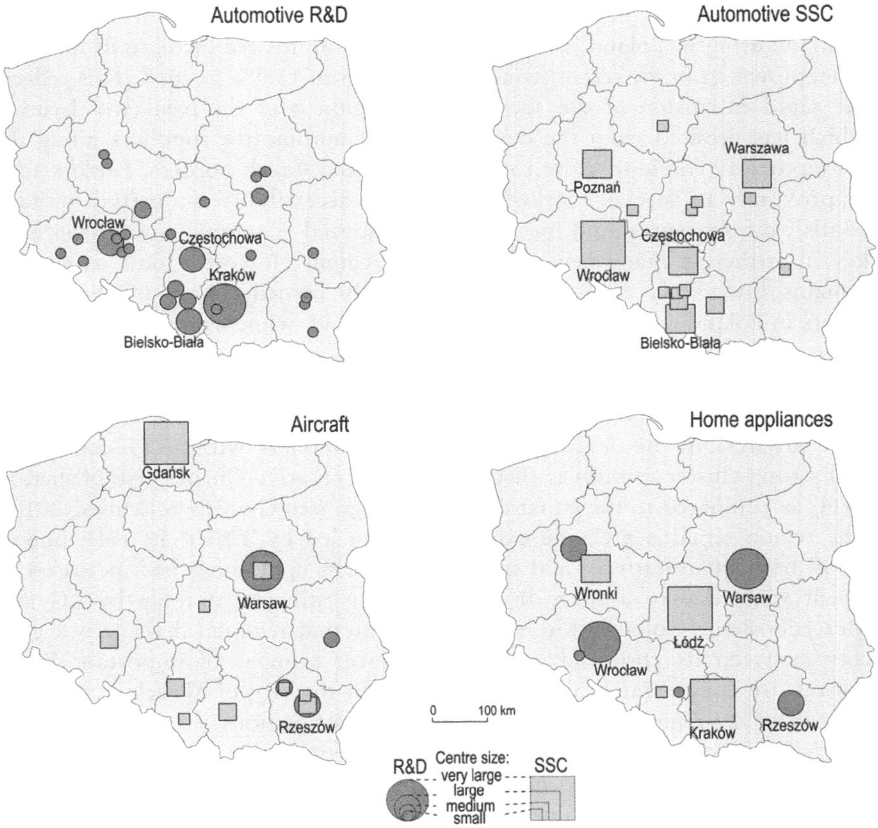

Figure 6.4 Distribution of R&D centres and SSCs in the automotive, aircraft and home appliance industries in Poland
Source: authors' elaboration.

Cluster. From a geographical perspective, it is worth highlighting the region's strong links with the automotive industry in the Silesian-Moravian region in Czechia and Žilina in Slovakia.

On the one hand, the rise of Upper Silesia-Małopolskie as a new automotive hub could be seen as a path-dependent process (Domański, 2003). The foundations of this development were laid by location decisions associated with Fiat's licensed car production in the 1970s, its subsequent successful privatisation and the establishment of the General Motors assembly plant in 1998. These milestones stimulated significant foreign investment in the region. On the other hand, this transformation represents a broader process of restructuring of an old industrial region by the automotive industry. This process of change can also be interpreted to some extent as a relatedness between the automotive industry and part of the region's former industrial base – in particular the machinery and metal industries (Otto & Weyh, 2014).

Dolnośląskie has benefited significantly from the growth of automotive manufacturing in Poland, as evidenced by the impressive increase in its share of employment in the sector from 7.8% in 1998 to 17.9% in 2018. This reflects the rapid expansion of the sector in the region over the past two decades, which has profited from the development of automotive suppliers along the A4 motorway corridor, close to the German and Czech borders. Factors such as proximity to foreign markets, good road accessibility, industrial heritage (skills), infrastructure and incentives from special economic zones have been key in attracting many new plants to the region. However, local ownership remains low. Only 6.3% of all domestically owned, IATF 16949-certified plants in Poland are concentrated in Dolnośląskie, while as much as 22.4% of the country's total of such certified plants with foreign capital are located in this region, illustrating the strong foreign presence in the region's automotive industry. It is also the most export-oriented region in Poland. There has been little progress in the development of Polish suppliers with IATF certificates and strong cluster initiatives (Dolnośląski Automotive Cluster, established in 2014) as compared to the situation 15 years ago (see Gwosdz & Micek, 2010). The region remains a classic export platform led by TNCs. Its role, understood both quantitatively and in terms of chain upgrading, has increased in recent years due to a surge in e-mobility investments, notably by LG and Mercedes-Benz. Dolnośląskie has a strong internal regional division – a contrast between its core and periphery. A large number of important R&D centres are concentrated almost exclusively in the city of Wrocław, whereas the rest of the region has mainly manufacturing functions.

Wielkopolskie holds an important position in the sector as the main location of Volkswagen's operations in the country. The share of employment in the Polish automotive industry increased slightly from 10.0% in 1998 to 11.3% in 2018, indicating relatively stable growth. The number of IATF 16949-certified plants is relatively low (56), of which 16% are Polish owned. However, the region has relatively fewer members of automotive cluster initiatives, suggesting less emphasis on formal collaboration in this region compared to others. The impressive investment by VW in recent years (a new greenfield plant in Września with a extensive supplier park nearby) has reinforced Wielkopolskie's character as a "hub-and-spoke" district, which typically consists of one or more hub firms around which smaller dependent firms (the spokes) revolve.

Podkarpackie is an interesting case in Central European automotive manufacturing. Historically, the region's competitive advantage was mainly based on its cheap but skilled labour force. This characteristic is still evident today, as reflected in the fact that Podkarpackie's share of total employment in the sector is higher than its share of revenues. Although the region's role in national employment has declined somewhat since the 1990s, it has been successful in attracting high-tech investors and significantly upgrading domestic firms. In particular, the region is home to two internationally successful manufacturers with Polish capital (Stomil Rubber and Bury Technologies). This development can be attributed to several factors: the availability of an industrial labour pool, good accessibility facilitated by the A4 motorway, and a much higher intensity of regional aid compared to western regions. A notable number of IATF-certified suppliers with Polish capital are located here (9% of the Poland total). This figure indicates a domestic production potential, which is further supported by the presence of two strong automotive clusters in the region: Polska Grupa Motoryzacyjna and the East Automotive Alliance. Podkarpackie is also characterised by a high level of social capital (Kwiatkowski et al., 2023). The importance of the automotive industry is also reflected in regional innovation policy. All these processes take place in a region that does not have a metropolitan centre, underlining the vital role of manufacturing in driving economic and technological progress.

In stark contrast to the success stories of other automotive regions, Mazowieckie has seen its role in the sector decline dramatically. Unlike Podkarpackie, which has managed to increase its automotive capacity, albeit less dynamically than south-western Poland, Mazowieckie has experienced a severe contraction of the automotive industry. Its share of national employment dropped from 13.3% in 1998 to just 2.7% in 2018. The region's diminishing position in the sector is mainly due to the demise of Daewoo, which previously controlled the key company FSO in Warsaw. The limited greenfield investment in Mazowieckie and central Poland in general is more difficult to interpret. Possible factors include the relatively late construction of the motorway, the high cost of land and labour in the fast-growing Warsaw metropolitan area, and the lower maximum regional aid intensity compared to other regions. Today, Mazowieckie's role in the sector is mainly determined by the still significant number of firms with Polish capital, the highest after the Upper Silesia-Małopolskie region. However, these companies specialise in labour-intensive products and only one of them has original design manufacturer capabilities. Furthermore, Mazowieckie has only three R&D centres and two producers participating in automotive cluster initiatives. The industry plays a negligible role in the regional labour market and is not listed as a "smart specialisation" in the Regional Innovation Strategy (RIS), suggesting that the sector is no longer a strategic priority here. However, the Warsaw metropolitan region has recently attracted new investments in the electromobility segment, which could herald a new chapter in the development of its automotive industry.

It is also worth looking at the differences between metropolitan and non-metropolitan areas. As expected, enterprises located in the former account for a larger share of total revenues than of employment in the country, 39.7% and 35.5%, respectively. Interestingly, there are no statistically significant differences between metropolitan and non-metropolitan areas for basic indicators such as the share of labour costs in total costs or the share of value added in revenues. Instead, at the regional NUTS2 level, a more pronounced division emerges, with the capital-intensive south-western regions standing out from the more labour-intensive remaining areas. In 2019, the share of labour costs was lower than the national average of 10.5% in all of Poland's main automotive regions located in the south-west and west of the country: Dolnośląskie, Wielkopolskie, Śląskie and Małopolskie.

The main difference between metropolitan and non-metropolitan areas is that the former attract R&D and shared service centres. However, as many R&D activities in the automotive industry in Poland are located together with manufacturing plants, the share of metropolitan areas is not dominant.

b The aircraft industry

Despite the significant expansion of the aircraft industry since the 1950s, its development in Poland has been markedly uneven, with a pronounced concentration in Podkarpackie (Figures 6.2 and 6.3). Notably, only this region recognises the aircraft sector as an integral part of its economic infrastructure and smart specialisation strategies (Kogut-Jaworska, 2015). In addition, it is of some importance in five other regions – Małopolskie, Śląskie, Dolnośląskie, Wielkopolskie and Lubelskie – but its presence there is overshadowed by the dominance of other industries. Nevertheless, each of the regions considered has at least one aircraft-related cluster or technology park.

The growth of the sector in Podkarpackie is remarkable: employment in the region has increased from 10,500 people in 2000 to 18,600 in 2019. About half of the Polish headquarters of aircraft companies with revenues exceeding PLN 20 million are located in Podkarpackie, and the region's share of total employment in the aircraft industry in Poland is as high as 44%. This development has its historical roots in the inter-war period, when aircraft (PZL Mielec) and engine (WSK PZL Rzeszów) plants were built.

There are four main centres of the sector in Podkarpackie. These include the regional capital Rzeszów and its agglomeration, as well as smaller towns such as Mielec, Krosno and Sędziszów Małopolski. Over the past two decades, a bipolar spatial pattern has gradually emerged around Rzeszów and Mielec, with additional locations such as Sędziszów Małopolski. There has also been a diffusion of development from Rzeszów to its surroundings. In particular, the Podkarpackie Science and Technology Park to the north of Rzeszów is the fastest-growing area, attracting numerous greenfield investments (Bodycote, McBraida, MTU AeroEngines, Zelnar) since its establishment in 2006 and hosting three new R&D and engineering centres with over 2,200 employees. In 2022, the ESA BIC incubator – a joint project of the European Space Agency and the Polish Industrial Development Agency – was opened there.

This development is inextricably linked to the region's human capital and R&D base. Rzeszów University of Technology has a wealth of technical and scientific resources in the aviation sector, including the NADCAP-accredited University Materials Testing Laboratory for the Aerospace Industry. Podkarpackie also has a long history of R&D collaboration, dating back to 2004 with the establishment of the Centre for Advanced Technologies Aeronet, a joint venture between Polish technical universities and the Aviation Valley Association. The region's human capital is further strengthened by the close cooperation between Aviation Valley companies and technical secondary schools specialising in the training of aircraft mechanics and avionics technicians in various Podkarpackie towns. The strength of the region is manifested in three regional cluster organisations, including the headquarters of Aviation Valley, the largest aviation cluster in Poland. Czakon's (2012) study (see also Czakon & Klimas, 2014) shows robust intra-regional trust-based networks between partners, with the former WSK PZL Rzeszów playing a central role.

In the other regions of Poland, there are individual locations rather than clusters of aircraft production centres. There are four such local concentrations, each situated in a different region.

The role of Lubelskie, which borders Podkarpackie and is the second-largest region in the country in terms of revenues, is determined by the helicopter manufacturer WSK PZL Świdnik – the first factory in this sector to be established in Poland after the Second World War. The importance of the aircraft industry in the region has been emphasised in the RIS with a separate sub-specialisation entitled "modern technologies and materials of the aircraft industry".

Warsaw has been a centre for the production of military aircraft and design offices since the 1930s and, after the Second World War, civil ones as well. In 2001, PZL Warszawa-Okęcie was acquired by the Spanish company CASA, part of the European Aeronautic Defence and Space (EADS) consortium, and subsequently became part of the Airbus Group, continuing the region's manufacturing and R&D traditions. Together with General Electric's operations and the Łukasiewicz Research Network – Institute of Aviation, it contributes to Warsaw's leading position in R&D employment in the sector in Poland, with more than 1,500 engineers (Figure 6.4). However, Mazowieckie has seen its share of national aircraft industry employment decline in recent decades, compared with absolute and/or relative growth in other areas.

The town of Kalisz in Wielkopolskie is another centre of aircraft manufacturing, with origins dating back to the post-war period and the supply of Russian-licensed small aircraft engines. Poland's second-largest aircraft engine manufacturer, WSK PZL Kalisz, went through a period of cooperation with Pratt & Whitney, culminating in the first foreign acquisition of an aircraft company in 1996. A well-established cluster of aircraft component suppliers continues to operate in Kalisz. Recently, the region updated its smart specialisation list to include aerospace technologies in the category of "specialised logistic processes". However, the focus of the RIS remains on space and satellite technologies rather than aircraft.

Wrocław, the capital of the Dolnośląskie region, has been a centre of aircraft manufacturing since 1947 with the establishment of the PZL airframe factory and associated design office. The city's role has grown significantly, especially since UTC acquired the former Hydral PZL Wrocław plant in 2010–2011. UTC R&D was also established there in 2014. Dolnośląskie has somewhat acknowledged the role of the aviation industry within its broader smart specialisation of "auto-moto-aero-space", but the focus here is on UAVs (drones) and spacecraft rather than aircraft and their components as smart solutions.

Finally, Bielsko-Biała in Śląskie is home to a cluster of glider, light and ultralight aircraft manufacturers whose traditions date back to the inter-war period. In recent years, however, some of them have faced declining demand, with the majority now only supplying spare parts for gliders and auxiliary services. The Silesian Aviation Cluster supports producers specialising in gliders, light and ultralight aircraft, drones, as well as modules for aircraft engines and composite structures. Since 2013, support has also been provided by one of the eight Regional Specialised Observatories located in the region. Over the past decade, UAV production has grown in other towns in Upper Silesia and Małopolskie with the emergence of new domestic manufacturers such as Flytronics.

Metropolitan areas have not been the main attraction for the aircraft industry, hosting only 23.2% of enterprises and 23.7% of employment. The majority of production is located in non-metropolitan areas, especially in medium-sized and small towns. In particular, two peripheral regions, Podkarpackie and Lubelskie, account for 64% of the revenues of Poland's large aircraft companies. The expansion of the sector in the eastern regions contributes to the reduction of territorial disparities. Overall, the historical centres of aircraft production (Mielec, Rzeszów, Świdnik, Warsaw), which developed on the basis of local skills and traditions, have remained largely unchanged. New factories have been located in the vicinity of existing facilities.

c The home appliance industry

The main centres of household appliance production were established in the 1950s and later, although some were based on earlier traditions of kitchenware and other metal and engineering production. The inherited spatial structure of the industry was stable until the 1990s. Most of the major domestic appliances were manufactured in three regions: Dolnośląskie, Wielkopolskie and Śląskie. By the end of the decade, Mazowieckie had emerged as a new player, partly due to the activities of Daewoo Electronics Manufacturing. Production of small domestic appliances remained dispersed, largely reflecting the configuration from the socialist era, except for the concentration processes triggered by the closure or insolvency of some producers.

This picture changed significantly at the beginning of the 21st century, with a marked shift of the sector towards the central and south-western parts of Poland. Dolnośląskie, Łódź and Wielkopolskie are now the country's main white goods production regions (Figures 6.2 and 6.3). The role of Mazowieckie has declined following the bankruptcy of Daewoo and the failure of companies in other historical centres, including Radom. Podkarpackie has also experienced a decline due to the reduced role of Zelmer and the fall in employment of several small domestic appliance manufacturers. Each of these regions' share of national employment has fallen dramatically from a dozen per cent to just 3%–5%.

The Łódź region has emerged as a new concentration of domestic appliance manufacturing in Poland, with the share of employment in final producers rising to 23%, a significant increase from 12% in 2006. Dolnośląskie remains the most important region with 26% of the total, and the third-largest manufacturer is Wielkopolskie. The latter's share of the OEM workforce has increased to over 18%. Śląskie and Podlaskie maintain relatively stable shares. In Śląskie this is due to the presence of large foreign-owned plants, which have replaced the legacy of Polish firms. In Podlaskie, on the other hand, the stability is due to the spread of a cluster of local producers specialising in small domestic appliances.

Despite its limited tradition in white goods production, Łódzkie benefits from its central location in the country near the junction of the W–E and N–S motorways, the availability of labour resources and close cooperation with local governments and the special economic zone. These were the key location factors for the greenfield plants of BSH, Whirlpool and luxury brand Miele, which are major foreign investors. The sector employs over 8,500 people in nearly 30 manufacturing companies, including suppliers, and investments exceed PLN 2.5 billion. R&D and shared service centres are expanding, particularly in cooperation with the Łódź University of Technology.

Dolnośląskie hosts factories of three TNCs: BSH and Whirlpool invested in privatised plants, whereas Electrolux built greenfield factories. The region also has a broad base of suppliers and non-production competences, including R&D centres in Wrocław. Diehl Controls and Jabil are examples of the development of non-manufacturing capabilities by key suppliers here. The region is a place of investment for many smaller firms, including several Italian ones, and companies from the region have strong links with Slovak and German enterprises.

Wielkopolskie is home to Amica, the largest locally owned household appliance manufacturer, which grew out of a privatised stove company and later sold two plants to Samsung. With 7% of the country's home appliance workforce, Amica has R&D centres in Wronki and Poznań, whereas Samsung's local presence is more focused on digital innovation. The specificity of the region is that it is located in a small town, independent of a local supplier network and somewhat remote from major highways.

The role of Podkarpackie in the sector has declined. Historically a centre for the production of small appliances, it now accounts for about 4% of employment in the industry, mainly at BSH, which manufactures small appliances at the former Zelmer plants in Rzeszów and Głogów Małopolski. BSH has recently expanded its activities by setting up an R&D centre for vacuum cleaners. There are also Polish-owned manufacturers in Sanok and Nowa Dęba.

Metropolitan areas dominate in terms of both number of enterprises and employment (61%). The influence of foreign-owned enterprises, especially OEMs, concentrated in Łódź and Wrocław, is particularly evident. Investment in privatised companies and new plants established by TNCs have significantly increased the importance of these regions. This trend is reinforced by the presence of suppliers close to their customers. Manufacturers located in metropolitan areas outperform their non-metropolitan counterparts in terms of productivity, with wages per employee 14% higher. However, the share of wages in total costs is greater in non-metropolitan areas, while there are no significant differences in export levels and the share of value added in revenues. Metropolitan areas are crucial in attracting non-production functions (Figure 6.4), concentrating over 90% of R&D and SSC employment.

Conclusions

Analysis of changes in the spatial structure of three industries reveals some sector-specific dynamics, but also allows the identification of certain more general patterns (Table 6.1).

From the point of view of spatial continuity or change, it is clear that each of the sectors studied has developed in a somewhat different way. The automotive and domestic appliance industries have formed new, strong spatial concentrations and their current geography is very different from the situation 30 years ago. A combination of three main factors – the availability of skilled labour, market accessibility and transport accessibility linked to the development of motorways – has been crucial to this shift. In contrast, the aircraft industry has consolidated its position in the historically established cluster in south-eastern Poland.

A common feature of all three sectors is that, at the regional level, they have all played the role of reindustrialisation rather than industrialisation. All the new clusters were formed in historically industrialised regions, especially in south-western Poland. In particular, the automotive and household appliance industries have had a significant impact on the economic restructuring of industrial towns and regions characterised by a sharp decline in previously dominant sectors: coal mining and basic metals in Śląskie (Upper Silesia), textiles, local coal mining and other sectors in Dolnośląskie (Lower Silesia) and textiles in Łódź voivodeship. Following the typology of "regional reindustrialisation patterns" recently proposed by Capello and Cerisola (2023), Dolnośląskie, Łódźkie and Śląskie can be classified as "reorientation of structures" (shrinking of the pre-existing industrial fabric towards a new specialisation). Podkarpackie, on the other hand, is an example of "upgrading", i.e. the strengthening of the existing specialised industrial structure, whereas Wielkopolskie corresponds to the "creation type", i.e. expanding the already diversified industrial base.[1] This demonstrates the possibility of multiple paths for the industrial development of Polish regions. For the majority of regions, generic capabilities associated with a broadly understood industrial culture have been more important than specific industrial capabilities.

In general, manufacturing activities have become a moderating force against strong metropolisation trends in the country. Despite the attractiveness of metropolitan areas for R&D and SSCs, the integral association of some of these functions with production facilities also anchors them in non-metropolitan regions. In addition, the location of non-production functions strengthens second-tier metropolises, especially in southern Poland – Kraków, Wrocław and the Upper Silesian agglomeration – thereby reducing Warsaw's dominant position in high-level business services.

Feature	*Automotive*	*Aircraft*	*Home appliances*
Main trends in spatial dynamics	shift towards south-western and western Poland together with the decline of the historically dominant region of Warsaw, more capital-intensive production in south-western Poland	strengthening of south-eastern Poland as a megacluster, limited role of metropolitan areas with declining role of Warsaw, strong position of smaller regional capitals and medium-sized towns that historically specialised in the sector	dominant role of metropolitan areas, creation of a new centre in Łódź, and its region, the strengthening of traditional production areas in Wrocław and Wronki, growing role of south-western Poland while diminishing of central and south-eastern regions except for Rzeszów
Distribution of non-production competences: R&D and SSCs	R&D is usually co-located with the largest plants, with stand-alone centres primarily located in some metropolitan cities, especially Wrocław and Kraków; SSCs are increasingly significant in metropolitan areas	R&D follow the distribution of factories with a larger role of metropolitan areas (especially Warsaw)	R&D tends to be co-located with major plants, with stand-alone centres concentrated in a few major cities, especially Wrocław, Łódź, Poznań and Warsaw; SSCs are increasingly significant in metropolitan areas (Kraków, Poznań)
Cluster initiatives	emerged relatively late from 2014, mainly in automotive regions, with the main concentration in Śląskie and Podkarpackie, followed by Dolnośląskie; there are few companies in cluster initiatives in other regions	developed relatively early with the dominance of the Aviation Valley initiative established in 2005, some follow-up effects in Dolnośląskie, southern Wielkopolskie (Kalisz) and Śląskie (Bielsko-Biała)	the sector has a strong national representation of manufacturers including the largest OEMs, but no clusters
Regional dynamics of the development of related industries	significant development of tooling and IT at the national level, co-location of related industries varies regionally – strong in Śląskie, Małopolskie, Wielkopolskie and Podkarpackie, weak in Dolnośląskie	significant development at the national level, including of tooling and IT, leading to varying degrees of co-location of accompanying industries across regions – strong in Podkarpackie, and to a lesser extent in Mazowieckie and Śląskie	linkages with other manufacturing industries (automotive, heating, ventilation and air conditioning HVAC) through a common supplier base (metal parts, plastics, rubber), creation of a recycling industry and impact on the circular economy
Dominant functional-spatial structures (ideal types)	evolution from TNC-led export platforms, through hub-and-spoke districts, to complex spatial structures	hub-and-spoke districts and complex spatial structures	mostly TNC-led export platforms

Source: authors' elaboration.

In a situation of significant changes in the spatial dynamics of some sectors, a particularly interesting question is whether there is an evolution in the territorial organisation of production that would indicate processes of industrial upgrading. This evolution could be evidenced by the transformation of simple spatial structures, such as TNC-led export platforms, into more complex systems, implying the increasing embeddedness of FDI-based firms and growing domestic manufacturers.

Indeed, the complexity of structures and the embeddedness of producers in regional economic structures are increasing, but this growth is highly spatially differentiated. The regions of Upper Silesia-Małopolskie, Podkarpackie and Wielkopolskie are relatively advanced in the development of a full-fledged cluster (in the sense of Enright's (2003) or Porter's (1998) typologies), whereas Dolnośląskie still represents a more typical TNC-led export platform. Moreover, the latter shows a very strong intra-regional contrast between the main city (Wrocław), which has dominated non-production functions, and the remaining areas. Such a significant difference is not observed in either Śląskie or Podkarpackie. The examples of these regions show that there is no universal path of upgrading. However, what seems to be central to this process is the simultaneous high attractiveness for external investors and the presence of local firms/industries (rooted in the region before 1989), including those in technology-related sectors. This underlines the importance of absorptive capacity, i.e. "the ability of local firms to recognise, assimilate and apply external knowledge" (Hansen & Schaumburg-Müller, 2006, p. 21). This process takes place over a considerable length of time, typically measured in decades rather than shorter periods. The development of the automotive industry in Upper Silesia-Małopolskie and aircraft manufacturing in Podkarpackie suggests that a critical number and specific types of companies are required as a precondition for more advanced territorial concentration and the emergence of economies of scale and diversity. The position of firms in the value chain and the set of local skills and competences are important.

In addition, Podkarpackie provides evidence that significant upgrading can take place in non-metropolitan areas. Conversely, Dolnośląskie illustrates how a newly emerging export platform can generate strong core–periphery effects. The latter could be attributed, at least in part, to the changing role of geographical proximity. In today's environment, it is not essential for related industries, such as tooling companies or providers of Industry 4.0 technologies, to be located close to the concentration of manufacturing plants. Instead, their growth depends on other factors that may not be present in an emerging TNC-led platform. These include a dense network of related firms, R&D centres and educational institutions that foster the necessary skills and entrepreneurial spirit critical for such upgrading. Path dependencies can also serve as explanatory factors, as in the case of the Polish tool industry. The high concentration of the sector in Kujawsko-Pomorskie, a region that is rather unimpressive in terms of the automotive industry (which is one of its main customers), is due to the presence of a large state-owned enterprise that existed there before 1989.

Looking to the future, a pertinent question arises: will the accelerated digitalisation of industrial activities (Industry 4.0), coupled with the ongoing hybridisation and servitisation of manufacturing (Baines et al., 2009; Paschou et al., 2020), lead to advanced industrial territorial structures? There is also the question of whether it will only strengthen metropolitan areas, which are currently at the forefront according to the incubation hypothesis (see Gwosdz et al., 2022), or will also facilitate functional upgrading in other areas.

Note

1 Surprisingly, Capello and Cerisola (2023) classify the analysed regions quite differently: Śląskie as "creation", Łódzkie as "diversification" and Wielkopolskie as "upgrading", while Dolnośląskie falls into a separate category of "deindustrialization".

References

Baines, T.S., Lightfoot, H.W., Benedettini, O., & Kay, J.M. (2009). The servitization of manufacturing: A review of literature and reflection on future challenges. *Journal of Manufacturing Technology Management*, 20(5), 547–567.

Baron, M. (2016). Open innovation in old industrial regions: Does old mean closed? In *The International Society for Professional Innovation Management Conference Proceedings* (pp. 1–9). Manchester: ISPIM.

Capello, R., & Cerisola, S. (2023). Regional reindustrialization patterns and productivity growth in Europe. *Regional Studies*, 57(1), 1–12. doi:10.1080/00343404.2022.2050894.

Churski, P., & Kaczmarek, T. (Eds.) (2022). *Three decades of Polish socio-economic transformations: Geographical perspectives*. Cham: Springer. doi:10.1007/978-3-031-06108-0.

Czakon, W. (2012). *Sieci w zarządzaniu strategicznym*. Warsaw: Wolters Kluwer.

Czakon, W., & Klimas, P. (2014). Innovative networks in knowledge-intensive industries: How to make them work? An empirical investigation into the Polish Aviation Valley. In D. Jemielniak (Ed.), *The laws of the knowledge workplace* (pp. 133–158). Farnham: Gower Publishing.

Domański, B. (2003). Economic trajectory, path dependency and strategic intervention in an old industrial region: The case of Upper Silesia. In R. Domański (Ed.), *Recent advances in urban and regional studies* (pp. 133–153). Warsaw: Polish Academy of Sciences, Committee for Space Economy and Regional Planning.

Domański, B. (2015). Współczesne procesy przemian regionalnych przemysłu Polski. *Studies of the Industrial Geography Commission of the Polish Geographical Society*, 29(4), 40–53.

Enright, M.J. (2003). Regional clusters: What we know and what we should know. In J. Brocker, D. Dohse, & R. Soltwedel (Eds.), *Innovation clusters and interregional competition* (pp. 99–129). Berlin: Springer.

Gwosdz, K., & Micek, G. (2010). Spatial agglomerations in the Polish automotive industry. *Przegląd Geograficzny*, 82(2), 159–190.

Gwosdz, K., Sobala-Gwosdz, A., & Hetmańczyk, K. (2022). Cyfrowi przedsiębiorcy przemysłu 4.0 w przestrzeni Polski. *Przegląd Geograficzny*, 94(3), 327–349.

Hansen, M.W., & Schaumburg-Müller, H. (2006). *Transnational corporations and local firms in developing countries: Linkages and upgrading*. Copenhagen: Copenhagen Business School Press.
Kogut-Jaworska, M. (2015). Identification of smart specialisations in Polish regions in the context of the EU's new financial perspective 2014–2020. *Oeconomia Copernicana*, 6(2), 23–36. https://journals.economic-research.pl/oc/article/view/171.
Kwiatkowski, T., Micek, G., & Łapczyński, M. (2023). Perceived social capital and institutional environment's impact on the success of regional cluster policies. *Central European Economic Journal*, 10(57), 198–218.
Micek, G., Gwosdz, K., Kocaj, A., Sobala-Gwosdz, A., & Świgost-Kapocsi, A. (2022). The role of critical conjunctures in regional path creation: A study of Industry 4.0 in the Silesia region. *Regional Studies, Regional Science*, 9(1), 23–44. doi:10.1080/21681376.2021.2017337.
Otto, A., & Weyh, A. (2014). Industry space and skill-relatedness of economic activities: Comparative case studies of three eastern German automotive regions. IAB-Forschungsbericht, No. 8/2014. Nürnberg: Institut für Arbeitsmarkt- und Berufsforschung (IAB).
Paschou, T., Rapaccini, M., Adrodegari, F., & Saccani, N. (2020). Digital servitization in manufacturing: A systematic literature review and research agenda. *Industrial Marketing Management*, 89, 278–292.
Porter, M.E. (1998). *On competition*. Cambridge, MA: Harvard Business Review Press Books.

7 Labour

Labour plays a fundamental role in economic development. Analysis of the growth of the Central European manufacturing sector requires a closer look at labour conditions, both as a determinant of this growth and as a social consequence of economic processes. It is generally believed that the availability of a large pool of relatively cheap skilled labour was one of the decisive factors attracting foreign investors and supporting the development of local companies (Pavlínek & Ženka, 2011; Pavlínek, 2018; Zavarská et al., 2023). OECD (2015) and ILO (2016) point to an increase in contingent forms of work in both advanced and emerging economies. Poor working conditions are particularly associated with export-oriented manufacturing sectors dominated by foreign firms in low-cost countries. This is reflected in job insecurity, flexible work arrangements and the persistence of low wages. The segmentation of the labour market with a high reliance on temporary and foreign workers can lead to competition with permanent workers and thus to a race to the bottom in working conditions (Waterman, 2014; Clibborn, 2015; Buckley et al., 2017; Jürgens & Krzywdzinski, 2016; Reber, 2021; Scott & Visser, 2022). Various aspects of the labour situation in CE countries are discussed in this context by Drahokoupil et al. (2015, 2016), Parteka and Wolszczak-Derlacz (2015), Mrozowicki and Trappmann (2021) and others.

Thus, the main question posed here is whether the spectacular growth of the Polish manufacturing sector has been accompanied by an improvement or deterioration of working conditions. Several detailed questions can be asked in this context. How have the availability of labour and its characteristics affected the development of Polish industry over three decades? How do wages in three manufacturing industries compare with wages in manufacturing as a whole and in the economy as a whole? How do wages compare with Western Europe? Has there been real growth in wages? What is the relationship between wage growth and productivity? Are employment and working conditions improving? What is the role of temporary and migrant workers, the reasons for their use and their impact? What is the position of trade unions? Finally, what is the relationship between industrial upgrading processes on the one hand and employment conditions and labour market trends on the other?

DOI: 10.4324/9781003430117-8

Dynamics and forms of employment

The shock of post-socialist transformation was reflected in the explosion of unemployment in Poland in the early 1990s. The decline in the number of jobs was particularly sharp in the manufacturing sector, which inherited overstaffed factories from the socialist era. Unemployment reached 16.5% in 1994, then fell with economic growth to 10.2% in 1998, but rose again to 20.0% in 2002 as large numbers of young people born in the early 1980s entered the labour market. Poverty rates, including in-work poverty, were above the European average, particularly high among those working in agriculture, and low-paid workers were also concentrated in the service sector (Lewandowski & Kamińska, 2014). Further economic growth, which created new jobs, and migration to Western Europe led to a radical improvement in the labour market situation in the following years. The unemployment rate in Poland and Czechia is now the lowest in the EU (2.6%), reflecting the general shortage of labour (see Chapter 2).

After a sharp decline in manufacturing output and employment (around 20%) between 1989 and 1992, production began to grow in 1992. This was achieved through productivity gains without an increase in employment, which remained at a level of 3.0–3.1 million until 1998. At the turn of the century, intensive restructuring took place, with extensive privatisation of state-owned enterprises and outsourcing of non-production activities (maintenance, transport, catering etc.), and the number of jobs in manufacturing fell to 2.4 million in 2005. Since then, Poland has been the country with the highest increase in manufacturing employment in the EU (see Chapter 2). It has been particularly rapid in recent years: 25% growth during 2013–2021, reaching 2.9 million employees. This contrasts with a decline in most European countries, including Czechia, Slovenia and Romania. The most spectacular rise in the number of jobs took place in the automotive industry, where it reached around 70% over the period 2005–2021, more than in any other EU country, although it grew in all CE economies. The total number of people employed in manufacturing is actually higher, as employment statistics do not include temporary agency work, which will be discussed below. Employment also increased in other sectors: 13% in aircraft and household appliances since 2008, and even faster in Polish furniture, metal products, rubber and plastic products. The gender composition of the workforce differs between sectors, with women accounting for 36% of the workforce in the automotive industry and 43% in the manufacture of electrical equipment, which includes domestic appliances.

The key issue in industries dominated by foreign investors is the stability of jobs. Large TNCs are often accused of "nomadic" behaviour – moving their operations from one peripheral country to another in search of lower costs and tax incentives. The impact of FDI on the number of jobs was different in the post-socialist transformation period until the early 2000s compared to later. The introduction of better organisation of production and new technologies by investors taking over state-owned enterprises meant that fewer people were needed, and hence redundancies. The extent and level of financial compensation depended on employment guarantees that were part of privatisation contracts negotiated with the government and negotiations with trade unions, discussed later in this chapter. Some investments of the 1990s ended in failure, e.g. Siemens in Elwro (electronics) and ABB in Dolmel in Wroclaw (locomotive engines) ceased production when the local market shrank. Massive layoffs were carried out as state-owned companies lost their market position and/or went bankrupt. At the same time, newly established Polish private companies and greenfield FDI created new jobs.

As shown in the previous chapters, plant closures due to the short-term commitment of investors and their relocation of production from Poland to other countries have been very rare, in contrast to what has happened in several Western European countries in recent decades. Nevertheless, some plants were closed as a result of company restructuring and the concentration of production in fewer large factories. There were a few cases of temporary assembly, e.g. Ford vans in Płońsk in the 1990s, as well as bankruptcies, the most spectacular being that of Daewoo.

The increasing demand for labour in the context of a shrinking working-age population due to demographic trends has led to labour shortages over the past decade. Recruitment difficulties are now faced by the majority of employers and are often perceived as an obstacle to further development. This is documented in JETRO's annual reports on 850 Japanese manufacturing companies surveyed in 22 European countries. In recent years, the issue of "securing human resources" has become the second most frequently cited operational challenge across Europe, and a predominant one in CE. In the 2021 survey, it was cited by 92% of Japanese affiliates operating in Hungary, 79% in Czechia and 71% in Poland. This is well above the European average of 43%.

JETRO's reports also provide an interesting insight into the types of employees being sought. According to the latest report (JETRO, 2023), 65% of Japanese companies in CE are looking for factory workers, 53% for engineers and 20% for Internet of Things (IoT)/AI specialists, while in Western Europe, 53% indicate a need for managers, 38% for engineers, 26% for IoT/AI specialists and far fewer for factory workers.

A weakness in Poland's economic development is the high share of non-standard employment as defined by the ILO (including fixed-term contracts, part-time work and civil/commercial contracts), which reached 25% in 2014[1] (ILO, 2016), similar to Spain and well above the EU average (15%), and was particularly high in eastern rural areas of Poland (Kapitsinis & Gialis, 2023). This reflects the popularity of civil/commercial contracts, which account for around 10% of the workforce, mainly in services. Their role in manufacturing is less than 5%. Krzywdzinski (2017) has shown that automotive suppliers from CE are more likely to use precarious employment contracts than factories in Germany. The particularly vulnerable group that deserves more attention is temporary agency workers, including a growing number of immigrants. The latter became an important part of the Czech labour market much earlier, when the country faced difficulties in recruiting workers.

The use of agency workers became popular in Poland after 2000. Their number increased from 433,347 in 2010 to 863,825 in 2017, when it started to decline to 651,369 in 2021 (Ministerstwo Rodziny i Polityki Społecznej, 2023). They represent about 0.7% of total employment in the country in full-time equivalent terms, compared with 2.9% in the UK, 2.3% in France and 1.7% in Germany (World Employment Confederation, 2022). Their prevalence can still reach 25%–35% in some large domestic appliance assembly plants during peak production periods. It is usually less than 10% in car component manufacturing and is now almost non-existent in large car assembly plants, although it was often higher in the past. Very few temporary workers are found in aircraft manufacturing (up to 3%). Sectoral differences can be explained by lower technological complexity (simpler tasks) and greater seasonal variations in sales in the domestic appliance industry than in the automotive and especially the aircraft sector. The general, radical decrease in all forms of precarious work in Poland in 2018 and 2020 compared to 2008 and 2014 and other countries is shown in the recent detailed study of EU regions by Kapitsinis and Gialis (2023).

The detailed study shows that the proportion of permanent and temporary workers also reflects company strategies and management practices. Companies that are most concerned with cutting costs tend to use more temporary workers. This is because temporary workers can work more flexible hours and longer hours than permanent employees. In addition, limited wage increases in the company lead to higher turnover and recruitment difficulties, so agency workers fill the gap. Thus, according to many of the managers and trade union leaders interviewed, "contrary to a popular image, the extensive use of temporary workers does not reduce labour costs per se, but is caused by the preoccupation with low costs" (Domański et al., 2024, forthcoming). Interestingly, the increase in production in 2021 occurred without the use of temporary workers returning to pre-pandemic levels in many companies. According to several interviews with employment agencies and HR managers, temporary workers are increasingly being used to select people who can be offered training and employment contracts in the firm.

Poland has historically been a labour exporter, whereas in recent years it has become a destination for a significant inflow of foreign workers. In 2021, 1.5–1.7 million foreigners were legally working in the country (around 10% of total employment). One-quarter of the work permits issued to non-EU nationals in the EU were issued in Poland (0.5 million), but more people worked on the basis of the so-called simplified procedure, i.e. declarations of assignment of work to people from Eastern European countries submitted by employers to labour offices (see Chapter 8). Ukrainians are a dominant group (more than two-thirds before the Russian invasion of Ukraine), and Belarusians are the second-largest group. About one-third of Ukrainians are employed in manufacturing, while the large number of female war refugees find jobs in the service sector. According to Exact Systems (2023), in 2022, 75% of car factories in Poland employed Ukrainians, with a similar proportion in Czechia and even higher in Slovakia (88%). Eastern Europeans are attracted to Poland by higher wages, a low language barrier and geographical proximity, which makes it easier to travel home. Classic chain migration occurs when migrants bring in relatives and friends. For employers, migrants fill the gap in the labour market, accepting simple tasks and working longer hours in search of higher earnings. Single foreigners from Eastern European countries are also more geographically mobile than local workers, as they can easily decide to move to other locations in search of better wages. Many interviewed managers and trade union leaders argue that foreigners tend to be more motivated and have lower absenteeism than the few Polish jobseekers available on the labour market; however, some claim that Ukrainians have a lower work ethic. Recently, there has been an increase in the recruitment of workers from Asia, especially India, Nepal, the Philippines, Indonesia and Uzbekistan.

Despite a growing number of Ukrainians with permanent contracts, the vast majority of immigrants are temporary workers (49% of temporary workers are foreigners), i.e. they represent the lower, insecure segment of the labour market. Language barriers and difficulties in the formal recognition of qualifications for the operation of some equipment in Poland limit the vertical mobility of foreigners. Many managers and trade union representatives interviewed believe that foreign workers are a must in the current labour market situation (household appliance manufacturers: "We could not function without them"; "There is no other way but to rely on immigrants"). This is confirmed by a recent national survey, according to which only 21% of Poles agree that Ukrainians "are taking our jobs". And only 14% of Ukrainian workers say they encounter negative attitudes from their Polish colleagues, while 45% describe them as neutral and 35% as positive (Personnel Service, 2023). Nevertheless, foreign agency workers do not necessarily integrate with the rest of the workforce on the shop floor. On the one hand, there may be a certain reluctance and lack of acceptance of "others" who speak a different language, while on the other hand, in the case of Ukrainians, limited cultural barriers are generally emphasised. The wages and working conditions of foreign and temporary workers will be discussed later.

Wages

At the end of state socialism, there was a huge gap in wage levels between Central and Eastern Europe and Western Europe. At the beginning of the 1990s they were about ten times lower in Poland. Since then, they have grown faster than in the West, so the wage gap has narrowed, especially in purchasing power parities (PPPs). However, the difference in nominal terms remains substantial, with Polish manufacturing workers earning about half what their Italian counterparts do on an annual basis and 43% on an hourly basis. Nominal wages in Poland are lower than in the other CE countries, with the exception of Romania, but in PPP terms they are the second highest in the region after Slovenia.

Lower nominal wages are reflected in the level of labour costs per employee (full-time equivalent), which are well below the EU average in the CE manufacturing sector. They represented 71% of this average in Slovenia, 48%–51% in Czechia and Slovakia, 40% in Hungary, 38% in Poland and 25% in Romania in 2021, with a similar picture in different sectors. As a result, several authors have pointed to the slow convergence of nominal wages between East and West (Parteka & Wolszczak-Derlacz, 2015; Piątkowski, 2018). While the share of labour costs in production value has not changed significantly in Western Europe since 2005, it has gradually increased in CE to 15.6% in Romania, 14.8% in Czechia and 13.8% in Poland, compared to 16.0%–16.1% in Spain and Italy. It is lowest in Hungary and Slovakia (12.5%–12.7%), while in Slovenia (22.1%) it is similar to that in France and above the EU average of 18.9%. In the CE automotive industry, Slovenia, Poland and Romania report the relatively highest share of labour costs in production (12.6%–13.4%), above the Spanish level (11.8%) and higher than in Czechia (9.9%), Hungary (8.2%) and Slovakia (11.8%), but below the EU average (16.9%). High labour cost growth is consistently reported by Japanese companies in CE more often than in Western Europe, and the rate of growth is also higher (JETRO, 2023). Despite rising labour costs, the shortage of human resources is now seen as the main operational challenge.

Most importantly, there has been an increase in real wages, e.g. in Poland they increased by almost half (48.7%) in the decade 2009–2019 (Figure 7.1). This compares with an average real growth of 8.4% in the EU, an increase of around 10% in Germany and France and a decrease in Italy and Spain (ILO, 2021). In addition, the total wage bill loss during the COVID-19 pandemic in Poland in 2020 was among the lowest in Europe.

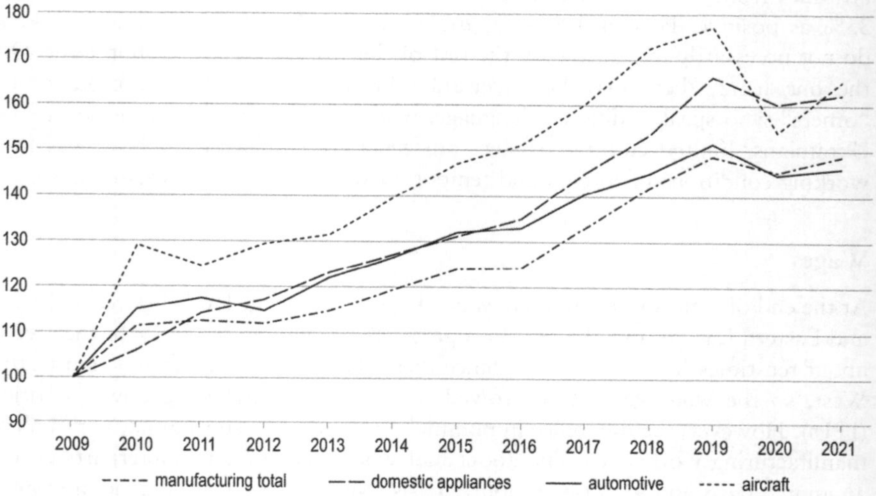

Figure 7.1 Real wage growth in Poland's manufacturing, 2009–2021 (2009 = 100)
Source: authors' calculations based on Eurostat data.

Faster wage growth and the narrowing gap between Central and Western European economies are particularly evident in PPPs. According to OECD data, wages in Slovenia were already higher than in Italy and only 10% lower than in France in 2022, while Polish wages were 10% below the Japanese level and 14%–18% below those in Spain and Italy (Table 7.1). The difference between Czechia and Italy was 25%, while it was greater in Hungary and Slovakia (37%–41%). All CE countries show a significant increase in wages during 2005–2022 in constant prices at 2022 USD PPP. This growth is most pronounced in Poland (49%) and Slovakia (39%) and relatively less dynamic in Hungary (16%), which is still higher than in Germany and France. At the same time, wages have remained almost unchanged in Spain and have even fallen since 2005 in Italy. The trends in CE contrast with those in North America, where wages in Mexico have not improved in PPP terms and the gap with the USA has widened significantly instead of narrowing. The countries of South-East Asia, such as Vietnam, Thailand and Indonesia, have shown rising wages over the last decade, although they are significantly lower than in CE.

All three sectors analysed in detail here have wages above the average for manufacturing in both Poland and the EU. The aircraft industry is characterised by significantly higher wages than the other two sectors – almost 40% higher than in the EU's automotive sector; the difference is less pronounced in Poland (14%). Wages in Poland's automotive and domestic appliance industries are

Table 7.1 Average annual wages in selected countries, 2000–2022 (constant prices at 2022 USD PPPs)

Country	*2000*	*2005*	*2010*	*2015*	*2020*	*2022*	*Change 2005–2022 (2005 = 100)*
Germany	51,344	52,378	52,912	57,431	60,309	58,940	113
France	43,694	46,824	49,926	51,415	50,550	52,764	113
Slovenia	33,203	38,510	42,846	42,482	48,605	47,204	123
Italy	45,290	46,654	47,629	46,103	44,246	44,890	96
Spain	43,029	42,437	46,538	44,957	43,828	42,859	101
Japan	41,428	41,936	40,999	40,062	41,442	41,509	99
Poland	23,770	24,682	28,091	29,635	37,325	36,897	149
Czechia	20,070	25,914	28,648	30,224	35,552	33,476	129
Portugal	30,975	30,886	31,589	29,448	31,300	31,922	103
Hungary	17,969	24,492	24,005	23,140	27,588	28,475	116
Slovakia	16,381	18,907	22,642	23,676	27,052	26,263	139
Mexico	17,311	18,778	17,618	17,730	17,467	16,685	89

Source: OECD.

similar, as are those in Italy and Spain, while in the EU the automotive sector pays around 20% more on average. In all three sectors in Poland, real wage growth during 2009–2019 was stronger than in total manufacturing; the highest was in the aircraft industry (77.4%), and since 2017 it has been faster in the domestic appliances sector than in the automotive sector.

A comparison of wages and salaries in large enterprises shows that foreign-owned companies offer significantly higher earnings than domestic firms (Table 7.2). They can afford to do so because they achieve greater productivity, thanks in part to economies of scale and technological advantages; this allows them to attract the best staff. The gap is particularly pronounced in the automotive industry, where it reaches 23%, compared with only 10% in domestic appliance manufacturing and even less in the aircraft industry.[2] There is also a significant difference in wages between motor vehicle and engine manufacturers on the one hand and automotive suppliers on the other: in 2019, earnings in 12 OEMs in Poland reached PLN 100,800, while they were 30% lower in suppliers. Small and medium-sized employers in manufacturing tend to pay less.

Overall income inequality in Poland, as measured by the Gini coefficient, increased from the 1990s until 2008, when it began to fall and is now among the lowest in the EU, according to Eurostat. The same applies to the gender pay gap (4.5% in Poland), which is similar to that in Slovenia and well below the levels in Germany, France, Czechia and Hungary, as well as the EU average of 12.7%. A recent international study by Lewandowski et al. (2023) suggests that participation in global value chains is negatively associated with wage inequality in most low- and middle-income countries that receive offshored jobs, and positively associated in high-income countries that send jobs offshore. In Poland, the share of people living in poverty has fallen from 18.1% in 2005 to 6.5% in 2021.

Table 7.2 Wages and salaries per employee in three manufacturing sectors in Poland, 2007, 2012 and 2019 (in PLN)

Sector	*Ownership*	*2007*	*2012*	*2019*
Automotive	Total	43,060	54,360	72,330
	Foreign-owned	43,880	54,900	73,460
	Polish-owned	33,760	46,840	56,730
Home appliance	Total	36,590	42,500	59,370
	Foreign-owned	39,020	42,400	60,910
	Polish-owned	26,810	39,510	54,920
Aircraft	Total	43,470	67,190	79,110
	Foreign-owned	44,210	67,960	77,950
	Polish-owned	40,510	64,780	84,220

Source: authors' calculations based on financial statements of the 287 largest enterprises with revenues exceeding PLN 50 million (about €10 million).

It is often believed that immigrants enable labour costs to be reduced. Under Polish law, temporary and foreign workers are paid the same as local employees, although they are not entitled to severance pay. Nevertheless, the presence of foreigners can slow down the pace of wage increases as they are willing to accept lower wages. Public opinion in Poland is divided on this issue: 41% of people think this is the case, while 36% disagree (Personnel Service, 2023); most of the union leaders interviewed deny this in the current situation of widespread difficulties in recruiting labour. There are also additional costs for employers of temporary and foreign workers. Constant turnover means the need for repeated training of newcomers, and immigrants also have to receive instruction in foreign languages. For the majority of foreign workers in Poland, the cost of accommodation is covered by the employment agency (Otto Work Force, 2022), which further increases the total cost of their deployment. All this can be afforded by large manufacturing companies, much less by smaller ones, which is why the latter use temporary and foreign workers to a lesser extent. The common complaint of local employees, especially team leaders, voiced by the unions, is that they deserve higher pay for the extra responsibility of supervising foreign workers on the shop floor. There may be a general envy that the latter earn the same or even more for working longer hours.

The relationship between wage dynamics and productivity is particularly important from an economic perspective. During the transformation period 1992–1998, real wage growth in Polish manufacturing was 50%, but productivity increased by 87%. The same is true for the following decade, when wage rises did not keep pace with productivity growth. The more limited convergence of wages than of productivity confirms the fact that the competitiveness of Polish manufacturing was based on cost advantages (Piątkowski, 2018). The situation started to change in 2010. Wages grew by 49% in real terms during 2009–2019, while labour productivity increased by 35%. At the same time, wages in the EU27 rose by 8% and labour productivity by 12% (ILO, 2021). The difference was even greater in the Polish automotive industry, where a 52% increase in earnings was accompanied by a 22% growth in productivity. If this trend continues, it will mark a new stage in the country's development, which may be linked to a fundamental change in the labour market situation: from the wide availability of labour in the past to its increasing scarcity.

Many managers interviewed, both foreign and Polish, emphasise that Poland is no longer a low-cost country, although it retains a general comparative advantage of lower costs compared to Western Europe. Technical culture and high-quality permanent staff are systematically gaining in importance with advanced technology, eliminating low-skilled, low-paying jobs.

Time regime and working conditions

The annual number of hours worked by an employee in manufacturing in Poland and Hungary in 2021 was 4%–8% higher than in Italy and Spain, similar to France, and 16%–21% higher than in Germany, while in Czechia and

Slovakia it was slightly lower than in Italy and Spain. The longest working hours in Europe are characteristic of Romania and Slovenia, where they exceed the Italian and German levels by 13% and 27%, respectively. The divergence in the length of working hours is particularly marked in the aircraft and automotive industries. In the former, Romanian and Polish employees work 18% more hours than their Italian counterparts, while the French and Czechs work 14% and 8% more hours, respectively, than the Italians. The number of hours worked in the automotive sector in Romania is 15% higher than in Italy, while in Hungary and Poland it is 8% greater than in Italy, and in France it is 12% higher. Interestingly, working hours in the manufacture of domestic appliances in most CE countries are similar to those in Italy and Spain, but 20%–27% longer than in Germany, with the exception of Romania, where they are 13% longer than in Italy.

There is a general trend of employers seeking labour market flexibility in both advanced and emerging economies (OECD, 2015; ILO, 2016). In Poland, too, flexible working arrangements have become an area of conflict (Mrozowicki & Maciejewska, 2013). Many employers would prefer their personnel to work overtime and/or on weekends (even at higher pay) rather than increase employment at a time of rising demand for their products. This is increasingly unpopular with workers, especially young people. Thus, employers' quest for numerical and time flexibility may be the main motivation for using temporary agency workers, especially in the case of seasonal and sudden production peaks. The predominant financial motivation of migrants and the low wage rate lead many of them to seek long hours as agency workers. They may also be more willing to work flexible hours, e.g. to come to work at short notice. On the one hand, this is in line with employers' demand for flexibility, but on the other hand, it contradicts the prevailing attitudes of the company's employees. The expectation of Ukrainians to work longer hours has "disrupted our system", as one manager of an automotive supplier put it. Most foreigners work in unskilled jobs. Their long-term employment prospects depend on both enterprise policy and the attitudes of migrant workers. The expectation that immigrants will work longer hours to earn more money may discourage some of them from seeking permanent contracts with companies. There is no doubt that workers from Asia are most likely to be unfairly treated and exploited by some employers and/or labour agencies – language barriers, lower geographical mobility and lack of support from wider social networks make them particularly vulnerable.

As far as other working conditions are concerned, including safety, tools, protective clothing, noise control, quality of rest areas, lockers, showers etc., the main improvement occurred after the privatisation of enterprises. This reflects the fact that under state socialism there were never enough resources for these provisions, while the improvement was part of the overall modernisation of the factories (Domański, 2001). Moreover, a large part of manufacturing activity now takes place in newly built plants. On the whole, working standards are viewed positively by the trade unionists interviewed.

Widespread labour shortages facilitate higher turnover. To make matters worse for employers, the attractiveness of manufacturing jobs to young people is generally considered by managers and trade unionists to be low. The key question, therefore, is: what are now the main factors influencing the choice of employer? The latest Randstad survey (Randstad, 2023) shows that attractive pay and benefits are still considered the most important factor, although less so than in the past. The role of a friendly atmosphere, opportunities for development and the reputation of the employer are more important than before, and job stability remains essential. This is in line with the opinion of the union leaders interviewed. The importance of permanent contracts is emphasised in particular by representatives of the white goods industry, which is characterised by a greater use of temporary workers, but also by some large automotive companies. Permanent contracts not only reduce job insecurity but can also provide access to housing loans. Less than one-fifth of workers in Poland (19%) are now worried about losing their jobs, including 9% who are very worried, according to the national survey (Personnel Service, 2023). Interestingly, some trade unionists suggest that a good working atmosphere, linked to the general attitude of management towards employees, can be crucial in the decision to stay with the current employer. Managers also point to advanced technology, good work organisation, company and personal development prospects and the employer's reputation. However, wages appear to play an important role in both retention and recruitment. Trade union leaders representing some companies claim that they have no difficulty in recruiting because they offer high wages. The CEO of a global domestic appliance manufacturer stated that, "to win business, the company has to be the best choice for employees; it depends on what economic conditions it offers along with other benefits, but also what the city offers."

The Randstad (2023) study ranks the most attractive industrial and service sectors and employers in Poland. The automotive industry is at the top of the list and the household appliance industry is in fifth place. In the company ranking, Volvo was among the top four employers in 2021, 2022 and 2023, Toyota Motor Manufacturing in the top six, VW Poznań in ninth place and Pratt & Whitney Rzeszów in tenth place in 2023. In the home appliance sector, BSH, Electrolux and Whirlpool are the most popular.

Trade unions

Trade union representation and activity are protected by law, so they are present in most large and medium-sized manufacturing companies in Poland, including Asian subsidiaries, which is not necessarily the case in Czechia and Hungary. However, union membership is on the decline. There are usually two or three unions in a large company, affiliated to national confederations such as Solidarność and OPZZ. In TNCs employees have representatives in European Works Councils. In most CE countries, including Poland, collective bargaining takes place at company level, where trade union organisations sign agreements with management.

The role of trade unions in the privatisation process was unique. The privatisation contract between the government and the investor had to include a social pact signed with the trade unions, providing for job guarantees for company employees and/or severance pay in excess of the statutory three months' compensation in the event of redundancy. Guarantees of two or three years were typical in the 1990s. It sometimes happened that long employment guarantees demanded by the unions deterred the investor, e.g. GM from taking over the car manufacturer FSO. Some investors sought to reduce employment by offering generous compensation to people who left their jobs voluntarily (Domański, 2001).

It is interesting to note the main concerns and complaints of trade unions today. Wage increases have been the central expectation since the early post-socialist period, reflecting the widespread feeling among workers that they are not being satisfactorily rewarded for their work. As shown earlier, this corresponded to the fact that productivity grew faster than real wages in Polish manufacturing until 2010. Several of the trade union representatives interviewed still emphasise that what people want most is higher wages. However, the experience of rapidly rising real wages in the last decade is also confirmed. Trade unionists in one of the large household appliance companies are happy that they have managed to double wages in five to six years, albeit from a low level; in an automotive OEM there is an opinion that "wages will undoubtedly continue to grow"; the trade union leader in one of the largest automotive suppliers even said that "wages are growing by themselves". The impact of government increases in the minimum wage is sometimes highlighted as an argument in negotiations with management.

Time flexibility seems to be one of the most contentious issues and areas of conflict in industrial relations in Poland today. There is strong trade union opposition to flexible working arrangements, which they have fought with varying degrees of success. In one of the foreign household appliance companies they managed to stop working 12 hours 6 days a week before the pandemic. However, there is room for numerical flexibility in the form of agency workers, especially during peak production periods and/or at weekends (sometimes called "weekend workers"). Trade union attitudes to the use of agency workers are generally negative, although some acknowledge that they are sometimes indispensable; "without them, production would have stopped", as a representative of a domestic appliance manufacturer put it. Some unions have concluded company agreements on the limits of temporary labour. They try to avoid differentiating between agency workers and company employees in terms of working conditions and financial remuneration (e.g. by placing the former in a lower wage bracket), and thus to avoid competition between them. Nevertheless, there are considerable sectoral and company differences, confirming the findings of Drahokoupil et al. (2015) that flexibility issues are handled differently even between plants of the same automotive TNCs in CE.

Unsurprisingly, trade union representatives believe that their organisations are important for workers and negotiate collective agreements that cover pay, benefits, promotion and working hours. They make it possible to achieve better conditions than the minimum requirements laid down in national legislation. There have been attempts to sign a sectoral agreement in the aircraft industry, but these have failed because of significant regional wage differentials. The general position of trade unions in the country is considered to be relatively weak, although some trade union colleagues are described as "fat cats", referring to those in the state-owned coal industry in Upper Silesia. Again, there are significant differences between companies in terms of management–union relations, with unions feeling marginalised by some employers. This may depend on the general company strategy, but even more on the personal characteristics and attitudes of managers, which are reflected in mutual trust, the union's access to information etc. Collective disputes are most often about pay. Industrial action such as strikes is rare, although it does take place; for example, at the bus manufacturer Solaris in 2022.

The level of wages and salaries differs between foreign-owned and nationally owned manufacturers. The former also use more temporary workers, but this may be related to their larger size. The origin of the TNCs also matters. In general, German employers seem to have the best industrial relations, whereas Korean employers have a worse reputation. This was also illustrated by Maciejewska (2016), who showed serious labour disputes, extensive use of temporary labour recruited in areas of high unemployment, and anti-union behaviour in the LG electronics assembly in Poland a decade ago.

Employment conditions and upgrading processes

Industrial upgrading should be linked to a strong permanent workforce and broad skills development. Both interviewed managers and trade union leaders emphasise that skilled labour, both factory workers and engineers, is the main strength of manufacturing firms and the key factor of their economic success in Poland. Thus, product and process upgrading can manifest itself in companies' labour policies. This link is even more evident in the current situation of labour shortages. It takes a long time to train employees in factories with advanced technology that manufacture complex products, and stabilising and recruiting a quality workforce requires attractive wages and other benefits, personal development prospects and good industrial relations. At the same time, there is less need for unskilled and semi-skilled labour in such plants. On the other hand, there may be little or no upgrading, with greater reliance on substitutable temporary workers. This was expressed by a trade union representative from the automotive supplier in Lublin: "There are companies that want to invest in their employees and keep them, while others take people from work agencies without any ties to the plant." The CEO of a manufacturer of premium household appliances said that if you rely on low-cost temporary and immigrant labour, then "in the medium and long term you are preventing yourself from developing more automated and sophisticated production".

There are obvious differences between industrial sectors in this respect, reflecting their technological and market characteristics. The dominance of a "high road" of development, combined with extensive training and on-the-job learning of a stable workforce, is most evident in the aircraft industry and some automotive manufacturers. In domestic appliance manufacturing, Miele and

Diehl stand out in this regard. There is also considerable variation according to company strategy. "There is no place in the company strategy for temporary workers," said a manager in an aircraft supplier. Several trade union leaders argue that the difficulties in the labour market make employees more important, which helps in negotiating wage increases. The response to labour shortages can include increased investment in advanced technology, greater automation and skilled workers, but sometimes also continued efforts to cut costs by seeking new low-cost labour and thus limited upgrading.

The link between industrial upgrading and the use of temporary and foreign labour in automotive firms in Poland was examined by Domański et al. (2024). They used stepwise regression and independent variables representing firm-specific characteristics (e.g. firm size, ownership, production and non-production competences, management strategies) and location-specific characteristics derived from a CATI questionnaire survey conducted in 2020 among 197 automotive firms (the sampling frame included 855 firms, the response rate was 23%). The average share of temporary workers in the sample was 7.4% and of foreign labour 8.7%. The analysis confirms that large and foreign-owned enterprises tend to hire more temporary workers. Their share decreases with the increasing role of automation and robotisation, as well as with the impact of EU environmental policy on companies' operations in Poland. Unexpectedly, managers' belief in the importance of Industry 4.0 solutions is positively correlated with the use of temporary workers, which may be due to the fact that they are both typical of large firms. More foreign workers are found in large enterprises and in those that emphasise the strong influence of the policy of the entire corporation on activities in Poland, which may imply pressure on low costs. On the other hand, higher levels of automation and robotisation, higher quality requirements, broader competences in product design and supplier management, and a greater share of exports are associated with fewer foreign employees. Surprisingly, the location in metropolitan and non-metropolitan areas is not significant. However, the share of temporary workers is higher in companies located in major urban agglomerations, where competition among employers is more intense. But this is not the case for foreign workers.

Overall, both quantitative and qualitative analyses confirm the interdependence between industrial upgrading and the limited use of temporary agency workers at company level. The employment of foreign workers is also linked to company characteristics and strategies.

Conclusions

The attributes of the labour force have been important determinants of FDI and the growth of Polish and CE manufacturing. They offered a wide availability of well-qualified and motivated labour, the cost of which was significantly lower than in the West, while allowing a steady increase in productivity and high product quality. However, there have been significant changes in the labour market situation in recent decades.

The post-socialist transformation in Poland, which lasted about 15 years, involved radical economic restructuring that led to the loss of many manufacturing jobs. The relative ease of finding workers at a time of high unemployment allowed manufacturers to benefit from faster productivity than wage growth. This, together with employers' drive for flexibility, also encouraged the emergence of temporary work.

Today's conditions are fundamentally different. The country has the highest increase in manufacturing jobs in the EU, very low unemployment and real wage growth well above productivity gains. So, there is no race to the bottom in wages and industrial relations, which is often attributed to growing emerging economies. This is underpinned by a widespread labour shortage in Poland, which means that employers have to compete for workers; trade union activity also plays a role. Moreover, foreign companies by and large represent the upper segment of the labour market in terms of pay and working conditions. All this applies to large and medium-sized manufacturers; conditions in small enterprises may be different.

Yet there are temporary agency workers who form the inferior, insecure segment of the labour market, where an increasing number of immigrants are filling the gap. Their weaker position is manifested in a lack of job security, long working hours and time flexibility, rather than in lower pay. The competition between domestic and foreign workers is not so much over jobs, but over the scope of responsibilities and the time regime. Time regime is an important area of conflict in many companies.

There are, of course, differences between sectors and companies. The aircraft, automotive and household appliance industries tend to be among the better employers, while electronics may offer less favourable conditions, where extreme reliance on agency workers has previously been documented in several countries, including Hungary and Poland (Maciejewska, 2016; Schipper, 2016). Meszmann's (2019) study of Ukrainian workers in Hungarian electronics showed their tendency to work long hours, which has been confirmed by our research in Poland. Krzywdzinski (2017) found significant differences in skill requirements and forms of employment contracts between German and CE automotive suppliers in 2015–2016, while Olejniczak (2019) demonstrated long-term employment, skill development and positive image among Japanese automotive subsidiaries, especially in Poland.

A "high road" in terms of employment conditions, expressed in a large, stable core of production workers and better pay, tends to be associated with greater industrial upgrading of sectors (mainly aircraft and, more selectively, automotive) and firms. In contrast, extensive use of temporary agency workers is an element of a "low road", which can undermine a move towards high value-added products and non-production competences, and hence the long-term competitiveness of manufacturing firms.

All in all, the expansion of Polish manufacturing in recent decades and its increased role in European production networks have been closely linked to the employment situation. Employers have found favourable labour conditions for their development in Poland, which initially entailed high unemployment and precarious forms of work, but in the long run has also proved beneficial for the vast majority of manufacturing workers, as reflected in job stability and real wage growth. Therefore, industrial development here cannot be considered to rest on social dumping. Nevertheless, there are significant differences between sectors and companies in this respect. This is also evident in the relationship between industrial upgrading processes and employment conditions in different firms, confirming the interdependence between economic and social upgrading (Barrientos et al., 2011) and the crucial role of company strategies (Fold & Nylandsted Larsen, 2011; Drahokoupil et al., 2016). The competitiveness of Polish manufacturing based on low costs is gradually disappearing, even though wages are still nominally well below Western levels. Several authors have emphasised that labour costs are becoming a less important determinant of development in CE with more advanced technology and higher capital costs (Drahokoupil et al., 2015; Szalavetz & Sass, 2023). Labour scarcity leads to increased recruitment of women as well as migrant workers in manufacturing jobs, and its impact on future investment and development is particularly interesting in this context.

Notes

1 The non-standard forms of employment were perceived as a business-friendly solution in CE countries and could be accompanied by circumvention or violation of labour code by some employers (Muszyński, 2020), in construction and services in particular (Keryk, 2017).

2 The picture for the two latter sectors may be distorted by a small number of large Polish firms.

References

Barrientos, S., Gereffi, G., & Rossi, A. (2011). Economic and social upgrading in global production networks: A new paradigm for a changing world. *International Labour Review*, 150(3–4), 319–340.

Buckley, M., McPhee, S., & Rogaly, B. (2017). Labour geographies on the move: Migration, migrant status and work in the 21st century. *Geoforum*, 78, 153–158.

Clibborn, S. (2015). Why undocumented immigrant workers should have workplace rights. *Economic and Labour Relations Review*, 26(3), 465–473.

Domański, B. (2001). Poland: Labour and the relocation of manufacturing from the EU. In G. Gradev (Ed.), *CEE countries in EU companies' strategies of industrial restructuring and relocation* (pp. 21–49). Brussels: European Trade Union Institute.

Domański, B., Micek, G., & Świgost-Kapocsi, A. (2024). Temporary and foreign labourforce vs. industrial upgrading in the semi-periphery: High or low road of Polish manufacturing? *Prace Geograficzne*, forthcoming.

Drahokoupil, J., Andrijasevic, R., & Sacchetto, D. (Eds.). (2016). *Flexible workforces and low profit margins: Electronics assembly between Europe and China*. Brussels: European Trade Union Institute.

Drahokoupil, J., Myant, M., & Domonkos, S. (2015). The politics of flexibility: Employment practices in automotive multinationals in Central and Eastern Europe. *European Journal of Industrial Relations*, 21(3), 223–240.

Exact Systems. (2023). *MotoBarometer. Moods in the automotive industry in Europe*. Częstochowa: Exact Systems. https://motobarometer.com/.

Fold, N., & Nylandsted Larsen, M. (2011). Upgrading of smallholder agro-food production in Africa: The role of lead firm strategies and new markets. *International Journal of Technological Learning, Innovation and Development*, 4(1–3), 39–66.

ILO. (2016). *Non-standard employment around the world: Understanding challenges, shaping prospects*. Geneva: ILO.

ILO. (2021). *Global Wage Report 2020–21: Factsheet for the European Union*. Geneva: ILO.

JETRO. (2023). Survey on business conditions of Japanese-affiliated companies in Europe. Tokyo: Japan External Trade Organization (JETRO) Overseas Research Department. https://www.jetro.go.jp/ext_images/en/reports/survey/pdf/2022/Europe2022_EN.pdf.

Jürgens, U., & Krzywdzinski, M. (2016). *New worlds of work: Varieties of work in car factories in the BRIC countries*. Oxford: Oxford University Press.

Kapitsinis, N., & Gialis, S. (2023). The spatial division of precarious labour across the European Union regions: A composite index analysis of the 2008/2009 global economic crisis effects and COVID-19 initial implications. *European Urban and Regional Studies*, 30(4), 380–403.

Keryk, M. (2017). Working in Poland: Violations of the labour rights of Ukrainian migrants in the construction and services sectors. Visegrad Fund and Government of the Netherlands.

Krzywdzinski, M. (2017). Automation, skill requirements, and labor use strategies: High-wage and low-wage approaches to high-tech manufacturing in the automotive industry. *New Technology, Work and Employment*, 32(3), 247–267.

Lewandowski, P., & Kamińska, A. (2014). *In-work poverty in Poland: Diagnosis and possible remedies*. Warsaw: Institute of Structural Research.

Lewandowski, P., Madoń, K., & Winkler, D. (2023). The role of global value chains for worker tasks and wage inequality. IBS Working Paper, 05/2023. Warsaw: Institute of Structural Research.

Maciejewska, M. (2016). 'Union busting is disgusting': Labour conflicts at LG Corporation in Poland. In J. Drahokoupil, R. Andrijasevic, & D. Sacchetto (Eds.), *Flexible workforces and low profit margins: Electronics assembly between Europe and China* (pp. 187–203). Brussels: European Trade Union Institute.

Meszmann, T. (2019). Snakes or ladders? Job quality assessment among temp workers from Ukraine in Hungarian electronics. *Central and Eastern European Migration Review*, 8(1), 75–93.

Ministerstwo Rodziny i Polityki Społecznej. (2023). *Informacja o działalności agencji zatrudnienia w 2022 r*. Warsaw: MRiPS.

Mrozowicki, A., & Maciejewska, M. (2013). Conflicts at work in Poland's new capitalism: Worker resistance in a flexible work regime. In G. Gall (Ed.), *New forms of expression and conflict at work* (pp. 191–211). Basingstoke: Palgrave Macmillan.

Mrozowicki, A., & Trappmann, V. (2021). Precarity as a biographical problem? Young workers living with precarity in Germany and Poland. *Work, Employment and Society*, 35(2), 221–238.

Muszyński, K. (2020). Liberalization without major reforms: The destandardization of employment relations in Central Eastern European countries. In J. Wratny & A. Ludera-Ruszel (Eds.), *New forms of employment. Current problems and future challenges* (pp. 53–78). Wiesbaden: Springer VS.

OECD. (2015). *In it together: Why less inequality benefits all*. Paris: OECD.

Olejniczak, T. (2019). *Japońskie fabryki hybrydowe w Polsce i Europie Środkowo-Wschodniej*. Warsaw: Poltext.

Otto Work Force. (2022). *Jak pracownicy z Ukrainy oceniają pracę w Polsce?*Wrocław: Otto Work Force.

Parteka, A., & Wolszczak-Derlacz, J. (2015). Integrated sectors – diversified earnings: The (missing) impact of offshoring on wages and wage convergence in the EU27. *The Journal of Economic Inequality*, 13(3), 325–350.

Pavlínek, P. (2018). Global production networks, foreign direct investment, and supplier linkages in the integrated peripheries of the automotive industry. *Economic Geography*, 94(2), 141–165. doi:10.1080/00130095.2017.1393313.

Pavlínek, P., & Ženka, J. (2011). Upgrading in the automotive industry: Firm-level evidence from Central Europe. *Journal of Economic Geography*, 11(3), 559–586. doi:10.1093/jeg/lbq023.

Personnel Service. (2023). *Barometr Polskiego Rynku Pracy*. Wrocław: Personnel Service. https://personnelservice.pl/.

Piątkowski, M. (2018). *Europe's growth champion*. Oxford: Oxford University Press.

Randstad. (2023). *Employer brand research*. Warsaw: Randstad.

Reber, L. (2021). The cramped and crowded room: The search for a sense of belonging and emotional well-being among temporary low-wage migrant workers. *Emotion, Space and Society*, 40, 100808.

Schipper, I. (2016). Electronic assembly in Hungary: How labour law fails to protect workers. In J. Drahokoupil, R. Andrijasevic, & D. Sacchetto (Eds.), *Flexible workforces and low profit margins: Electronics assembly between Europe and China* (pp. 131–152). Brussels: European Trade Union Institute.

Scott, S., & Visser, M.A. (2022). Constraining labour: The integration dynamics of working-class horticultural migrants in rural areas of Norway, the UK and the US. *Sociologia Ruralis*, 62(1), 112–130.

Szalavetz, A., & Sass, M. (2023). Disentangling the semi-periphery: Evolutionary trajectories and perspectives of the Austrian and Hungarian automotive industries. *Post-Communist Economies*, 35(3), 211–235. doi:10.1080/14631377.2023.2171179.

Waterman, P. (2014). The international labour movement in, against and beyond, the globalized and informatized cage of capitalism and bureaucracy. *Interface*, 6(2), 35–58.

World Employment Confederation. (2022). *Economic report 2022*. Brussels: World Employment Confederation.

Zavarská, Z., Bykova, A., Grieveson, R., Hanzl-Weiss, D., & Sankot, O. (2023). Industrial policy for a new growth model: A toolbox for EUCEE countries. Research Report, No. 469. Vienna: The Vienna Institute for International Economic Studies.

8 Public Policies

Public policies provide the framework for and create the business environment, which can be defined as the set of conditions outside a firm's control that have a significant impact on how companies behave throughout their life cycle (World Bank, 2004). They are undoubtedly crucial to the upgrading processes discussed in this book. These policies are part of a wider institutional environment consisting of organisations (actors), formal institutions, legal and regulatory systems, and other "soft" elements such as norms, values or customs (North, 1990). A broader institutional perspective indicates that these conditions vary considerably not only between countries but also within them (see Chapter 6). In an evolutionary context, they are also subject to continuous change. Effective and development-friendly institutions are a necessary condition for high efficiency and competitiveness of economies (Acemoglu & Johnson, 2005).

The chapter does not attempt to give a systematic and comprehensive review of all policies and conditions. The aim is to outline public policy and the regulatory environment in post-socialist Poland related to manufacturing activity, with a particular focus on the functioning of the three industries analysed in this book. The chapter begins with an outline of the shaping of the general regulatory framework in the country, then a description of trade and foreign investment policies, with a closer look at special economic zones (SEZs) as a major incentive in this area. This is followed by a discussion of industrial, innovation and cluster policies, and then infrastructure development. Energy and environmental regulations, as well as labour and immigration policies, are considered separately. This leads to a final discussion on policy complementarities and interdependencies, prospects and challenges.

General regulatory framework

As emphasised in Chapter 2, the early post-socialist reforms implemented since 1989 proved to be crucial in the process of CE's transition from state socialism to a market economy. A new institutional order was forged through processes of liberalisation, privatisation and internationalisation, underpinned by political democratisation. These are considered to be the cornerstones of Poland's

DOI: 10.4324/9781003430117-9

economic growth since 1992 and are described in detail by Balcerowicz (1994), Kołodko (2000) and Koźmiński (2008).

Another fundamental institutional change was accession to the European Union. The process of adopting Community law took place before the formal accession in 2004, and made Poland part of the broad common regulatory framework that provides stability for economic activity. In addition, the effective use of EU funds required the development of appropriate institutional structures at national, regional and local levels (due to the decentralisation of the distribution and implementation of these funds in Poland) and was associated with the raising of accounting, legal and auditing standards, as well as the strengthening of evaluation and monitoring processes. This contributed to the general professionalisation and improvement of the quality of public authorities at all levels, creating a better investment climate in the country (Medve-Bálint & Šćepanović, 2020). At the same time, the Polish government's room for manoeuvre has been reduced in many areas, and companies operating in Poland are subject to regulations introduced at the EU level, even if they are contested locally. Since 2015, there has been greater government intervention in the national economy, including changes in tax regulations and increased social spending at the expense of lower investment in recent years (Naczyk, 2022; Feldmann & Popa, 2022).

Trade, foreign investment and SEZs

Poland had been a member of the General Agreement on Tariffs and Trade (GATT) since 1967 (from which it had withdrawn in 1950 under the influence of the Soviet Union, at which time it also gave up its membership of the World Bank and the IMF). Poland's main goal in its relations with the GATT after 1989 was to replace the 1967 accession rules with classical schedules of concessions and to include these concessions in the final agreements of the round, thus allowing Poland to join the new organisation on full terms. This happened in 1995, when the Polish Parliament passed a law ratifying the Agreement Establishing the World Trade Organisation. Formal WTO membership ended a period of incomplete and unclear presence in the GATT. WTO membership allowed Poland to develop foreign trade under rules respected by more than 160 countries. Since 1995, Poland has participated in the second phase of the Uruguay Round, accepting all the conditions resulting from its conclusion. These conditions included a reduction of the overall level of tariff protection for industrial products by at least one-third by the end of 1997 and a reduction of tariffs on agricultural and food products by 36% by the end of 2000. EU accession changed Poland's formal situation in the WTO, transferring responsibility for trade policy-making from the national to the European level. This means that negotiations with third countries and WTO members are conducted by the European Commission (Directorate General for Trade) (Skrzypczyńska, 2018).

The meandering nature of Polish trade policy before EU accession can be illustrated by the changing rules governing the car market. The opening of the

Polish economy led to huge imports of used cars in 1990–1991 in response to unmet demand for cars. In response, and in an attempt to protect the domestic market to attract foreign automotive investors, tariffs on imported cars were raised to 35% in 1992 when Fiat acquired FSM. At the same time, a small duty-free quota of 30,000–40,000 cars was introduced. The restrictive customs policies of the 1990s had to disappear with the implementation of the EU Association Agreement, but there was continued protection of local manufacturers through the imposition of excise duties on imported used cars and stricter emission standards (Kudłak et al., 2023). These barriers disappeared when Poland joined the EU. All subsequent parliamentary initiatives to curb the inflow of used cars on the basis of technical standards failed, although they were implemented in several other CE countries. This is reflected in the structure of the Polish car market, where 4.8 million new cars were registered between 2004 and 2019, while around 12 million used vehicles were imported during the same period (Kudłak et al., 2023).

Participation in the European Single Market is generally considered to be the main economic benefit of Poland's EU membership. It is estimated that the Single Market contributed an additional 1.6–2.1 percentage points of GDP growth per year in the period 2004–2020, compared to an impact of about 0.3–0.5 percentage points in the case of EU funds (Orłowski, 2020). This was mainly due to an increase in trade and an improvement in its balance (see Chapter 2). EU membership also meant the free flow of capital, which led to a reduction in its cost and greater investment. FDI brought additional capital, participation in global production networks, new technologies and management practices (Jirasavetakul & Rahman, 2018; Bruno et al., 2021).

At the beginning of the economic transformation in 1989, a government agency for attracting investment was established, which was transformed into the Polish Foreign Investment Agency in 1992 and continues to operate today under the name of the Polish Investment and Trade Agency. It worked through foreign missions to promote investment opportunities in Poland and later assisted investors in their dealings with other authorities and institutions. In the early 1990s, Poland concluded bilateral investment treaties and agreements on avoidance of double taxation with most of its major partners.

The overall pace of privatisation of state-owned enterprises, and hence the influx of foreign investors, was slower in Poland than in Hungary in the 1990s (World Bank, 1996). In some sectors, such as oil refineries, steel and pharmaceuticals, there were initial restrictions on private capital, which were later lifted. This was also the case in the financial sector, where foreign banks became an important element of its modernisation and stability, supporting the development of the Polish economy, including during the period of the 2008 financial crisis (Polański, 2017). In 2017, one of the major banks was bought back by state-controlled entities, and the same happened with some power plants. The purchase of land by foreign companies has long been subject to government approval.

Companies with foreign capital were eligible for three-year tax holidays granted by the Ministry of Finance until 1996. High unemployment, combined with painful industrial restructuring and massive layoffs, encouraged the Polish government to introduce a new regionally oriented instrument of SEZs, aimed at attracting greenfield manufacturing investment to troubled areas. The zones initially offered corporate tax exemptions for up to ten years. Other important factors that attracted foreign and domestic investors to the zones were the availability of land with infrastructure, the growing organisational efficiency of the SEZ management bodies over time and the presence of other investors. The first SEZ was established in the town of Mielec, which was plagued by unemployment after the collapse of a major aircraft manufacturer, WSK PZL-Mielec. This was followed by an SEZ in the coal and steel region of Upper Silesia. A total of 14 SEZs were created, but a change in the law in 2000 made it possible to create subzones in many other parts of the country, so they were no longer an instrument of regional policy. At the end of 2009, SEZ subzones were located in 186 towns and 311 rural municipalities. Companies operating in SEZs (2,392 permits) employed 338,000 people and invested €29.3 billion, with one-quarter of the expenditure going to the automotive industry (Ministry of Development, 2020). The largest investments came from Polish companies (23.3% of the total), followed by those from Germany (20.9%), the Netherlands (7.1%), Luxembourg (5.6%) and the USA (5.6%).

In 2018, a new instrument, the Polish Investment Zone (PIZ), was established to replace the SEZs. Since then, SEZs have not issued any new permits, and existing ones remain valid until the end of 2026. The main difference between PIZs and SEZs is that the former are not territorially limited to specific areas. The amount by which the investor can reduce its corporate income tax liability during the exemption period depends on the amount of the investment (i.e. the value of the investment expenditure or two years' labour costs), the size of the investor itself and the location. The Polish government has adopted the Guidelines on Regional State Aid for 2022–2027, which the European Commission introduced in 2021 in the form of a map specifying maximum levels of support in various regions. According to the map, state aid may vary from 0% in the city of Warsaw to 50% in the eastern regions of Poland. Decisions on support within the framework of the PIZ are taken by the managers of the existing SEZs.

Infrastructure development

One of the major challenges facing Poland at the end of state socialism was its poor transport, municipal and energy infrastructure. Substantial resources were invested in their development and modernisation, recognising their crucial role in the country's economic development and living standards. Initially, the investment was financed from national and local government sources, and then mainly from the EU Structural Funds. Poland has been the largest net beneficiary of EU funds. According to the Polish Ministry of Development Funds and Regional Policy (2022a, 2022b), between 2004 and 2022 the country received €158 billion under the Cohesion Policy and €74 billion under the Common Agricultural Policy (at the same time it contributed €77 billion to the EU budget). Most of the EU funds have been allocated to the Operational Programme Infrastructure and Environment. Political interference in the judiciary has been at the root of the Polish government's conflict with the EU in recent years and has resulted in limited access to funds, particularly under the National Reconstruction Plan.

The changes are illustrated by the growth of selected parameters of infrastructure in Poland and the associated development of housing (Table 8.1).

In the early years of transformation, limited resources for investment and other challenges (economic restructuring, unemployment) meant that most infrastructure development during this period took place at the regional and municipal levels. Local governments were involved in the construction of water supply and sewerage systems, and wastewater treatment plants. Some of them started to invest in infrastructure development in local industrial zones attracting greenfield investments, which accelerated with the availability of EU funds. The Structural Funds became the main source of financing for nationwide programmes and investments in the construction of new roads and motorways. The following years also saw investment in the modernisation of the railway network. As a result of these initiatives, Poland is now crossed by two east–west transport axes (A2 and A4 motorways) and three north–south axes (A1 motorway, S7 and S3 expressways), with further extensions underway. The construction and modernisation of national roads and motorways are defined by the National Road Construction Programme (currently in force until 2030 with a perspective until 2033). Similarly, investments in railways are outlined in the National Railway Programme until 2030 with a perspective until 2032. In contrast to the earlier focus on building transit corridors through Poland, the current programmes emphasise internal connections between sub-regional centres. In addition, the Via Carpathia transport corridor is under construction, which, while connecting Lithuania to Romania via Slovakia and Hungary, is important for stimulating growth in eastern Poland. The construction of

Table 8.1 Development of infrastructure in Poland, 1990–2022

Infrastructure	*Units*	*1990*	*2000*	*2010*	*2022*
Motorways and expressways	km	381	592	1,560	4,887
Passengers served at airports	million	2.9	5.8	20.4	41.0
Dwellings	thousand	11,022	11,845	13,470	15,575
Water supply network	thousand km	93	212	273	338
Sewage network	thousand km	26	51	108	178

Source: GUS and Civil Aviation Authority.

bypasses around many towns is currently playing an important role. EU funding has also contributed to the development of local and regional roads through regional operational programmes.

There has been a major expansion of Polish airports. As a result, the main airports in Warsaw, Kraków and Gdańsk now have multiple daily flights to all major European hubs (Frankfurt, Munich, Hamburg, London, Vienna, Zurich, Milan), significantly increasing the attractiveness of Poland, especially its metropolitan areas, for the location of non-production functions of large companies and BPO/SSC, where Poland has become a European leader. The flagship project of the outgoing government was the Central Communication Port 80 km west of Warsaw, including the construction of a new airport (for 40 million passengers by 2028) and 10 new railway lines (so-called railway spokes) converging at this location. With a change of government in December 2023, the future of this project is uncertain.

The development of maritime infrastructure is covered by A Development Programme for Polish Seaports until 2030. In 2007, the Baltic Hub Container Terminal (formerly DCT Gdańsk) was opened, which, after being expanded to a capacity of 3 million Twenty-foot Equivalent Units (TEUs), is the largest terminal on the Baltic Sea, serving large container ships and regular ocean routes, e.g. to Shanghai. After taking over some of Ukraine's foreign trade, its throughput proved insufficient, so it was decided to expand it to 4.5 million TEUs by 2024.

In 2006, it was decided to build the Liquefied Natural Gas (LNG) reloading and regasification terminal in Świnoujście, which opened in 2015. The current handling capacity of the Polish LNG terminal is 6.2 billion cubic metres per year (compared to Poland's gas consumption of 20 billion cubic metres). The terminal is being further expanded to meet growing demand. The construction of the Baltic Pipe gas pipeline connecting Poland to Denmark and Norway with a capacity of 10 billion cubic metres, which opened in 2022, as well as additional gas connectors to Germany and Slovakia contribute to increasing energy security.

As GDP and incomes have risen, so has the construction of new housing, much of it by the private sector in larger towns and their suburbs. The government supports this mainly through tax breaks, guarantees and credit subsidies. What has been lacking is an effective housing policy for low-income groups.

Reindustrialisation, sectoral and innovation policies

What we are now witnessing in Europe is a resurgence of industrial policy, understood as measures and efforts to support the development of selected industries that are considered vital for long-term economic competitiveness and/or security (Benner, 2019). This is driven by the recognition that market forces alone will not be able to meet the challenges posed by global warming and/or the growing dominance of China (Casanova & Miroux, 2020), and is also stimulated by the consequences of the COVID-19 pandemic, which require active public intervention. The renaissance of industrial policy is also linked to the pace of technological change and the growing dependence of competitiveness on innovation, which are closely linked to the scientific world and more generally to the public sphere. This brings us to innovation policy, which can be seen as a form of industrial policy. The success and technological progress of Chinese companies, strongly supported by the state, have led to the belief that industrial policy and state support can ensure continued competitiveness (Terzi et al., 2022). One of the most significant consequences of the COVID-19 pandemic was the disruption of supply chains, raising awareness of the dangerous dependence of the European and American economies on Asian (mainly Chinese) suppliers. Difficulties in the supply of microchips and shortages of essential components for pharmaceutical production reinforced the idea of reindustrialisation, which has become increasingly prominent in contemporary discourse and planning in the developed world (Ambroziak, 2015). The result is, among other things, huge subsidies offered by some governments for new industrial projects, such as the gigafactories for electric car batteries and electronics plants in Germany, made possible by the recent liberalisation of EU state aid policy.

Three main stages of industrial policy can be identified in post-socialist Poland. The foundations of a new social and economic system were laid in the early 1990s. They were mainly horizontal in nature, while industrial policy was largely focused on supporting shrinking traditional sectors, mainly coal mining, as well as some forms of market protection, e.g. for the automotive industry. The latter was abandoned with EU accession, whereas the former has survived. In the period 2004–2015, no specific industrial policy for manufacturing was introduced at the national level, but general investment incentives in the form of tax exemptions in SEZs and infrastructure provision continued. What was important during this period, however, was the integration of Polish academic institutions and companies into the European research area. Since 2016, new reindustrialisation and innovation policies have emerged.

The Strategy for Responsible Development adopted by the Polish government in 2017 outlined eight key industries for targeted development and investment incentives: aviation, defence, automotive parts manufacturing, shipbuilding, information technology, chemicals, furniture manufacturing and food processing. The plan announced the reindustrialisation of Poland and increased support for innovation. This was elaborated in the Polish Industrial Policy 2021, which was preceded by the White Paper on Industrial Development, which identified the main obstacles to industrial activity. Specific objectives include preparing a skilled workforce for the needs of a digitalised economy, automation, robotisation and digitalisation of enterprises, increasing the intensity of knowledge and technology use in the economy, and developing an algorithmic data-based economy. Special emphasis is placed on the development of artificial intelligence technologies and their implementation in key sectors of the economy. Triggering innovation processes includes the creation of regional competence centres that support networking and training activities, while the Incubator of Industry Leaders 4.0 is designed to promote collaboration with technical universities. SEZs have changed their function from being mainly developers providing land and technical infrastructure to innovation brokers. Financial support for clusters has become an important element of innovation support in Poland. There are also special programmes for selected manufacturing sectors; for example, Innomoto provides financial support for the implementation of R&D projects in the automotive sector. Another important area is labour policy, with various training programmes. Direct tax incentives for innovators include the "IP Box" tax treatment for patent and licence income, as well as tax relief for R&D expenditure, innovative employers, robotisation and prototype development. Other incentives include tax breaks for expansion, consolidation, initial public offerings and corporate philanthropy. The IP Box reduces the tax rate applicable to income derived from intellectual property rights to 5% and is expected to significantly increase private sector R&D activity (EY, 2021).

Clusters have become an important component in the implementation of territorial policies in the EU. Especially in the second half of the 2000s, the cluster concept was integrated into the mainstream strategies for promoting economic development and innovation (European Commission, 2008). The development of cluster policy in Poland is closely linked to the inspirational influence of the EU. This includes the transfer of knowledge and experience and the provision of support funds and programmes. The official governmental strategic document *Directions and Assumptions of Cluster Policy until 2020*, introduced in 2012, is acknowledged as the formal start of an autonomous cluster policy in Poland (Kryjom, 2019), which was previously considered only an element of a broader innovation policy (Dzierżanowski, 2011). As highlighted by Kwiatkowski (2023, p. 99), "two fundamental recommendations for cluster policy emerge from this document: first, to focus support on networks with the highest potential for development and economic specialisation; and second, to coordinate various development policy instruments around these networks."

An example of cluster activity related to the industries analysed in this book is Aviation Valley. Established in 2003 by leading aircraft companies with financial support from Pratt & Whitney, it has grown to include almost all major aircraft manufacturers in Poland. Aviation Valley currently comprises some 180 companies employing 35,000 people (about 83% of total employment in the Polish aircraft industry). It is a good example of a bottom-up approach that originated in south-eastern Poland and is focused on promoting the aircraft industry, supporting cooperation with universities and other research centres, and protecting the sector. Aviation Valley's short- and medium-term goals include improving the existing domestic suppliers to create a strong network of subcontractors. In addition to attracting further investment, the cluster aims to develop relationships with other European aircraft hubs.

The impact of cluster policy on the transformation of manufacturing industries varies. Joint research and development initiatives are the key aspect of the policy.

However, the effectiveness of such initiatives depends on the specific sector and cluster. Results are influenced by both formal structures and informal interactions within clusters. Similarly, although joint strategies in product distribution, service sales and collective procurement of raw materials and services are encouraged, the actual impact on operational efficiency and cost savings may vary. Undoubtedly, the policy enables broader promotional campaigns, can contribute to increased market visibility of industries and provides a platform for the exchange of ideas. Therefore, the overall impact of cluster policy presents a nuanced picture, reflecting a mix of potential benefits and specific sectoral and regional challenges (Grashof, 2021; Horzela & Olko, 2021).

National lobbying organisations play an important role in supporting and promoting the development of individual sectors in Poland. In the automotive industry this is the Polish Chamber of Automotive Industry (Polska Izba Motoryzacji) and in the household appliances sector it is APPLiA. The Polish branch of the European Committee of Domestic Equipment Manufacturers (CECED) was established in 2004. It is a Brussels-based organisation that has represented the interests of the home appliance industry since 1958. In 2018 its name was changed to APPLiA. Its members include 35 companies representing not only manufacturers, but also the distributors, of household appliances in Poland. The organisation has a particularly strong dialogue on the circular economy, energy efficiency and the impact of EU policies on the domestic market. Other important tasks include representing the industry in standardisation committees and running awareness-raising campaigns. In response to the Waste from Electrical and Electronic Equipment (WEEE) Directive, the organisation established ElektroEko S.A. Organizacja Odzysku Sprzętu Elektrycznego i Elektronicznego to manage the recycling of household appliances in the country. APPLiA's objectives include improving existing domestic suppliers to create a strong network of subcontractors by building relationships between OEMs and suppliers via, e.g. the Business Mixer during APPLiA congresses.

Energy and environmental policies in Poland

Poland is among the countries with the highest dependency on energy produced from fossil fuels in the EU, especially coal (both hard coal and lignite). The installed energy capacity of coal-fired power stations (21 GW) is second only to Germany's. Due to the influence of the strong coal-mining lobby on successive governments, the transition away from fossil fuels has been significantly delayed. Nevertheless, renewables now account for 43% of installed capacity (29 GW) and represented 24% of total electricity generation in 2023 (compared to the EU average of 35%). This illustrates the rapid pace at which the green transition is currently taking place. Much of this is the result of private investment in wind and solar photovoltaic (PV), despite formidable barriers of insufficient grid capacity to connect new dispersed energy sources and restrictive distance rules for wind turbines from 2016 (with some relief in 2023).

According to the Energy Policy of Poland until 2040 (PEP2040), the country aims to increase its energy independence by accelerating the growth of renewable energy sources, including offshore wind turbines and PVs, accompanied by the construction of nuclear power plants. The cost of investment in new power generation capacity is expected to reach nearly $170 billion by 2040. The policy is a response to historical dependence on fossil fuels and to rising energy costs associated with increasing emissions charges. Failure of this policy or a delay in its implementation could jeopardise further development and reduce Poland's attractiveness for industrial activity.

In addition to the investment required for energy production, huge sums are needed to develop the transmission networks. This is due both to the need for modernisation and to changes in the direction of energy transmission. Historically, power generation capacity has been concentrated in southern Poland, reflecting the distribution of fuels and the concentration of municipal and industrial consumers. Currently, wind farms are being built and planned mainly in northern Poland, including the Baltic Sea coast, due to more favourable wind conditions and lower population density. For the same reason, nuclear power plants will also be located here. This implies the need to transport energy from the north to the south of the country. And the implementation of wholesale energy market integration at EU level is underway, requiring the upgrading of the national grid. In addition, the increasing role of prosumers in electricity production (mainly PV) requires the development of local grids and the management of temporary energy surpluses. There is a risk that the costs of the energy transition will only be partly covered by EU funds and government resources, with the rest being borne by energy consumers. Given the tendency to protect households from rising energy prices, the increase is likely to fall more heavily on commercial consumers. This may encourage even greater investment in wind and PV farms, which provide cheaper electricity for large manufacturing users but which smaller companies cannot afford, making them more vulnerable to high energy prices.

Despite official media and political controversy in Poland over EU energy and climate policy in recent years, the country is adopting regulations and amending relevant laws to implement EU directives. Since November 2023, the amended Renewable Energy Sources Act (RED III) has been in force, which promotes renewable energy. Among other things, it defines and facilitates the operation of energy clusters, which are recognised as an effective way of supporting decentralised energy. These are associations of energy producers and local government units that are exempted from the renewable energy levy, the cogeneration fee and the obligations related to certificates of origin of electricity within the support system. There are already over 70 such clusters in Poland, and it is estimated that their number will exceed 300 by 2029. The regulations also support the construction of power plants based on renewable energy sources. This is an important step in line with the EU's Fit for 55 package, which aims to reduce net greenhouse gas emissions in Europe by at least 55% by 2030, as confirmed by the REPowerEU plan.

Climate policy and its challenges are intertwined with the issue of electromobility. The Electromobility Development Plan announced by the Polish government in 2017 set a target of one million electric vehicles (EVs) on Polish roads and 6,000 charging points by 2025, with at least 30% of the value added in the production of EVs generated domestically, together with the expansion of the manufacturing and use of electric buses. The plan included several groups of actions and intentions. The Electromobility and Alternative Fuels Act was passed. Changes in the law were intended to encourage individual purchases of electric cars, including VAT exemptions, higher depreciation allowances, the ability for electric cars to use bus lanes and their free parking in paid parking zones. In 2021, subsidies for the purchase of electric vehicles were introduced as part of the My Electric Car programme – around €6,000 for private buyers and up to €16,000 for businesses (including light commercial vehicles (LCVs)). At the same time, however, the maximum purchase price of a new vehicle that qualifies for support has been set at such a low level (recently around €60,000) that most customers who can afford such a purchase cannot benefit from these subsidies when buying mid-range or premium cars. The programme has had a relatively limited impact: only 42,600 battery electric vehicles (BEVs) were registered in Poland by July 2023, and their sales accounted for only 5% of the new car market. The Green Public Transport programme, which allows municipalities to receive a subsidy of up to 90% of the cost of purchasing a new electric or hydrogen bus, has proved more successful, leading to the purchase of 530 such vehicles. Additional generous support is also available through regional programmes using EU cohesion funds. As a result, public transport in many cities already has a significant share of zero-emission vehicles. The government's ambition was also to start production of a Polish electric car, the Izera. This is the task of ElectroMobility Poland, a new company set up by state-controlled energy corporations. After several deadline extensions and delays, the current status of the project is that the car will be redesigned by Italy's Pinifarina and manufactured on the platform provided by China's Geely. The construction of the plant in Jaworzno in the Śląskie voivodeship had not begun by the end of 2023.

Other important EU-level regulations affecting the functioning of the manufacturing sector that are already in force or will come into effect in the near future include the Emissions Trading System (ETS) and the related Carbon Border Adjustment Mechanism (CBAM). The recently announced ETS II Directive changes the rules for monitoring emissions from 2025 and introduces higher emission charges from 2027, when it will be fully operational. It also establishes new rules for auctioning allowances, reduces the number of exemptions and extends the charging system to air and maritime transport and small industrial enterprises. In addition, part of the fees will go to the EU-managed Social Climate Fund, rather than to the budgets of the contributing countries. The aim of the ETS II is to reduce greenhouse gas emissions by 42% by 2032 compared to 2005 levels. This is linked to the introduction of the CBAM scheme from 2026. The CBAM is designed to levy charges on imports into the

EU of raw materials and components associated with significant emissions of pollutants, such as cement, steel, aluminium, fertilisers, hydrogen and electricity. This measure aims to prevent importers, as a way to avoid such charges, increasing the share of imports of energy-intensive semi-finished products from countries with weaker environmental legislation. Importers will have to pay the same amount per tonne of CO_2 emitted as if the goods were manufactured in the EU. The price of the allowances will be determined by the average weekly cost of the auction of emission allowances under the ETS. However, this regulatory framework may be extremely unfavourable to some industries that currently rely on such supplies for a variety of market reasons. The imposition of charges on components, while exempting finished assembled products, may lead to a shift in the location of production. Instead of sourcing steel, aluminium and other materials outside the EU, it may become more profitable to manufacture and assemble finished products there and import them into the EU. This is known as "carbon leakage". This regulation would be particularly challenging for domestic appliance manufacturers, certain segments of the automotive industry and producers of construction materials. APPLiA puts the potential cost of the proposed regulation at €580 million per year in the EU, while the CEPII think-tank suggests that this could rise by 30% by 2040 if all ETS sectors are covered by CBAM. The industry's access to steel, which is the main input in the production of household appliances, is also seen as problematic. The caps within the ETS are seen as too low, forcing producers to pay a 25% out-of-quota levy (APPLiA, 2023a).

Regulations on recycling (WEEE), ecodesign and fluorinated gases (F-gases) are important for the manufacture of domestic appliances. The first version of WEEE legislation, introduced in 2003, places the responsibility for managing waste from electrical and electronic equipment on the manufacturer or distributor of such equipment. It requires them to set up a collection infrastructure for WEEE in such a way that "users of electrical and electronic equipment from private households should have the possibility of returning WEEE at least free of charge". APPLiA Polska members are responsible for organising and financing the collection of approximately 75% of the WEEE market in Poland. However, there are concerns about this system because WEEE is being channelled through only a few large retailers. This leads to inequality and high prices for WEEE. In addition, the industry is starting to compete with others (e.g. producers and importers of PV panels) for waste equipment. Waste PV panels will only be available for recycling in a few years and the producers and importers can fulfil their WEEE collection obligations by collecting household appliances. In addition, the Ecodesign for Sustainable Products Regulation (ESPR) (European Commission, 2022) aims to ensure that ecodesign principles contribute to sustainability, with an emphasis on circularity. It will further strengthen ecodesign requirements related to material efficiency, including durability, reliability, reparability, upgradeability, recyclability, hazardous substances, recycled content and design for disassembly. The ongoing evaluation of these directives and the announced increase in recycling targets are causing concern among European appliance manufacturers (APPLiA, 2023b). The industry is already struggling to meet current standards at a lower level and there are fears that this could lead to increased imports of household appliances from outside the EU, undermining local production.

Labour market and immigration policies

One of the main concerns of public policy in the early period of post-socialist transformation in the 1990s, when massive unemployment occurred, was the number of jobs. This was reflected in regulations aimed at protecting jobs through employment guarantees and levels of financial compensation in the event of redundancy (see Chapter 7), and at encouraging the creation of new jobs. The latter included measures to support local entrepreneurship and incentives for large investors, such as the SEZs in high-unemployment areas discussed above.

The opening up of the EU labour market to people from the new member states resulted in a large labour migration to Western Europe. In the short term, this eased pressure on the Polish labour market, helping to reduce unemployment, and provided financial transfers from Poles working in Germany, the UK and other countries, estimated at €3.5–4.5 billion per year according to the Polish National Bank. In the longer term, return migration, especially of educated people who have acquired new skills and work experience, enriches the Polish labour market. On the other hand, the outflow of mainly young people has exacerbated the demographic crisis and the current labour shortage.

At the same time, the mass participation of young people and students in the Erasmus/Erasmus+ academic exchange programmes has also promoted education and knowledge transfer. In 2019 alone, 45,688 students studied abroad through this programme. Labour and educational migration contributes to the creation of networks and connections, as well as to the reduction of cultural distance, which can have a positive impact on upgrading processes in various economic activities. Last but not least, EU funds support the development of human capital through a wide range of educational projects, skills development and entrepreneurship initiatives.

Poland's immigration policy tends to support the labour market with three-year and five-year work permits (one-quarter of all work permits in the EU for non-EU nationals are issued in Poland) and a simplified procedure. Since 2015, the latter has allowed people from six Eastern European countries (Ukraine, Belarus, Russia, Armenia, Moldova and Georgia) to be employed for up to two years if the employer submits an ex-post declaration to the local labour office on the assignment of work to a foreigner. The 2018 revision also introduced a new work permit, the seasonal work permit, which allows legal employment for up to nine months in sectors such as agriculture, horticulture, tourism and related industries. In March 2022, a law on support for Ukrainian citizens in light of Russia's invasion of Ukraine came into force. The law grants legal residence and employment rights in Poland for up to 18 months to Ukrainian citizens displaced by the conflict. Employers are now only required to notify regional authorities when hiring Ukrainian workers. Between February 2022 and September 2023, the Ministry of Family and Social Policy reported over 900,000 cases of use of the procedure to facilitate access to the labour market for refugees from Ukraine.

Trade union activity is guaranteed and protected by law, but strike rules are more prohibitive than in some Western countries. Successive Polish governments have been criticised for liberalising the labour market, which has allowed the widespread introduction of non-standard forms of temporary employment, and for weak labour inspection mechanisms (Muszyński, 2020). On the other hand, employers' associations have complained about significant increases in the minimum wage in the country in recent years.

Conclusions

The development of the Central European economies and the growth of their manufacturing industries are the result of numerous internal and external factors. Institutional conditions play a very important role. They are part of a complex system of interdependencies in which factors, instruments, policies and regulations at different scales, from global to local, are intertwined. What have proved crucial for Poland and other CE economies have been the creation of an enabling environment for their development within a pluralistic political system, stability and access to the EU's large Single Market, and improvements in infrastructure. Horizontal policies have been crucial, while industrial (sectoral) policies have been of secondary importance. However, appropriate sectoral policies are likely to play an increasingly important role in the future.

It should be recognised that different policies – energy, migration, education, taxation, trade, climate, innovation etc. – are interlinked and their priorities can sometimes coincide and sometimes diverge. Moreover, the interests of producers do not necessarily coincide with those of consumers, and certain horizontal solutions may benefit one industry but harm others, or benefit large companies but disadvantage small ones. It is therefore essential for governments and regulators to be aware of the need for complementarity between these policies. From the perspective of companies and their operational strategies, navigating in an environment of multiple policies and increasing fragmentation in a once globalised world will require even greater consideration of different country contexts and constraints, and tailoring approaches to fit those markets. One size fits all will become much more difficult. Under these conditions, the development and successful cross-border expansion of firms may be an indicator of industrial upgrading in the future. What should distinguish core economies from the periphery is precisely the ability to design and implement appropriately complementary policies that take into account many dimensions of the complexity of the surrounding world. The best test of such policies is sustainable development, leading to higher living standards, inclusive growth, a better environment and resilience.

The continuation of Poland and Central European economies on their current development path – in the context of emerging geopolitical, energy or technological challenges – is by no means an obvious scenario. On the one hand, these challenges may open up new opportunities (e.g. reindustrialisation, nearshoring, green economy), but on the other hand there is a risk that the CE countries are not fully prepared for them, among other things in terms of regulation. This is where the crucial role of well-targeted policies and their instruments comes into play, enabling several challenges to be addressed in the longer term: the growing role of electromobility and its impact on the shape and functioning of the automotive industry; the progress of digitalisation and robotisation (Industry 4.0); the green transformation and the quest for climate neutrality; the dramatic demographic changes (ageing societies, migration) and their impact on the labour market (European Commission, 2020; Landesmann & Stöllinger, 2020). These challenges in countries that owe their development to industrial specialisation are particularly serious and perhaps only comparable to those faced by the German economy, to which the economies of Poland and the CE countries are strongly linked (Leal et al., 2019). Well-designed public policies also need to take into account various local, European and global contextual factors – especially in light of China's industrial expansion, which is becoming a major player and is establishing a foothold in Europe, especially in CE. National policies should aim at enhancing the innovation potential and human resources for modern industries and the research sector. This can be done directly by allocating funds for these purposes, and indirectly by fiscal policies that encourage companies to invest in modern solutions, research and skills development, as well as through immigration policies. Finally, a rapid energy transition to renewable energy sources is a must for maintaining and further upgrading Poland's manufacturing sector in the coming decade.

References

Acemoglu, D., & Johnson, S. (2005). Unbundling institutions. *Journal of Political Economy*, 113(5), 949–995.

Ambroziak, A.A. (2015). Europeanization of industrial policy: Towards re-industrialisation. In P. Stanek & K. Wach (Eds.), *Europeanization processes from the mesoeconomic perspective: Industries and policies* (pp. 61–94). Kraków: Uniwersytet Ekonomiczny w Krakowie.

APPLiA. (2023a). Joint industry statement calling for termination of EU steel safeguard measures. APPLiA Policy Papers. Brussels: APPLiA. Retrieved November 20, 2023, from https://www.applia-europe.eu/policy-papers-applia/joint-industry-statement-calling-for-termination-of-eu-steel-safeguard-measures.

APPLiA. (2023b). How the ESPR can shape the next generation of sustainable products. Brussels: APPLiA. Retrieved November 20, 2023, from https://www.applia-europe.eu/applia-event-reports/how-the-espr-can-shape-the-next-generation-of-sustainable-products.

Balcerowicz, L. (1994). Understanding postcommunist transitions. *Journal of Democracy*, 5(4), 75–89.

Benner, M. (2019). Industrial policy in the EU and its neighbourhood: Learning from policy experimentation. *Economies*, 7(2), 44. doi:10.3390/economies7020044.

Bruno, R.L., Campos, N.F., & Estrin, S. (2021). The effect on foreign direct investment of membership in the European Union. *JCMS: Journal of Common Market Studies*, 59(4), 802–821.

Casanova, L., & Miroux, A. (2020). *The era of Chinese multinationals: Competing for global dominance*. Elsevier: Academic Press. doi:10.1016/C2018-0-01595-9.

Dzierżanowski, M. (2011). *Raport otwarcia nt. polskiej polityki klastrowej opracowany na potrzeby prac Grupy roboczej ds. polityki klastrowej w ramach przedsięwzięcia Polskiej Agencji Rozwoju Przedsiębiorczości „Polskie klastry i polityka klastrowa"*. Warsaw: Polska Agencja Rozwoju Przedsiębiorczości.

European Commission. (2008). *Communication from the Commission to the European Parliament, the Council, the European Economic and Social Committee and the Committee of the Regions: Towards world-class clusters in the European Union* (SEC (2008) 2637). Brussels: European Commission.

European Commission. (2020). *Communication from the Commission to the European Parliament, the Council, the European Economic and Social Committee and the Committee of the Regions: A new industrial strategy for Europe* (COM(2020) 120 final). Brussels: European Commission.

European Commission. (2022). *Communication from the Commission to the European Parliament, the Council, the European Economic and Social Committee and the Committee of the Regions: On making sustainable products the norm* (COM(2022) 140 final). Brussels: European Commission.

EY. (2021). Ernst & Young tax news update, global edition November 24, 2021: 2021-6251. Warsaw: EY Doradztwo Podatkowe Krupa sp.k. Retrieved November 20, 2023, from https://globaltaxnews.ey.com/news/2021-6251-poland-new-tax-incentives-package-for-investments-in-poland-from-1-january-2022.

Feldmann, M., & Popa, M. (2022). Populism and economic policy: Lessons from Central and Eastern Europe. *Post-Communist Economies*, 34(2), 219–245. doi:10.1080/14631377.2022.2029253.

Grashof, N. (2021). Putting the watering can away – Towards a targeted (problem-oriented) cluster policy framework. *Research Policy*, 50(9), 104335. doi:10.1016/j.respol.2021.104335.

Horzela, A., & Olko, S. (2021). The role of cluster policy in shaping regional competitiveness: The case of Poland. *European Research Studies Journal*, 24(4), 444–463.

Jirasavetakul, L., & Rahman, J. (2018). Foreign direct investment in new member states of the EU and Western Balkans: Taking stock and assessing prospects. IMF Working Paper WP/18/187. Washington, DC: International Monetary Fund.

Kołodko, G.-W. (2000). *From shock to therapy: The political economy of post-socialist transformation*. Oxford: Oxford University Press.

Koźmiński, A.-K. (2008). *How it all happened. Essays in political economy of transition*. Warsaw: Difin.

Kryjom, P. (2019). *Raport polityka klastrowa wdrażana w regionach w latach 2014-2019; na potrzeby grupy roboczej ds. polityki klastrowej*. Warsaw: Polska Agencja Rozwoju Przedsiębiorczości.

Kudłak, R., Kołsut, B., & Kisiała, W. (2023). Driving gears of car ownership transformation. In B. Kołsut & T. Stryjakiewicz (Eds.), *The economic geography of the car market: The automobile revolution in an emerging economy* (pp. 24–43). London: Routledge.

Kwiatkowski, T. (2023). *Kapitał społeczny i wyposażenie instytucjonalne jako czynniki sukcesu regionalnych polityk klastrowych*. Kraków: Institute of Geography and Spatial Management, Jagiellonian University.

Landesmann, M.A., & Stöllinger, R. (2020). The European Union's industrial policy. In A. Oqubay, C. Cramer, H.-J. Chang, & R. Kozul-Wright (Eds.), *The Oxford handbook of industrial policy* (pp. 621–660). Oxford: Oxford University Press. doi:10.1093/oxfordhb/9780198862420.013.23.

Leal, J., Lehmann, R., Marc, B., Wollmershäuser, T., & Wozniak, P. (2019). The weakness of the German car industry and its sectoral and global impacts. EconPol Policy Brief 18-2019. Munich: IFO Institute – Leibniz Institute for Economic Research at the University of Munich.

Medve-Bálint, G., & Šćepanović, V. (2020). EU funds, state capacity and the development of transnational industrial policies in Europe's eastern periphery. *Review of International Political Economy*, 27(5), 1063–1082. doi:10.1080/09692290.2019.1646669.

Ministry of Development. (2020). *Informacja o realizacji ustawy o specjalnych strefach ekonomicznych. Stan na 31 grudnia 2019 r.* Druk sejmowy 397. Warsaw: Sejm Rzeczypospolitej Polskiej.

Ministry of Development Funds and Regional Policy. (2022a). *Impact of cohesion policy on the socio-economic development of Poland and regions in the years 2004–2020*. Warsaw: Ministry of Development Funds and Regional Policy.

Ministry of Development Funds and Regional Policy. (2022b). Summing up 2022: More than EUR 76 billion from the cohesion policy, approval of programmes by the EC and disbursement of advances. Warsaw: Ministry of Development Funds and Regional Policy. https://www.gov.pl/web/funds-regional-policy/summing-up-2022-more-than-eur-76-billion-from-the-cohesion-policy-approval-of-programmes-by-the-ec-and-disbursement-of-advances.

Muszyński, K. (2020). Liberalization without major reforms: The destandardization of employment relations in Central Eastern European countries. In J. Wratny & A. Ludera-Ruszel (Eds.), *New forms of employment: Current problems and future challenges* (pp. 53–78). Wiesbaden: Springer VS.

Naczyk, M. (2022). Taking back control: Comprador bankers and managerial developmentalism in Poland. *Review of International Political Economy*, 29(5), 1650–1674. doi:10.1080/09692290.2021.1924831.

North, D.C. (1990). *Institutions, institutional change and economic performance*. Cambridge: Cambridge University Press.

Orłowski, W.M. (2020). Trajectories of the economic transition in Central and Eastern Europe. In G. Gorzelak (Ed.), *Social and economic development in Central and Eastern Europe* (pp. 11–34). London: Routledge.

Polański, Z. (2017). Stabilization policies and structural developments: Poland and the crises of 1929 and 2008. CASE Working Papers 9. Warsaw: CASE – Center for Social and Economic Research.

Skrzypczyńska, J. (2018). Polska w GATT/WTO. *Przegląd Politologiczny*, (1), 83–91.

Terzi, A., Singh, A., & Sherwood, M. (2022). Industrial policy for the 21st century: Lessons from the past. European Economy - Discussion Papers 157. Brussels: Directorate General Economic and Financial Affairs (DG ECFIN), European Commission.

World Bank. (1996). *World development report: From plan to market*. New York: World Bank.

World Bank. (2004). *World development report 2005: A better investment climate for everyone*. Washington, DC: World Bank.

9 Industrial Upgrading

Factors, Mechanisms and Effects

The fundamental question of the changing role of Polish manufacturing in global production networks (GPNs), which is discussed in the book, requires addressing three main issues. Firstly, the extent to which the processes of change observed in recent decades and their effects represent a continuation of existing structures and mechanisms of development or their radical transformation. The central question posed in this context is whether these processes can be regarded as upgrading towards the manufacturing of more sophisticated high value-added products, new technologies and the development of non-production functions. This is followed by the question of what economic, social and political factors underlie the reproduction of these structures and mechanisms or bring about major changes. The final problem is whether these can be explained in terms of the core–periphery dichotomy or its various elaborations.

With the end of state socialism, Central European countries were rapidly integrated into wider European and global production networks and then politically joined the European Union. This was reflected in capital transfers in the form of foreign direct investment (FDI) and, above all, in close trade links between Western Europe and Central Europe (CE). To what extent and how has this changed CE's peripheral position in the European economy and in manufacturing activity in particular?

We can begin by juxtaposing the characteristics of contemporary Polish manufacturing with those commonly ascribed to the periphery discussed in Chapter 1.

There is little doubt that the low density of economic activity, low level of supporting organisations and limited capacity of local firms, as well as limited economies of scale and scope (low diversity of products and services offered), are no longer representative of Polish manufacturing. As a result, disembedded foreign affiliates without local linkages and thus limited local content and multiplier effects, combined with the lack of an appropriate institutional environment for business services, are no longer typical. Specialisation in simple, low value-added activities, which was common in the 1990s, is still found in many firms, although there are many others manufacturing complex, high value-added products. Several sectors, including those analysed in detail in previous chapters, are dominated by foreign transnational corporations (TNCs),

DOI: 10.4324/9781003430117-10

implying dependence on external capital and imported technology. Outward FDI remains significantly lower than in Western European economies. At the same time, successful domestic brand-name manufacturers are among the leading firms in many industries, including export-oriented ones, such as the manufacture of furniture, food products, rubber and plastic products, chemicals, metal products, printing and the reproduction of recorded media. There has also been the endogenous development of a large number of small and medium-sized enterprises (SMEs), most of which serve the domestic market and some of which are integrated into wider globalising production networks. Research and development (R&D) activity, despite its dynamic growth in recent years, is clearly much less advanced than the country's production capacity. Labour costs are still significantly lower than in Western Europe in nominal terms, but this does not mean that the competitive advantages of Polish and, more generally, CE manufacturing are primarily based on low costs. Lower costs are part of a broader set of labour-related advantages, together with skills and motivation, as confirmed by numerous interviews with company managers and consultants to foreign investors. Much cheaper locations were available on the periphery of the EU, e.g. in Eastern Europe, Türkiye and North Africa. A race to the bottom in the form of lowering labour standards, curbing wage increases and trade union activity and/or cutting taxes in order to compete with other low-cost countries is clearly not the case in Poland; on the contrary, social upgrading has been observed in recent decades. The wider social benefits of the country's economic growth are reflected in radical reductions in the proportion of people living in poverty, income inequality and the gender gap, which are well below the EU average. All this takes place within a democratic system, and the regulatory and welfare functions of the state have been strengthened over the last decade. The social and political conditions in the CE countries are fundamentally different from those of many of the growing economies in Asia, which are characterised by income inequality, gender discrimination, child labour and lack of democracy and independent trade unions (Dünhaupt et al., 2022).

Overall, characteristics such as limited economies of scale, lack of high value-added activities, poor local linkages, together with low wages and taxes, are likely to result in limited local value creation and value capture in the periphery. Moreover, competitive advantages based on low costs are not sustainable in the long run and can easily be eroded, leading to relocation of production to other low-cost areas of the world at any time. In contrast, Poland and other CE economies have shown an impressive rate of investment in manufacturing over three decades (see Chapter 2), rising wages (Chapter 7) and increasing tax revenues. The level of reinvestment of profits by foreign investors in Poland has exceeded 40% in most years, reaching 53%–61% in 2020–2022 (Table 9.1). Moreover, there have been very few disinvestments and relocations out of the country. This indicates strong resilience despite the shocks of the 2008–2009 financial crisis, changes of government and related policy meanderings, the COVID-19 pandemic and the Russian invasion of Ukraine.

Table 9.1 Income from FDI in Poland, 2010–2022

Year	*Total income (bln PLN)*	*Share of FDI income (%)*		
		Reinvested profits	*Dividends*	*Interest*
2010	50.965	44.0	46.8	9.2
2011	54.104	39.9	50.4	9.7
2012	52.803	34.6	53.6	11.9
2013	58.236	25.3	62.3	12.4
2014	63.943	40.6	46.0	13.4
2015	67.507	43.2	44.6	12.3
2016	81.949	45.5	43.2	11.3
2017	81.220	48.1	40.5	11.5
2018	84.776	41.5	47.4	11.1
2019	89.479	48.9	41.7	9.4
2020	87.673	53.3	37.6	9.1
2021	120.464	60.6	32.7	6.8
2022	128.921	58.8	32.4	8.9

Source: authors' calculations based on National Bank of Poland data.

All in all, the current picture of Polish manufacturing in the face of the characteristics of the periphery is hardly simple and unambiguous (Table 9.2). On the one hand, the whole of CE is a large complex of different manufacturing activities, with a large number of lead firms now embedded in the region through an extensive network of suppliers. This is even more the case for Poland, which is larger and more diversified in its manufacturing than the smaller CE countries. Industrial growth has been accompanied by an increase in productivity and real wages, which has significantly narrowed the gap with Western Europe in purchasing power parity (PPP) terms. On the other hand, the gap still exists and the development of technological competences has not kept pace with the expansion of production and exports. This is related to the important role played by foreign-owned enterprises in several industrial sectors, which entails dependence on their decisions, capital and innovation.

In this context, we can address some common views and beliefs that provide simplistic and/or misleading interpretations of CE manufacturing. Manufacturing activity in the region often appears in popular narrative as a simple assembly of products, a kind of "screwdriver economy". There is also a belief that what really matter are the final products, such as cars and aeroplanes, while the production of their components is of secondary importance. In fact, the production of many parts, e.g. steering systems and aircraft engines, is a more complex process than final assembly. The repeated assumptions that foreign investment in CE is a temporary, disembodied "cathedral in the desert" based

Table 9.2 The attributes of the periphery versus the contemporary Polish economy

Periphery	*Poland*
low density of economic activity	high concentration of different economic activities
specialisation in standard low value-added activities	both low and high value-added activities
low diversity of products and services	diversified economic structure
less advanced technology	advanced and basic technologies
low productivity	narrowed but still existing productivity gap
poor quality of human capital	high quality of human capital
underdeveloped infrastructure	well-developed infrastructure
weak support organisations	wide network of support organisations
limited role of the state in regulatory and welfare functions	active role of the state in regulatory and welfare functions
low territorial embeddedness of foreign firms in the local economy	strong embeddedness of foreign firms in the local economy
low financial autonomy and hence dependence on foreign capital	dependence on foreign capital in some industries and dominance of local firms in others
low capacity to export capital through foreign investment	limited outward foreign investment
limited power to take strategic decisions	varying degrees of strategic decision-making power
weak ability to generate and absorb innovations	weak ability to generate innovations, but their rapid absorption
dependence on core countries for strategic functions	dependence on core countries in several manufacturing sectors
low wages	medium-high wages in PPP terms, but low in nominal terms
poor working conditions	improved labour conditions
high income inequality in the population	low income inequality in the population

Source: authors' elaboration.

on low costs and a "race to the bottom" are myths that, as we have seen, now have little empirical support in reality. The issues of the relevance of lower labour costs and the impact of foreign investment deserve a broader discussion.

Lower nominal labour costs than in the world's high-income countries are often cited as a defining characteristic of the periphery. The question is whether this is the intrinsic shortcoming of fast-growing emerging economies or rather one of the factors that can help them catch up. If we agree that the fundamental economic weakness of less developed countries is significantly lower productivity, then raising productivity becomes crucial to their success. Rising productivity allows for wage growth without compromising economic efficiency. This is the process that has been observed in manufacturing in the CE countries in recent decades. From the point of view of the local workforce, what matters is a real increase in incomes in terms of PPP, which in Poland, according to the Organisation for Economic Co-operation and Development (OECD), had reached almost 90% of the Japanese level by 2022.

What is the impact of foreign investment on Polish manufacturing? There is little doubt that FDI has become an important factor facilitating the growth of production and exports by providing capital, bringing technological change, better organisational culture and skills development. This is also a common view among the managers of both Polish and foreign-owned companies and trade union leaders interviewed. The interesting question is what other options for the development of the manufacturing sector without the extensive involvement of FDI were possible in post-socialist countries, which were lacking in capital, market economy experience and European-level brand manufacturers. The only two other ways found were continued reliance on state-controlled enterprises and the development of private oligarchic monopolies. The former has been observed in coal mining and partly in energy production in Poland, and more recently in the attempt to start production of the Polish electric car; neither of these is considered economically efficient and successful. Oligarchic industrial conglomerates have emerged in Russia and Ukraine with obvious negative social and political consequences (Kryshtanovskaya & White, 2005; Novokmet et al., 2018). Last but not least, EU membership eliminated any barriers to capital flows.

The benefits of FDI do not mean that the small number of large domestic manufacturers and the consequent dependence on foreign decision-makers in many sectors are favourable in the long run. On the one hand, the external control of economic activity by large TNCs is a typical feature of the contemporary world economy, including many regions in the advanced countries, where branch plants of companies from other regions and/or countries play an important role. This means that strategic decisions about what, how and with which suppliers to produce are taken elsewhere. The power of individual nation states vis-à-vis large corporations has been reduced, especially within the European Union, and the national origin of companies has generally become less important in today's economy of networks rather than hierarchies. This is reflected, among other things, in the development of advanced R&D activities in CE countries in recent years. On the other hand, locally owned firms that are successful in international markets may not only be a source of national pride but also bring real economic and social benefits. They may show greater autonomy in their decisions, have a stronger influence on national policies and are likely to bring with them enhanced non-production competences, including design, marketing and purchasing skills, which may lead to a wider use of local suppliers. And domestic companies operating only in the country generate higher tax revenues due to the absence of transfer pricing.

The development of Polish manufacturing raises the question of the extent to which the trends observed can be considered upgrading. There is no doubt that all the dimensions of economic upgrading distinguished in Chapter 1 are taking place in the country. GPN upgrading (Blažek, 2016) can be observed in the household appliance and automotive sectors, where the entire GPN tends to move towards more demanding market segments. As was discussed in Chapters 2 and 6 and summarised above, the role of the studied industries in the national and regional economic structures has also grown, illustrating the upgrading of the industrial structure. Moreover, path upgrading (Grillitsch et al., 2018; Blažek et al., 2020) has occurred in the case of south-eastern Poland in the aircraft industry. When taken together with the developed education and knowledge system, it simultaneously represents cluster upgrading. All the aforementioned dimensions of upgrading would not have been observed if firm-level upgrading had not taken place in all the studied sectors, in both foreign and domestic firms. Firm-level upgrading, however, depends on the upgrading of the entire economic, social (including changes in the quality of life and consumption models and the transformation of the labour market), institutional and technological environment. This environment forms a complex network system that makes industrial upgrading possible.

In terms of the four types of firm-level upgrading (Humphrey & Schmitz, 2002; Gibbon & Ponte, 2005), product upgrading[1] is highly visible among manufacturers of household appliances, such as washing machines and refrigerators. The same is true for the automotive and aircraft industries, where upgrading is most pronounced among component manufacturers. Factories operating in Poland tend to make more advanced and sophisticated products than they did a decade or two ago. This reflects the general tendency of foreign companies to move in this direction; a similar process is taking place among many domestic producers.

Process upgrading is largely a result of company strategies and is observed in all industries studied, in both domestic and foreign firms. It is illustrated by increasing automation and robotisation, especially among foreign original equipment manufacturers (OEMs) and Tier-1 suppliers. Many domestic producers of metal and mechanical components, as well as plastic and rubber parts, also show process upgrading.

Both product and process upgrading are clearly evolutionary in nature. In the first phase of the post-socialist transformation, simpler products were made using less advanced technologies than in Western Europe. At present, most production comes from newly built or expanded and modernised factories.

Functional upgrading, understood as the emergence of R&D and advanced service functions, has been accelerating in Polish manufacturing for more than a decade as a result of the development of some successful Polish firms and the offshoring of non-production competences by foreign companies. It is a more selective process, taking place mainly among some Tier-1 suppliers and to a lesser extent among OEMs. Overall, product and process upgrading have so far been much stronger than functional upgrading.

Overall, two main mechanisms of upgrading at the firm level can be observed. There is a top-down pressure for process, increasingly product and sometimes functional upgrading that lead firms exert upon their suppliers in GPNs. As a result, Tier-1 suppliers appear to be the most advanced in this area, while lower-tier suppliers may be lagging behind. This also means that large companies, among which foreign-owned firms predominate in the three sectors studied in detail, tend to show greater upgrading. Nevertheless, many TNCs are initiators and facilitators of the upgrading of their suppliers through their strategy of increasing local content in order to reduce costs throughout the supply chain, which involves supporting the development of the production capabilities of firms operating in Poland and/or encouraging them to locate here. Increasing quality requirements for manufacturers integrated into GPNs are the main driver for process upgrading. In addition, there is a mechanism of bottom-up development of Polish-owned companies with product, process and, more rarely, functional upgrading. The latter is a key element in the successful expansion of some domestic manufacturers into international, and especially global, markets.

What are the external factors behind the changing position of Polish manufacturing in GPNs and, in particular, its upgrading? And to what extent have these factors changed since the 1990s?

As shown in the previous chapters, the initial factors favouring the dynamic development of Polish manufacturing in the post-socialist period were the availability of a skilled but relatively cheap labour force, its motivation, including the acceptance of long working hours and time flexibility, opportunities to acquire existing production facilities during privatisation, public support for infrastructure development and tax incentives for greenfield investors in special economic zones, and local entrepreneurship. This made it possible to stimulate product upgrading and achieve good product quality together with productivity growth. The relatively large size of the Polish market compared to other post-socialist countries was an advantage for both domestic producers and foreign investors, as was its geographical proximity to Germany. Rapid market reforms, together with the harmonisation of legislation with that of the EU, provided the necessary institutional framework.

While the stable institutional environment of the EU, proximity to Germany, the size of the domestic market and local entrepreneurship are still relevant today (Fortwengel, 2011; Pipkin & Fuentes, 2017), some other conditions have changed and new significant determinants have emerged. Most importantly, the labour market situation is now fundamentally different as a result of sustained economic growth and new job creation in a context of demographic decline. Widespread labour shortages have arisen with a growing role of immigrant labour, rapid wage growth outstripping productivity gains, and higher expectations. The investment incentives granted by the Polish government are hardly competitive with those offered by

Western European governments. There are many complaints about government bureaucracy and frequently changing tax regulations. The availability of electricity from renewable sources (wind and solar) is becoming a must, which requires massive public investment in the grid and may lead to more expensive energy. In addition, close integration with the German manufacturing sector means a strong dependence on its future performance.

At the same time, there are new factors that could sustain the further development of manufacturing in the country. The growing economies of CE, in both manufacturing and services, together with the increasing purchasing power of the population, are creating an expanding regional market. The efficiency (profitability) of large modern plants offering internal economies of scale, coupled with increasing agglomeration economies (external economies of scale), may encourage further investment here, which may be reinforced by the greater role of Polish subsidiaries and local managers within TNCs. Product and process upgrading, as well as the gradual development of non-production competences, should have the same effect. Finally, the general business environment in Poland has improved considerably compared to two or three decades ago. This includes a much better technical infrastructure, in particular an expanded network of motorways and good roads, as well as the development of a wide range of producer services, e.g. IT, tool and equipment manufacturers, repair services and so on. There are also more and better support institutions and initiatives, more experienced partners in local authorities, cluster organisations, centres of excellence, research grants etc. All these factors create a favourable environment for industrial upgrading.

The enhanced role of Polish manufacturing and its upgrading processes reflect the co-evolution of firms and industries on the one hand, and the milieu in which they operate (territory) on the other. What we have witnessed in recent decades is the transformation of both the former and the latter. Industrial change does not take place in a vacuum and cannot be understood without taking into account its interdependence with the evolution of a broader economic, social and institutional context. Thus, processes of upgrading do not simply involve the advancement of manufacturing per se, but the upgrading of the whole system (as in the urban context, see Bulu, 2014). These dynamic relationships between economic activities and the territory in which they are located can be interpreted in terms of localised capabilities.

According to the evolutionary competence theory of the firm, companies forge their competitive advantage by developing distinctive competences on the basis of assets they derive and/or control, which occur in particular places (Maskell, 2001). Consequently, firm competences are built on dynamic localised capabilities, i.e. tangible and intangible assets embodied in the relationships between different stakeholders in a given territory (Domański & Gwosdz, 2009). They include the attitudes and skills of entrepreneurs, managers, engineers and workers, the reliability of suppliers, the behaviour of consumers, the performance of government agencies and local authorities, the activities of business associations and NGOs. All of these have evolved – have been eroded, reproduced or strengthened – under the influence of the development of different industries, as well as national and global political, social and macroeconomic changes, rising living standards and consumption models, decreasing availability and changing characteristics of the workforce (which is more skilled but less willing to work long hours and in flexible time arrangements), the development of clusters etc. At the same time, the localised capabilities have an impact on the development of companies' competences and their strategies.[2] They also contribute to the positive image of the country, which is a prerequisite for trust in producers based in Poland. On the whole, the dynamic localised capabilities are shaped by the interaction of economic activities and the evolving milieu of various stakeholders. There have been interrelated, far-reaching changes in the manufacturing activities themselves, including selective industrial and functional upgrading, as well as in their environment, which has become conducive to further development. It can be argued that localised capabilities are an element of sunk cost and thus a mediating factor in the territorial embeddedness of manufacturers, which hinders their relocation out of the country (Domański & Gwosdz, 2009). This is connected to their involvement in the extensive network of relationships, especially those related to labour and supplier linkages.

The question is to what extent the development of Polish manufacturing in sectors with a strong presence of TNCs can be considered as strategic coupling (Yeung, 2015), which is a set of relationships between technological, organisational, political and social regional assets (affine localised capabilities) and GPNs. It can be argued that both regional and industrial (GPN) dynamics are complementary and interact in CE, leading to successful strategic coupling of foreign firms. According to this perspective, manufacturing in CE, and in Poland in particular, has largely shifted from the production platform model, which was evident in the 1990s and early 2000s and is still present in the household appliance sector, to the international partnership model of strategic coupling, which can be observed to some extent in the aircraft and automotive industries.

In the relational perspective, three dimensions of economic peripherality appear essential to the functions of certain countries in GPNs and thus their dominance and/or dependence on other economies:

- the power to make strategic decisions,
- generation of innovation,
- the provision of products and services.

The previous analysis suggests that Poland, together with other CE countries, does not resemble most of the characteristics associated with peripherality in terms of manufacturing activities and the wider socio-economic system. They have increased their connectivity in GPNs and thus become more central in relational terms, which is considered crucial in the contemporary network economy (see Zöllner et al., 2023). There are clear processes of industrial upgrading and surprising evolutionary resilience to political and economic shocks (crises). Nijkamp (2022) goes further and argues that despite some problems with demographics and low innovation, the Polish transformation can be seen as a good example of successful prosilience. In contrast to resilience, prosilience is a proactive change leading to a deep and radical recovery in a different and more robust form. In other words, the country should not be considered a periphery in this respect,[3] and its evolution could be seen as a move towards stages three and four in Friedmann's (1972) model of the development of the space economy, i.e. the emergence of spatial integration of interdependent and relatively well-developed territorial units. It is in line with Piątkowski's (2018) diagnosis of Poland's rise from the economic periphery to its "golden age" and Kordalska et al.'s (2022) findings of growing functional diversification of CE economies.

The position of CE is more ambiguous in terms of decision-making power. There is no doubt that in several industrial sectors, such as the three examined in detail in this book, Poland is heavily dependent on strategic decisions made by corporate headquarters located elsewhere. However, the overall dependence of Polish manufacturing on foreign-owned enterprises is significantly lower than in other countries in the region, and lower than or similar to that in several Western European countries, such as Sweden, Belgium and the Netherlands; it is the only CE economy, apart from Slovenia, where domestic producers dominate in terms of both value added and employment (see Chapter 2). This is even more true if we look at the country's overall business economy. The fundamental weakness of Polish manufacturing remains its limited potential for product innovation, which makes it dependent on R&D activities carried out abroad.

As the book shows, the processes of change in Polish manufacturing in recent decades represent its profound transformation and selective upgrading. The characteristics of industrial activities and their wider environment are in many respects different from those of the past. New and/or significantly changed patterns and mechanisms of development have emerged. At the same time, elements of continuity are evident, i.e. the processes of change cannot be understood without a longer historical perspective. From an international perspective, this is reflected in the generally better economic performance of the CE manufacturing sector than that of the Balkan and post-Soviet states, which is underpinned by both pre-socialist and socialist legacies of economic, institutional and cultural structures. The role of early post-socialist institutional reforms as a precondition for subsequent economic growth and structural change is also crucial. The broadly understood path-dependent nature of industrial development is also evident in the impact of industrial traditions and labour skills on the development of particular sectors, as well as regions and towns, e.g. the growth and upgrading of the aircraft industry in south-eastern Poland. Most importantly, industrial upgrading has been accompanied by social upgrading with real wage growth, low income inequality and improved employment conditions.

Notes

1 It must be borne in mind that product upgrading observed in a number of enterprises belonging to the same production chain may constitute the upgrading of whole GPNs (GPN upgrading).
2 This can be illustrated by the development of cooperation between manufacturing companies and local technical schools and universities.
3 This is also true of the notion of the "integrated periphery", which is presented as sharing all the main characteristics of the periphery except for having stronger trade links with the core. The social conditions and the impact of manufacturing growth in the CE countries make them very different from some other emerging economies classified as the integrated periphery, such as Mexico and South-East Asia (Covarrubias, 2020; Teipen et al., 2022).

References

Blažek, J. (2016). Towards a typology of repositioning strategies of GVC/GPN suppliers: The case of functional upgrading and downgrading. *Journal of Economic Geography*, 16(4), 849–869. doi:10.1093/jeg/lbv044.

Blažek, J., Květoň, V., Baumgartinger-Seiringer, S., & Trippl, M. (2020). The dark side of regional industrial path development: Towards a typology of trajectories of decline. *European Planning Studies*, 28(8), 1455–1473. doi:10.1080/09654313.2019.1685466.

Bulu, M. (2014). Upgrading a city via technology. *Technological Forecasting and Social Change*, 89, 63–67. doi:10.1016/j.techfore.2013.12.009.

Covarrubias, A. (2020). The boom of the Mexican automotive industry: From NAFTA to USMCA. In A. Covarrubias & S. Ramirez (Eds.), *New frontiers of the automobile industry. Exploring geographies, technology, and institutional challenges* (pp. 323–348). Cham: Palgrave Macmillan.

Domański, B., & Gwosdz, K. (2009). Toward a more embedded production system? Automotive supply networks and localized capabilities in Poland. *Growth and Change*, 40(3), 452–482.

Dünhaupt, P., Herr, H., Mehl, F., & Teipen, Ch. (2022). Introduction: Governance, rent-seeking and upgrading in global value chains. In Ch. Teipe, P. Dünhaupt, H. Herr, & F. Mehl (Eds.), *Economic and social upgrading in global value chains. Comparative analyses, macroeconomic effects, the role of institutions and strategies for the Global South* (pp. 1–31). Cham: Palgrave Macmillan.

Fortwengel, J. (2011). Upgrading through integration? The case of the Central Eastern European automotive industry. *Transcience Journal*, 2(1), 1–25.

Friedmann, J. (1972). A general theory of polarized development. In N.M. Hansen (Ed.), *Growth centers in regional economic development* (pp. 82–107). New York: The Free Press.

Gibbon, P., & Ponte, S. (2005). *Trading down: Africa, value chains, and the global economy*. Philadelphia, PA: Temple University Press.

Grillitsch, M., Asheim, B., & Trippl, M. (2018). Unrelated knowledge combinations: The unexplored potential for regional industrial path development. *Cambridge Journal of Regions, Economy and Society*, 11(2), 257–274. doi:10.1093/cjres/rsy012.

Humphrey, J., & Schmitz, H. (2002). How does insertion in global value chains affect upgrading in industrial clusters? *Regional Studies*, 36(9), 1017–1027.

Kordalska, A., Olczyk, M., Stöllinger, R., & Zavarska, Z. (2022). Functional specialisation in EU value chains: Methods for identifying EU countries' roles in international production networks. Research Report 461. Vienna: Vienna Institute for International Economic Studies.

Kryshtanovskaya, O., & White, S. (2005). The rise of the Russian business elite. *Communist and Post-Communist Studies*, 38(3), 293–307.

Maskell, P. (2001). The firm in economic geography. *Economic Geography*, 77(4), 329–344. doi:10.1111/j.1944-8287.2001.tb00168.x.

Nijkamp, P. (2022). Spatial economic prosilience: A signpost framework for Poland. In P. Churski & T. Kaczmarek (Eds.), *Three decades of Polish socio-economic transformations: Geographical perspectives* (pp. 525–531). Cham: Springer.

Novokmet, F., Piketty, T., & Zucman, G. (2018). From Soviets to oligarchs: Inequality and property in Russia 1905–2016. *The Journal of Economic Inequality*, 16(2), 189–223.

Piątkowski, M. (2018). *Europe's growth champion: Insights from the economic growth of Poland*. Oxford: Oxford University Press.

Pipkin, S., & Fuentes, A. (2017). Spurred to upgrade: A review of triggers and consequences of industrial upgrading in the global value chain literature. *World Development*, 98, 536–554.

Teipen, Ch., Dünhaupt, P., Herr, H., & Mehl, F. (Eds.). (2022). *Economic and social upgrading in global value chains. Comparative analyses, macroeconomic effects, the role of institutions and strategies for the Global South*. Cham: Palgrave Macmillan.

Yeung, H.W.-c. (2015). Regional development in the global economy. *Regional Science Policy & Practice*, 7(1), 1–23. doi:10.1111/rsp3.12055.

Zöllner, S., Heidinger, M., Sager, S., Lüthi, S., & Thierstein, A. (2023). Advanced producer services in Germany: A relational perspective on spatial core–periphery structures, 2009–19. *Regional Studies, Regional Science*, 10(1), 347–368. doi:10.1080/21681376.2023.2185536.

Conclusions

Central European manufacturing in general has shown a remarkable **evolutionary resilience** over more than 30 years. A large diversified industrial complex of growing complexity has emerged, playing an increasing role in global production networks (GPNs). None of the shocks – EU accession and the introduction of the euro in some countries, the financial crisis of 2008–2009, the COVID-19 pandemic and changes in political elites – have slowed its growth. Contrary to some views, this growth has not proved to be temporary. There has been a sustained high level of reinvestment of profits in domestic and foreign manufacturing companies, the location of new products, the construction of greenfield plants and the expansion of existing factories, with very few relocations to other countries.

The improved position of Central European countries in European manufacturing has been accompanied by an apparent, albeit selective, industrial upgrading. The in-depth analysis of three export-oriented industrial sectors in Poland reveals a significant role of **GPN upgrading** in this process. The close integration of manufacturers operating in Central Europe (CE) into GPNs through numerous lead firms brings about product and process upgrading at the company level, as they have to introduce more sophisticated, high value-added products and new technologies in their plants located here in order to face competition and meet consumer expectations. This stimulates further upgrading processes up the supply chain, especially among Tier-1 and Tier-2 suppliers, and may be associated with the gradual growth of non-production competences, i.e. functional upgrading. In this way, strategic coupling opens up opportunities for wider benefits for the development of CE, challenging a one-sided negative view of the impact of export-oriented foreign investment. **Firm-level upgrading** may be part of broader GPN upgrading processes, but it is also conditioned by company characteristics and strategies. The decisions of foreign transnational corporations (TNCs) as well as the ambitions and capabilities of domestic producers in different manufacturing sectors are crucial. A growing number of Polish-owned firms are expanding into international markets.

Another important mechanism of upgrading, which is often overlooked, is **the advancement of the entire socio-economic system of the country and/or region**. Industrial change does not take place in a vacuum. There is an

DOI: 10.4324/9781003430117-11

interdependence between the processes of industrial upgrading at GPN and enterprise level on the one hand, and the evolution of their economic, social and institutional environment on the other. This milieu forms a complex network system that makes industrial upgrading possible and can be seen as dynamic localised capabilities embodied in the relationships between different actors in a given area. They include the changing attitudes and skills of entrepreneurs, managers, engineers and workers; the reliability of suppliers; rising living standards and evolving consumption models; the development of business services; and the performance of public authorities. These localised capabilities are the tangible and intangible assets that firms use to build their competences and thus promote their territorial embeddedness in the Central European countries. However, they can vary considerably from one region to another. This can be illustrated by the upgrading of some regional clusters, such as the Upper Silesian automotive agglomeration and the Aviation Valley in south-eastern Poland. These bottom-up clusters build regional competitive advantages of some CE regions and improve the upgrading capabilities of individual firms.

The expansion of manufacturing activity has contributed to the overall economic development of the Central European countries and regions, generating multiplier effects in other sectors such as construction, transport, producer and consumer services. This is reflected in a significant narrowing of the gap with Western European economies in terms of GDP per capita and labour productivity, although the gap still exists. Importantly, it has also had a positive **social impact**. The myth of development based on a "race to the bottom" no longer finds empirical support in CE. There is no doubt that the post-socialist transformation of the 1990s had considerable social costs, especially in terms of high unemployment. Unemployment in Poland was still high at the beginning of the 21st century and was accompanied by a large labour force with insecure employment conditions (fixed-term and civil/commercial contracts, temporary work). Since then, the number of manufacturing jobs in Poland has been on the rise, in contrast to their decline in most European countries, including Czechia and Romania, and unemployment has fallen to record lows, indicating a growing labour shortage. In addition, there has been a radical reduction in precarious work combined with a rapid increase in real wages, which has significantly narrowed the gap with Western Europe in terms of purchasing power standards and quality of life in general. Income inequalities in Polish society are among the lowest in the EU, and the welfare functions of the state have been strengthened. Thus, Poland and other Central European countries are undergoing not only economic upgrading but also social upgrading. What is more, this is taking place under conditions of democracy, political rights and civil liberties. All this makes CE fundamentally different from some other fast-growing, export-oriented emerging economies that are categorised as the "integrated periphery", such as South-East Asia and Mexico.

The concept of **periphery** does not seem satisfactory to capture the current position of Central European economies in GPNs. It can be argued that the core and periphery debate is partly ill-conceived and has significant limitations in explaining development processes that naturally change over time. It can lead to a teleological interpretation of the economic development of countries or regions as a process of imitating the characteristics and trajectories of areas defined as the core, when in fact there are different development paths and development does not mean moving towards a predefined state. Moreover, general conclusions should not be drawn on the basis of studies of individual sectors, ignoring a broader context, including complex network relations and interdependencies in the contemporary economy and changes in the entire socio-economic system.

There is no doubt that a long-term **evolutionary and relational perspective** is needed to understand development processes. **Three types of functions** can be seen as crucial in defining the position of countries and/or regions in GPNs and hence their **dependence** on other countries and/or regions: the capacity to provide high-quality products and services, the power to make strategic decisions and the capacity to generate innovation.

The profound transformation and selective upgrading of Central European manufacturing in recent decades mean that it no longer exhibits the typical features of **production activities** in the periphery: low density and diversity, lack of internal and external economies of scale, low productivity, narrow specialisation in low value-added activities and weak territorial embeddedness due to poor local linkages, hence limited local value creation and value capture. Whereas in the early stages of the post-socialist transformation CE countries often specialised in the production of mature, standardised products that were relocated from the core (where new products were introduced at the same time in line with **product life-cycle theory**), their current position is much more complex. The location of large, modern, and sometimes the only EU production facilities of certain TNCs in CE means that they are increasingly entrusted with the manufacturing of new generations of products. Extensive supplier networks, reinvestment of profits, and rising wages and salaries indicate increasing value added and value capture.

Slovakia, Hungary, Romania and, to a lesser extent, Czechia show a high degree of **dependence on foreign-controlled enterprises** in many sectors of their manufacturing industries. This implies relatively weak economic power and dependence on strategic decisions taken elsewhere. This dependence is much lower in Poland and Slovenia, where it is similar to that in Sweden, Belgium and the Netherlands. Domestically owned enterprises predominate in most sectors, although foreign-owned enterprises dominate in such important industries as motor vehicles and electrical equipment.

A major weakness of manufacturing in all Central European countries remains their limited potential for product **innovation** and hence their **dependence** on research and development (R&D) activities carried out in the core economies. Despite the rapid growth of such activities and design competence in Central European manufacturing in recent decades, the level of R&D is disproportionately low in relation to their production capacities and lags significantly behind that of the major Western European countries.

The final question is how the characteristics of Polish manufacturing and the factors that underpin it might affect its further development. It is necessary to consider the impact of wider processes of political, economic, environmental and technological change. The higher level of development and changing internal and external conditions mark new challenges to be faced. These include shifts in global markets and supply chains, environmental imperatives and EU policies, the demographic crisis and ever-increasing labour costs, new technologies called Industry 4.0 and the slowdown in German manufacturing, which is highly integrated with producers operating in Poland. The upgrading processes in other countries, such as China, South-East Asia, Türkiye and Romania in the immediate vicinity, should also be taken into account, because these will result in increased competition. On the other hand, the potential for greater integration of Ukraine into European economic and political structures could be an opportunity for Polish-based companies to develop in this market, facilitated by geographical proximity and existing links.

Three scenarios for the future development of Polish manufacturing over the next decade can be considered (see Figure 10.1). The first is a gradual erosion of the competitive advantages of Polish and, more broadly, Central European manufacturing. This would result in a stagnation of production volumes and/or their gradual decline with decreasing investments and relocation of some activities to other countries. The second is a kind of continuation of growth based on predominantly foreign investment in some sectors and domestic producers in others, with limited functional upgrading. The last scenario is a more rapid selective upgrading with the development of R&D competences and Polish OEMs and large suppliers expanding on global markets in the coming decades.

The diminished position of Central European manufacturing in GPNs in the future may be part of a wider process of Europe's declining role as a market and as a place of production in the world economy. The shrinking European market and ageing societies may have a particularly negative impact on the production of durable consumer goods, such as domestic appliances and motor vehicles, but may support some other sectors, e.g. pharmaceuticals. This decline may be facilitated by further growth in production capacity and upgrading of manufacturing in competing countries, both nearby (e.g. Türkiye, Morocco) and more distant (e.g. China). Less attachment to traditional brands may favour producers from outside the EU, and the post-pandemic fall in transport costs may encourage greater imports from Asia. In addition, radical technological changes may reinforce the dominant position of a few economies with the strongest R&D, and the costly adjustment to strict environmental regulations will be easier in the wealthier economies of Western Europe than in CE, partly because of rising energy costs and the risk of a delayed transition to renewable energy sources. Massive subsidies as part of the reindustrialisation policies of national governments in Germany, France etc. will facilitate investment in these countries, while rising labour costs and difficulties in recruiting labour in CE may discourage further investment in the region.

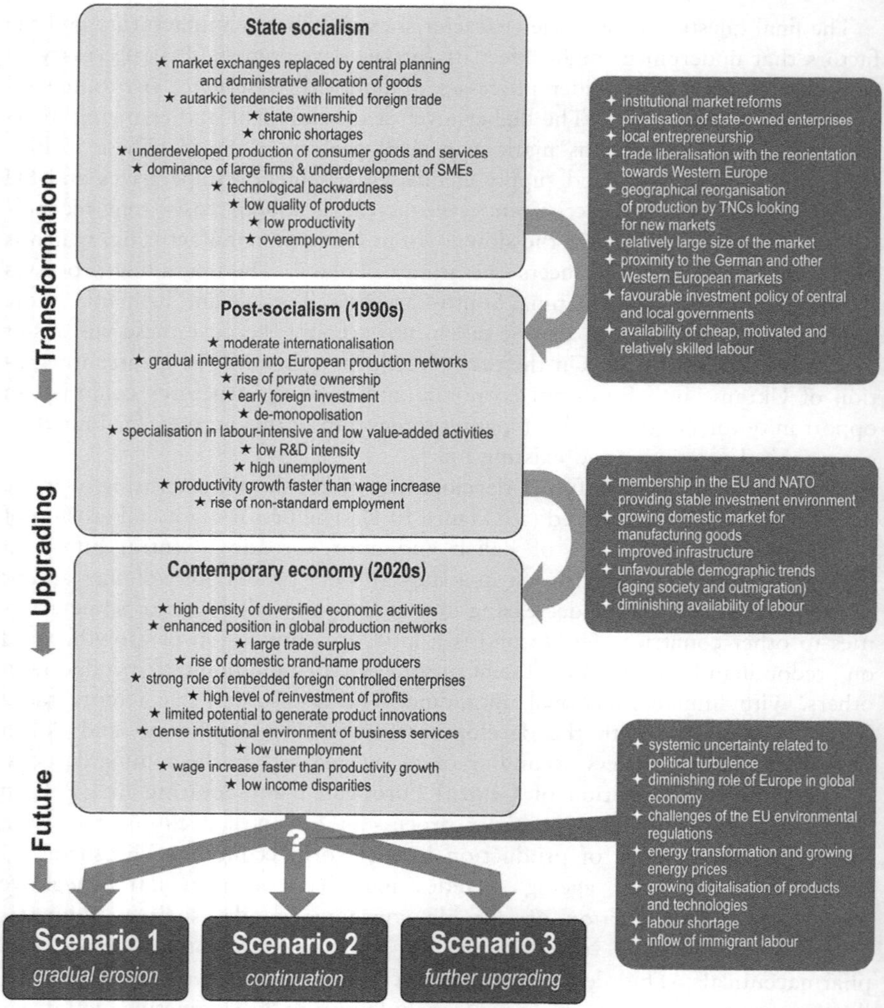

Figure 10.1 The evolution of Poland's manufacturing: features and factors
Source: authors' elaboration.

The question is whether the potentially declining role of CE should be interpreted in terms of **the middle-income trap.** If the concept is understood in terms of GDP and income per capita, this is not the case, as the CE countries are already classified as high-income economies by the UN and the World Bank. However, if we define it as a form of lock-in mechanism, the slowdown or gradual decline in manufacturing production can be seen as the wearing out of the existing development model. This model has enabled the significant catch-up with advanced economies since the 1990s, but may not be sufficient to reduce the remaining gap.

At the same time, several features of Central European manufacturing and their broader socio-economic systems, together with some of the trends described, may support **further industrial development**. It may be fostered by the diversified manufacturing base with a large number of lead firms and a wide range of products, large production capacity of mostly new and expanded plants offering economies of scale, high product quality and the extensive supplier network. The current emphasis on shortening supply chains in Europe may benefit countries with developed manufacturing capabilities, while growing cost pressures may encourage further relocation of production capacity from Western Europe to CE, where wages are still nominally lower in the European context, i.e. offer a favourable productivity/labour cost ratio. Higher transport costs due to stricter environmental regulations may also help to shorten supply chains. Global geopolitical instability may further strengthen the role of institutional trust in the political and business environment of EU countries. In addition, rising defence spending in Europe may support the growth of military-related manufacturing sectors, such as aircraft and chemicals. However, the historical dependence on foreign technology in many sectors may hamper the faster development of innovation capabilities and functional upgrading. Domestically owned producers face particularly strong barriers due to limited access to capital and the lower technological competences of SMEs. They will also be more affected by increasing difficulties in recruiting labour and by rising wages, as they often cannot afford to pay as much as TNCs to attract the most talented people.

Further progress and industrial upgrading may be facilitated by the size and diversification of Poland's manufacturing sector, with a greater role of domestically owned firms than in other smaller CE economies. The larger domestic market is supporting the gradual organic development of Polish-owned manufacturers, some of which have been successfully expanding globally for more than a decade. Rapid growth in R&D expenditure and employment has been observed in recent years, underpinned by the good skills of engineers and the growing role of local managers in foreign affiliates. Poland's strong IT sector can foster the development of indigenous innovation as industrial products and technologies become increasingly digitalised. Last but not least, there is an improved innovation ecosystem with public support policies as well as a growing financial market in Poland providing easier access to external financing.

Overall, there is no doubt that strengthening the domestic innovation potential is crucial for the further development and upgrading of the Polish manufacturing sector. What matters is how many domestic and foreign-owned companies are willing and able to expand their R&D capabilities, create their own branded products, use advanced technologies and gain a reputation as good employers, which will increase their competitiveness in the situation of labour shortages, higher wages and new challenges. Thus, the high road of development within the GPNs must combine enhanced innovativeness and further industrial upgrading with social upgrading that sustains inclusive growth of social well-being. Public policies are needed to support research activities, higher employment rates and standards, and the influx and integration of immigrants. There will certainly be different sectoral and regional paths.

It is not easy to cover all the issues of upgrading and peripherality in a book of limited size. There are many avenues for **future research**. More comparative studies of the similarities and differences in the scale and scope of industrial upgrading in different political and cultural contexts in Asia, Latin America, North America and Europe are essential to understand the development of specific countries and regions. In-depth research on upgrading in different Central European countries should be carried out, taking into account the dynamics and diversity of economic landscapes. Moreover, there is still a need to study the interrelations between economic and social upgrading and the evolution of regional structures. In other words, the co-evolution of industrial upgrading and the overall economic, social and institutional structures should be further explored. This could lead to a new conceptual framework of the relationships between firm-level upgrading and the broader social, economic and institutional system.

The consequences of economic upgrading are not yet fully understood. This is particularly important in the case of the relationship between industrial upgrading and the development of services. Therefore, the spillover effects of manufacturing growth into services need to be studied, perhaps using multiplier effects analysis. In addition, measures of industrial upgrading at the firm level should be examined more critically. Finally, the most important and challenging research challenge is to develop a new comprehensive perspective on the core–periphery dichotomy.

Index